THE ACCOUNTING RESPONSES TO CHANGING PRICES

Experimentation With Four Models

THE ACCOUNTING RESPONSES TO CHANGING PRICES

Experimentation With Four Models

By Task Force on
Conceptual Framework
for Accounting and
Reporting
American Institute of Certified
Public Accountants, *Task Force on Conceptual Framework for Accounting and Reporting.*

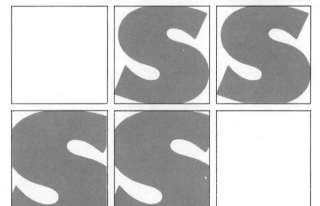

Contents

Preface

Past research and experimentation in accounting has usually been performed by the academics of the profession. Many of the articles and books published have used hypothetical circumstances in their modeling, and if actual financial reports have been used as a starting point, the companies affected have usually not been directly involved.

When in late 1975 the Securities and Exchange Commission proposed the requirement to disclose supplementary replacement cost data of the nature later specified in Accounting Series Release no. 190, members of the American Institute of Certified Public Accountants became concerned about the lack of experimentation by corporate managements in the area of price changes (other than supplementary general purchasing power statements). Failing an effort to deter the SEC until some empirical research could be undertaken in this area, they nevertheless proceeded to embark on a program of experimentation in which companies would attempt to recognize the effects of price changes by recasting actual financial statements based on a variety of premises then being proposed or discussed. A task force was organized to devise the nature of the experiment and to coordinate its efforts with the Financial Accounting Standards Board, which was then in the process of drafting its discussion memorandum on conceptual framework for financial accounting and reporting (published in December, 1976). This monograph is the result of the work of that task force.

Four different models of financial reporting (in addition to the conventional model) were designed to cover the gamut from historical cost to current value, and through the favorable intercession of the Financial Executives Institute, twenty-three major (unnamed) public companies agreed to recast all or a portion of their 1975 and 1976 financial statements on the basis of the four models. The objective was to provide the FASB with live research data to be used in resolving the conceptual, and particularly the measurement, issues involved in its project. The data in this book summarize the results of that experiment, but only two complete sets of financial statements are reprinted here.

It was recognized at the outset that no conclusions could be drawn from this experiment, since no absolute criteria exist to determine the usefulness of any particular model nor the extent to which any one might best portray economic reality. This is especially so since the FASB has not yet agreed on the basic objectives of financial reporting.

The AICPA task force makes no brief for any of the models and fully recognizes that the best answer may lie in a combination of approaches followed, or none at all. Likewise, it was not intended that the experiment should attempt to determine whether the present conventional (largely historical cost) model should be supplemented or replaced. Events here and abroad since the commencement of the experiment indicate that considerable shifting of sentiment in this area is continuing and that we are far from reaching a consensus on the answer to the problem of how accounting should deal with the effects of price changes, particularly in an inflationary period. Nevertheless, the task force believes that all elements of the profession will benefit from the exposure of the material presented in this monograph in keeping with maintaining the anonymity of the participants. Obviously more experimentation is needed in this area before the final solution is found, and the task force hopes that more will be undertaken. Researchers are invited to make use of the data provided and to offer their commentary and conclusions. Public corporations are invited to apply the models to their financial results to get a better appreciation of the problems involved. No doubt the FASB would be interested in any such results or opinions.

The task force wishes to take this opportunity to publicly thank the companies that volunteered to participate in this experiment for their interest in this cause, the many hours of professional time devoted to it, and their patience throughout. Also, it is grateful for the cooperation of the Financial Executives Institute and its committee on corporate reporting in furthering the project.

Task Force on Conceptual Framework for Accounting and Reporting (Models)

PHILIP L. DEFLIESE, *Chairman*	ROBERT HAMPTON, III
ROBERT W. BERLINER	THOMAS L. HOLTON
W. DONALD GEORGEN	ROBERT K. MAUTZ
WILLIAM D. HALL	KENNETH W. STRINGER

AICPA Staff

PAUL ROSENFIELD, *Director* Accounting Standards Division	LEONARD LORENSEN, *Manager* Technical Information Division

1

Model Development and Experimentation

Recent Developments in Accounting

Rapid development and changes in views regarding accounting theory beginning in 1975 have dramatically affected the thinking of all who are involved in financial reporting. Articles, proposals, and regulations from all quarters—academic, professional, and governmental—have proliferated. They suggest (and impose) new concepts designed to supplement or supplant the conventional financial accounting framework with which accountants have so long been familiar. Although there are deeper, long-standing roots underlying the interest in a new conceptual framework of accounting and reporting, the surging inflation of recent years—particularly overseas—has accelerated this trend.

The following summarizes recent developments:

- In March, 1976, the SEC issued ASR 190 requiring large enterprises to provide, in notes to financial statements for 1976 and thereafter, information on the replacement cost of inventories, cost of goods sold, plant and equipment, and related depreciation.

- In October, 1976, the Institute of Chartered Accountants in Australia and the Australian Society of Accountants issued a provisional standard encouraging the use of current cost accounting instead of historical cost accounting for financial reports for accounting periods beginning after June 30, 1977. (The implementation of this proposal has been delayed.) They had previously issued two contemporary exposure drafts proposing the use of general purchasing power and current value concepts.

- In November, 1976, the Accounting Standards Committee (ASC) of the Institute of Chartered Accountants in England and Wales and associated accounting organizations issued Exposure Draft 18, which proposed the adoption of current cost accounting for certain financial reports for accounting periods beginning after June 30, 1978. This followed a crash effort to implement the Sandilands report (1975), endorsed by the government, which was a response to the ASC's

1

provisional standard (1974) recommending general purchasing power information as a supplement to traditional financial statements. (This proposal has been withdrawn and alternative supplementary disclosures are being encouraged.)

- In December, 1976, the FASB issued a discussion memorandum—*An Analysis of Issues Related to Conceptual Framework for Accounting and Reporting: Elements of Financial Statements and Their Measurement* together with its *Tentative Conclusions on Objectives of Financial Statements of Business Enterprises*. Public hearings on the two documents were held in August, 1977, and January, 1978. The FASB had previously issued an exposure draft (1974) proposing general purchasing power information as supplementary to traditional financial statements but deferred action on that proposal until the issues on objectives and conceptual framework are resolved.

- In December, 1977, the FASB issued an exposure draft, *Objectives of Financial Reporting and Elements of Financial Statements of Business Enterprises*.

Development of the Models

The AICPA recognized that in the light of the SEC requirement, developments in other countries, and proposals by some major accounting firms, any consideration of the FASB discussion memorandum would be a serious undertaking of considerable magnitude. The Institute believed that it would be inappropriate for the accounting community to decide for or against any framework of accounting that departs radically from the present one without first undertaking substantial research to determine the results of applying the various proposals.

Accordingly, the AICPA appointed the task force on conceptual framework for accounting and reporting (models) to study the various proposals of concept and measurement, both existing and forthcoming. The task force decided to encourage experimentation with a minimum number of models formulated from the proposals, which would assist the FASB in its deliberations. The objective was to make available a small number of models for major companies to apply to their financial results for 1975 and 1976, which would incorporate the various measurement proposals. The task force developed four basic models as possible alternatives (or supplements) to present practice:

Model A. Condensed financial statements based on historical costs but stated in units of general purchasing power (general price-level statements).

Model B. Historical cost financial statements incorporating inventories based on LIFO and with depreciation based on the current cost of depreciable assets.

Model C. Financial statements based partially on historical cost and partially on current costs and values (generally relying on replacement costs) distinguishing between operating income and value changes. This model has many elements of the Australian and U.K. models.

Model D. Current value financial statements applying either replacement cost or current values to all resources and obligations as well as recognizing the effect of changes in the general level of prices on shareholders' equity.

The four models are composites of several alternative concepts and measurement bases and cannot be identified precisely with specific proposals previously publicized. The number of variations and permutations available could have produced a larger number of models but the task force felt that the experimentation should be limited to these four basic models. Consequently, within this set of four, variations are possible and perhaps desirable. The treatment of goodwill, deferred taxes, market values of monetary liabilities, to name a few, could vary within each model. Rather than increase the number of models, the task force decided that experimenters should be asked to suggest variations of each model they believed appropriate.

An accounting model that attempts to deal with the impact of changing prices on reported earnings usually raises the question of whether income taxes should be revised to make allowances for the effects of those changes. Much has been said in publications and the media of the need for such consideration, with arguments pro and con. The task force took no position on the desirability of any change in tax laws in this area but it recognized that possibility. The models are *financial accounting* models, that is, models of how to prepare general purpose financial information for investors, creditors, and others interested in the financial affairs of business enterprises. Whether and how the effects of changing prices should be treated for tax purposes should be determined based on considerations other than those under study by this experiment. The models vary in their approach to the accounting problem this presents.

The task force took no position on the desirability of any of the models and emphasized the experimental nature of this project. Furthermore, it took no position on whether the financial statements contemplated by the models should be supplementary to the present conventional statements (parallel presentation) or should (perhaps only ultimately) replace them. That is a difficult issue, which the task force believes should be addressed only after experimentation and study of views from the experimenters as to the practicability, desirability, and usability of any new concepts or framework. It was recognized that there are no undisputed criteria for evaluation. In the final analysis, only an unbiased consensus—the act of an independent body such as the FASB—can make the necessary determinations.

The Experiment

Twenty-seven companies volunteered to participate in the experiment conducted by the task force, of which twenty-three companies completed the experiment and four withdrew before completion. The majority of the operations of each company are in the following industries:

	Number of companies
Banking	1
Regulated utility	1
Retailing	1
Manufacturing	19
Transportation	1
Total	23

The participating companies are all publicly owned, and tend to be active in the development of accounting theory. Fifteen companies had previously participated in the FASB experiment on general purchasing power accounting. Ten had submitted comments to the FASB on the objectives of financial statements and on part I of the FASB discussion memorandum on a conceptual framework. Four had submitted comments on parts II and III of the discussion memorandum. One had previously published current value financial statements in its annual report to shareholders.

Seventeen participants applied the four experimental models to all or substantially all of their consolidated operations. Six applied the models to a "free-standing" segment of their operations, in most cases to the parent company.

All twenty-three participants applied all four models to their two most recent fiscal years, which for twenty companies ended on December 31, 1976, and for three companies in July or October, 1976. Each experimenter prepared five sets of financial statements, including related notes, for the reporting entity—(1) a set based on present generally accepted accounting principles and (2) a set of experimental statements for each of the four models—using the principles applicable to each model and including notes that either were peculiar to the statements for the model or differed from corresponding notes that were part of the statements based on present principles. Financial statements prepared by two participants are presented in chapter 11.

The participants were also requested to fill out answers to a written questionnaire. The questions dealt with preparation time, implementation problems, improvements suggested for the models, and the participants' evaluation of the usefulness of the models. A copy of the questionnaire is reproduced in the Appendix.

2

Choices for a Conceptual Framework for Accounting and Reporting

The structure of a financial accounting and reporting model depends on the nature of the conceptual framework that underlies it. Each of the four models developed by the task force is derived from a conceptual framework that differs from the frameworks from which the other three models are derived. This chapter discusses the choices involved in the development of a conceptual framework preparatory to model construction. The conceptual frameworks peculiar to each model are discussed in chapters 3 and 4.

An agreed conceptual framework for accounting and reporting would provide help in dealing with specific choices that are required in the design of a financial accounting and reporting system. Constructing such a framework involves identifying both the objectives of financial accounting and reporting and the choices required in the design of a system.

Identifying objectives requires determining the needs of the users of financial information and specifying the objectives of the information required to meet the needs, including desirable qualities of the information. Identifying the choices in designing a financial accounting and reporting system requires determining the various ways in which such a system can be designed and the decisions required to select one of those ways. The choices made in the design of a system should be compatible with the objectives identified.

The Study Group on the Objectives of Financial Statements (Trueblood committee) reported its findings on the objectives of financial accounting and reporting. On December 2, 1976, the FASB issued a document entitled *Tentative Conclusions on Objectives of Financial Statements of Business Enterprises*.

Also on December 2, 1976, the FASB issued a discussion memorandum identifying the choices required in the design of a system: *An Analysis of Issues Related to*

Conceptual Framework for Financial Accounting and Reporting: Elements of Financial Statements and Their Measurement.

Before the FASB issued its discussion memorandum, the AICPA task force identified thirteen choices that underlie a conceptual framework for accounting and reporting and determined the positions on those choices reflected in the four experimentation models it was preparing. This chapter states and discusses the thirteen choices, together with brief descriptions of answers provided by present practice, alternative answers that have been proposed, and implications of the various answers. (Each choice, of course, could be the subject of extended discussion, but this chapter is intended only to provide an overview.) Some of the choices are independent; for example, choices 5 and 8. Others are related; for example, whether choice 9 arises depends on the answer to choice 8.

The choices discussed in this chapter are not precisely the same as the issues discussed by the FASB. This chapter indicates the relationships between the choices identified by the task force and the issues presented in the FASB discussion memorandum.

Choice 1—Theory of the Entity

Should the entity be viewed as separate from its parties at interest (so-called entity theory), merely as the focus of the interests of its owners (so-called proprietary theory), or some other way?[1]

The theory of the entity is held to affect a number of accounting descriptions and decisions. Under the most extreme "entity theory," the firm is the sole focus of attention, and outsiders' interests, including stockholders', are viewed as essentially alike. Payments for dividends, interest, and income taxes are all considered to be similar distributions of net resources gained by use of the entity's resources. Maintaining and increasing productive capacity in physical terms is an example of a goal that would be especially appropriate to this theory.

The extreme version of the "proprietary theory" involves the assumption that the entity has no existence apart from its owners and that accounting for the entity really is accounting for the owners' resources and obligations. Under this theory, stockholders' equity is described as being the stockholders' property. The need to maintain or increase their property in terms of general purchasing power is especially appropriate to that description since stockholders are presumed to be primarily interested in the ability to buy a wide variety of goods and services.

Another theory of the firm that has been suggested has been called the "perspective theory," in which information about a separate entity and its resources and obligations and changes in them is designed from the perspective of the parties who have an interest in the entity.[2] Their perspective can come into play in the choices required in the design.

---

1. The FASB discussion memorandum states that "issues relating to the relative merits of the so-called proprietary and entity concepts are not raised in this Discussion Memorandum" but "are deferred to a later phase of the conceptual framework project" (p. 32).

2. The perspective theory was developed by Paul Rosenfield of the task force staff, who suggested the theory to the task force during the development of this chapter.

Choice 2—Articulation

Should financial statements that show position interlock with financial
statements that show changes in position (articulated financial
statements)?[3]

Financial statements under presently accepted accounting principles interlock in that the items included in the income statement and statement of changes in shareholders' equity represent changes in assets and liabilities that were included in the calculation of assets and liabilities for balance sheet purposes. Other statements could be used in addition to the income statement and statement of changes in shareholders' equity that interlock as a group with the balance sheet. For example, current market price could be used to quantify marketable securities in the balance sheet and unrealized gains and losses could be reported in a special statement.

It has been said that interlocking statements are wasteful since they are prepared on the same basis and are therefore redundant. Financial statements that do not interlock would permit various bases in various statements, to gain purported advantages without suffering purported disadvantages. For example, current market price could be used to quantify marketable securities in balance sheets but unrealized gains and losses would not need to appear in any statement of changes.

A substitute for noninterlocking statements would consist of presenting supplementary information that does not interlock with otherwise interlocking financial statement amounts.

Choice 3—Controlling Factors for Recognition and Measurement (Revenues and Expenses Approach vs. Resources and Obligations Approach)

Should the recognition and measurement of revenues and expenses
be controlling factors that dominate the recognition and measurement of
resources and obligations,[4] *or should the recognition and measurement*
of resources and obligations be controlling factors that dominate the
recognition and measurement of revenues and expenses?[5]

The present financial accounting system makes the recognition and measurement of revenues and expenses controlling factors that dominate the recognition and measurement of resources and obligations. In the main, revenues are proceeds from the sale of goods or the provision of services. Expenses are the historical costs of resources transferred or used up in the process of earning revenues. The historical costs of resources not yet transferred or used up are presented in balance sheets.

One approach to modifying the present system would retain the dominance of the recognition and measurement of revenues and expenses. The main change would be to substitute current cost for historical cost in the measurement of expenses. A question to be resolved would be the treatment of changes in costs of resources while they are held.

---

3. Issue no. 1 of the FASB discussion memorandum (pp. 48–53).

4. In this study, the terms *resources* and *obligations* include, but are not limited to, assets and liabilities that appear in balance sheets.

5. Issue no. 1 of the FASB discussion memorandum (pp. 38–40).

7

Another approach to modifying the present system would be to abandon the dominance of the recognition and measurement of revenues and expenses and make the recognition and measurement of resources and obligations the controlling factors. That approach basically starts afresh. Resources owned and obligations owed at the balance sheet date would be recognized and measured regardless of how they were acquired or incurred. Balance sheets would exclude deferred items that represent neither resources nor obligations. Revenues, expenses, value changes, and other causes of changes in shareholders' equity would be recognized and measured solely as a result of the recognition and measurement of changes in resources and obligations.

Choice 4—Individual Resources and Obligations

Should financial statements portray aspects of individual resources and obligations or aspects of the entity as a whole?[6]

At present, financial statements present amounts related to individual resources and obligations and no attempt is made to account for the value of the business as a whole. Academic literature sometimes states that accounting ideally should account for the value of the business as a whole and that attention to individual resources and obligations is only a fall-back position adopted because of the impracticality of the ideal approach. The current value approach that incorporates the concept of value of the entity is that which measures the amount of cash held plus the discounted amount of net future cash receipts.

Choice 5—Selection of Resources

Should all resources of the enterprise be included in balance sheets or only resources that are exchangeable separately from the business as a whole and from significant segments of the business?[7]

At present, resources that are obtained in transactions with outside parties (exchange transactions, issuance of capital stock, and so forth) are accounted for in balance sheets regardless of whether they are exchangeable separately from the business as a whole and from significant segments of the business. For example, goodwill is a resource that is accounted for in balance sheets if it is purchased, although it cannot be exchanged separately from the business as a whole and from significant segments of the business.

Some proposals would continue to account for resources regardless of whether they are exchangeable separately from the business as a whole and from significant segments of the business. Other proposals would account only for resources exchangeable separately; they would require, for example, that purchased goodwill be written off immediately.

---

6.   Paragraph 18 of the FASB's *Tentative Conclusions on Objectives of Financial Statements of Business Enterprises* states, "Financial accounting cannot directly measure the value of a business enterprise—the present value of its expected net cash receipts." Its exposure draft (December, 1977) makes the same statement (par. 33).

7.   Issue no. 2 of the FASB discussion memorandum (pp. 69–75).

Choice 6—History

To what extent, if at all, should financial statements reflect past events that affected the entity, past events that might have but did not affect the entity, or future events that have not yet affected the entity but are expected to affect it?[8]

Present accounting emphasizes the results of past events that affected the entity (for example, past sales) but also reflects estimates of future events that have not yet affected the entity but are expected to affect it (for example, termination of the usefulness of equipment). Current value systems vary in their emphasis on different types of events. Some approaches to current value include all relevant past events that affected the entity up to the balance sheet date but avoid all past events that might have but did not affect it and all future events that are expected to affect it.

Other current value systems emphasize past events that might have but did not affect the entity directly (for example, replacement cost accounting for long-lived assets that reflects line by line in the income statement the pro forma results that might have been obtained in the present period if the enterprise had used the latest equipment purchased currently instead of the equipment it did use and had resulting labor and overhead cost savings). Still other current value systems emphasize estimates of future events that have not yet affected the entity but are expected to affect it (for example, the "ideal" system—cash plus the discounted amount of net future cash receipts—or net realizable value).

Choice 7—Unit of Account

Should money (for example, dollars, pesos) be the basis of the unit used in accounting or should there be another basis for the unit of account (for example, general purchasing power)?[9]

The present unit used in accounting is defined in terms of money: costs, revenue, expenses, gains, losses, and so forth are stated in terms of numbers of dollars. Money has traditionally been used to define the unit of account since it is exchangeable for other resources and is simple to use since transactions, prices, values, and so forth in the world outside financial statements are stated in terms of money.

Selection of the basis to define the unit of account helps define success. For example, if money is used, success and failure are in terms of money.

General purchasing power can also be used to define the unit of account—then success and failure are defined in terms of general purchasing power. During inflation, success in terms of money can be accompanied by failure in terms of general purchasing power.

Choice 8—Types of Changes

Should events and changes reported be mostly confined to transactions and other changes in quantities of resources or obligations or also include others such as changes in prices or in prospects?[10]

---

8. This choice is not specifically discussed in the FASB discussion memorandum.
9. Issue no. 9 of the FASB discussion memorandum (p. 191).
10. Issue no. 9 of the FASB discussion memorandum (pp. 191–208).

Amounts in financial statements are quantities (monetary items) or the product of quantities times prices (nonmonetary items). At present, changes accounted for are almost exclusively transactions and other changes in the quantity factor and not changes in the price factor. The quantity of monetary items is the number of dollars they represent and changes are reported when the quantities change. Changes are reported for nonmonetary items when their quantities change—when they are bought or sold. Amortization (including depreciation) allocates the diminution of the quantity of service available (for example, months of insurance protection or years of useful life of equipment) over the periods in which it is used up.

Only in limited situations are changes now recorded based on changes in the price factor alone—essentially only to implement the lower of cost and market rules for inventories and marketable securities.

All current value methods add the recognition of changes in price to the recognition of changes in quantity.

A related question is whether changes in the amounts at which obligations can be refinanced or repaid (that is, in their current market value) before they are due should be recognized when they occur.

Choice 9—Types of Prices

Should the prices used be past, present, or future prices? Should they be buying prices or selling prices? [11]

At present, prices that enter the accounting system are mainly those attached to changes in quantities: when goods are purchased, their purchase price at that date is used; when goods are sold, their selling price at the date of sale is used.

If changes in price are to be recognized at times other than when quantities change, the types of prices must be selected. Prices vary in two important respects: time and market.

Time. Prices may be past prices, present prices, or future prices. Historical cost is a past (purchase) price; current replacement price and current selling price are present prices; net realizable value [12] and discounted future net cash receipts of the business as a whole involve future prices and prospects (the latter includes future quantities).

Market. Prices may be in the entity's buying markets or its selling markets. [13] Historical cost and replacement price are buying prices. Current selling price, current net realizable value, and net realizable value involve selling prices.

Various current value systems differ based on the time and markets of the prices they use.

---

11. Issue no. 9 of the FASB discussion memorandum (pp. 191–208).

12. The term *net realizable value* is defined in this study the same way it is defined in paragraph 429 of the FASB discussion memorandum—the amount of cash (or its equivalent) into which an asset is expected to be converted in due course of business less direct costs expected to be incurred in converting it to cash. The term *current net realizable value* is defined here as current selling price less expected direct costs of disposal.

13. Selling prices in orderly liquidation are different from selling prices in forced liquidation. In this study, the selling prices discussed are those in orderly liquidation.

Choice 10—Single Measurement Basis vs. Multiple Measurement Basis

Should the accounting and reporting system use a single basis for nonmonetary resources, such as selling price, or several bases? [14]

The present system is essentially a single basis for nonmonetary resources, since it emphasizes historical cost and uses market value only peripherally. Many proponents of current value accounting advocate single basis systems for nonmonetary resources, emphasizing either selling price or replacement cost or net realizable value, and so forth, to the exclusion of other bases. They contend that the single basis system can be better defended, its results better defined, and problems involving measurement and communication theory reduced.

Others advocate a multiple measurement basis for nonmonetary resources, which they contend is necessary because of the diverse characteristics of resources; for example, accounting for resources held for sale should differ from accounting for resources held for use.

Choice 11—Realized vs. Unrealized Gains or Losses

Should both realized and unrealized gains and losses be recognized and distinguished? [15]

At present, gains and losses are generally recognized when they are "realized"— for example, when nonmonetary items are exchanged for monetary items—or when they are used or lost. The gains and losses represent changes over time—the time span often began before the period in which the gain (and sometimes the loss) is reported. Some current value systems report gains and losses while resources are held (or obligations are owed) before they are sold—so-called holding (or owing) gains and losses. Whether gains and losses should be recognized before resources are sold, whether they should be included in income, and whether holding and owing gains and losses should be distinguished from gains and losses realized on sale regardless of when recognized are answered differently in designing proposed systems.

Choice 12—Starting Point to Determine Income (the "Capital Maintenance" Question)

If an income type concept is emphasized (for example, net income, operating results), from what starting point should it be measured? [16]

At present, income is measured in units of money from the starting point of stockholders' equity at the beginning of the period as reported, and the change is

---

14. This choice is discussed in paragraph 439 of the FASB discussion memorandum.

15. This choice is not discussed in the FASB discussion memorandum, although the term *realization* is defined (p. 30) and often used in the memorandum.

16. Issue no. 8 of the FASB discussion memorandum (pp. 123–144).

determined exclusive of dealings with the owners. Accounting in units of general purchasing power using the same type of starting point has been proposed. Income would be measured by starting with stockholders' equity at the beginning of the period as reported and determining the change exclusive of dealings with the owners. (Stockholders' equity at the beginning of the period would be restated, if necessary, for a change in the size of the unit, so that all items in the computation are stated in the same unit.)

Two types of starting points other than the type presently used have been advocated. Both are used in systems in which the accounting is in units of money. In one system, the starting point is the stockholders' equity at the beginning of the period, not as reported but in units of the general purchasing power of the unit of money at the end of the period—this method uses a so-called capital maintenance adjustment. (The net result is the same as if the accounting were done in units of general purchasing power at the balance sheet date and income were measured using the type of starting point presently used—but the income statement details to arrive at the net result are different.)

In the other system, the starting point is the stockholders' equity at the beginning of the period as reported in units of money adjusted for changes in the replacement cost of the productive capacity held at the beginning of the period. Income is measured starting from the point at which the productive capacity of inventories and long-term assets at the end of the period equals their productive capacity at the beginning of the period. Current replacement value accounting may use this starting point. Changes in the replacement cost of inventories and of the productive capacity of long-term assets held are recognized in the balance sheet and in computing cost of goods sold and depreciation but the changes are excluded from income.

Choice 13—Emphasis of Net Results

Should the net result of some of the changes that affected shareholders'
equity be emphasized, for example, by segregating them in a separate
statement, by labelling the net result "net income" or a similarly
emphatic label, or otherwise? [17]

At present, changes that affected shareholders' equity are presented in one or more statements. Virtually all changes that resulted from events other than transactions with owners are presented in the statement of income and the net result is emphasized with the label "net income." Changes that resulted from transactions with owners are presented in combined statements of income and retained earnings (for example, dividends), or in other statements such as statements of changes in capital accounts (for example, stock issuances and repurchases).

Proposals have been made to change the emphasis given in the statements, by changing the number or content of the statements of change or otherwise. For example, one proposal involves segregating some of the results of events other than transactions with owners in a separate statement of the results of ordinary operations. Another proposal involves combining all the results of events affecting share-

---

17. This choice is discussed in Appendix A of the FASB discussion memorandum: "Issues about form of financial statements are expected to be specifically raised in later phases of the conceptual framework project" (p. 259).

holders' equity in a single statement and segregating various types of changes within the statement, for example, ordinary operations, unusual transactions and events, value changes, and transactions with owners, and presenting an unlabelled subtotal of the results of all events other than transactions with owners.

3

Models A and B

Models A and B are similar to the conventional model in that assets and liabilities are stated at historical cost (although model A changes the unit of measure) and changes in their value are not explicitly recognized in the financial statements. Also, the financial statements presented under the two models do not essentially differ in form from those presented under the conventional model.

Model A

Model A incorporates the concepts presented in the FASB December 31, 1974, exposure draft entitled *Financial Reporting in Units of General Purchasing Power*, but it modifies both the methodology used and the form of presentation of supplementary general purchasing power information illustrated in the draft. The modifications are discussed below under "Departures From FASB Methodology" and "Form of Presentation."

Positions on General Choices

The positions model A incorporates as to each of the choices for a conceptual framework for accounting and reporting discussed in chapter 2, except for choice 7 (unit of account), are identical with those reflected in present generally accepted accounting principles. Differences between the amounts that appear in conventional financial statements and the corresponding amounts that appear in the supplementary general purchasing power information contemplated by model A arise solely because the latter amounts are restated to recognize changes in the general purchasing power of the dollar. That is, the position on choice 7 (unit of account) implied by present principles is that the unit of account is defined in terms of money. The position incorporated in model A is that the unit of account is defined in terms of general purchasing power.

Concepts Underlying Model A

Model A retains the historical cost basis but changes the unit of account by restating the amounts originally recorded in terms of dollars whose general purchasing power differ into units of account defined in terms of a single amount of general purchasing power. The following concepts underlie the model:

- The effects of inflation—the decline in the general purchasing power of money—should be measured, and information incorporating those effects should be presented to accompany primary financial statements that present either financial position at the end of a fiscal year or results of operations for a fiscal year.
- The impact of inflation can be reflected within the historical cost framework without changing present financial reporting. Enterprises may continue to keep their books and prepare their primary financial statements in terms of dollars.
- Even gradual inflation over a period of time has cumulative effects that are brought out by restating historical cost financial statements.
- Reporting the effects of changes in prices of particular goods and services (which may occur either more or less rapidly than changes in the general price level and may even be counter to them) is a separate issue, not to be confused with reporting the effects of inflation. Movements in specific prices are influenced by all the factors that affect both supply and demand for the particular items, and only by coincidence would the rates of specific price movements correspond with the rate of inflation.
- Restatement to units of general purchasing power is a process of translation, not of revaluation, and historical costs expressed in units of general purchasing power are still historical costs; only the unit of account is changed.
- Comprehensive restatement of the primary financial statements in terms of the general purchasing power of the dollar at the most recent balance sheet date is required.
- Partial restatement of only certain items in the primary financial statements is not sufficient and can be misleading.
- Information concerning losses on holding monetary assets and gains on owing monetary liabilities is necessary to evaluate the overall impact of inflation.
- The recoverability conventions presently existing under generally accepted accounting principles apply equally to model A. To the extent that generally accepted accounting principles require the use of a "value" lower than cost (for example, "market," "permanent impairment," and "realizable" value) such a requirement is equally applicable in model A. Restated cost should be written down to the applicable value if lower than restated cost.
- The gross national product implicit price deflator is the index to use in restatement.

Departures From FASB Methodology

One of the principal objections to the FASB exposure draft has centered on the time and expense required to apply the general purchasing power restatement procedures. Some critics have said that the FASB methodology swamps them in computations, many involving picayune amounts.

Implicit in model A methodology is the belief that neither the purpose of general purchasing power information nor the inherent limitations on its precision justify intricate restatement of every nonmonetary item. The model adopts the following from the U.K. provisional standard (Provisional Statement of Standard Accounting

Practice no. 7, *Accounting for Changes in the Purchasing Power of Money*, published by the Institute of Chartered Accountants in England and Wales in May, 1974):

> In applying these tests, and during the whole process of conversion, it is important to balance the effort involved against the materiality of the figures concerned. The supplementary current purchasing power statement can be no more than an approximation, and it is pointless to strive for over-elaborate precision.

Accordingly, developers of the model recommend the use of assumptions and short-cut techniques, applied with judgment and tested for propriety, to avoid striving for unattainable precision. That approach will likely produce results that approximate amounts derived by detailed computations.

The developers of model A assume that it is doubtful, for example, that the significance of general purchasing power results would change if routine recurring prepayments and deferred items were simply treated as monetary in order to avoid the extensive detail involved in treating them as nonmonetary. Both common sense and materiality come into play here, and specific circumstances will determine whether an item that is clearly nonmonetary in theory needs to be so treated in practice.

Deferred Income Taxes. Deferred income taxes deserve special note. The FASB exposure draft treats both deferred income tax charges and credits as nonmonetary items because they represent, respectively, deferred past costs and deferred past cost savings that will be amortized in future periods. That treatment accords with the principles for deferred income taxes under present GAAP. Those principles, however, are controversial. Another view is that deferred income tax items should be considered like receivables and payables. Model A treats deferred income tax items as monetary, in effect changing the principles on which they are stated before restatement, based on the view that the principle adopted is preferable and that fact becomes evident under general purchasing power accounting. Furthermore, there is a significant, practical benefit in eliminating the extensive computations otherwise needed to restate deferred taxes.

Foreign Currency Items. The FASB exposure draft provides that items are to be classified as monetary if they are "fixed in terms of numbers of U.S. dollars." Model A modifies the definition of monetary items by changing the expression to "fixed in terms of units of money," thereby making it unnecessary to treat items as nonmonetary merely because they are denominated in a foreign currency.

A change in classification of foreign currency items from nonmonetary to monetary affects the amounts presented in the restated income statement for *exchange gains or losses* and *general purchasing power gains or losses on monetary items* but does not affect restated net income. The change avoids the serious practical problems involved in segregating transactions and balances in dollars from those in other currencies. That benefit is considered to more than offset any loss in information caused by combining gains and losses on foreign money resulting from both domestic inflation and exchange rate changes with gains and losses on domestic money caused solely by inflation.

General Purchasing Power Gains and Losses. One of the concepts underlying the FASB exposure draft is that a general purchasing power income statement should measure and report as elements of net income the loss of general purchasing power as the result of holding monetary assets and the gain from owing money to others during inflation. Critics of the exposure draft have charged that this concept is unsound, particularly as to the recognition in income of the gains on long-term monetary obligations. Some have objected because highly leveraged enterprises would report substantial general purchasing power profits when, in fact, they might be illiquid to the extent of being in precarious financial condition.

Model A incorporates this concept of the FASB exposure draft under the rationale that such gains are economic benefits—that is, the liabilities will be liquidated with dollars having less general purchasing power than those received when the liabilities were incurred. Both in conventional financial accounting and in general purchasing power accounting, the income statement measures profitability and the balance sheet and statement of changes in financial position measure liquidity. General purchasing power gains do not represent inflows of cash, nor do general purchasing power losses represent outflows of cash. Even in conventional financial statements, immediate receipt of cash, or even imminent receipt of cash, is not a necessary condition to the recognition of income.

In response to the criticism of the FASB exposure draft in this regard, model A calls for separate disclosure of the portion of net general purchasing power gain or loss that is applicable to long-term debt in the supplementary income statement information (see "Form of Presentation," below). Other significant general purchasing power gains and losses might also be shown separately. Interest income and interest expense might be shown separately and might be associated with the related general purchasing power gains and losses.

Form of Presentation

Model A calls for condensed general purchasing power financial statements that would supplement primary financial statements prepared on the basis of unrestated historical cost. Since the general purchasing power statements would be supplementary, model A calls for presenting them as simply as possible. Condensed financial statements, confined to major balance sheet and income statement captions and expressed in round amounts, would highlight the effects of inflation without presenting an apparently competing set of primary financial statements. Information from the statement of changes in financial position would not be part of the general purchasing power information. If the primary financial statements are in comparative form, the model calls for presenting statements in comparative form. Although condensed general purchasing power statements are illustrated, a full set of financial statements could be prepared based on model A for presentation as the basic statements or as supplementary statements and they could be presented if that is desired.

In response to the objections that have been raised about the general purchasing power gains on debt (see "General Purchasing Power Gains and Losses," above), model A segregates the general purchasing power gains on long-term monetary obligations from other general purchasing power gains and losses and reports both in the supplementary income information following income from operations. This disclosure (beyond that required by the FASB exposure draft) would enable financial statement users to accommodate the information to their own views on the nature of those gains and losses.

Furthermore, model A provides for presentation of a reconciliation between unit-of-money income and general purchasing power income, rather than making this optional as did the FASB exposure draft. Under the usual format of general purchasing power reporting, financial statement users tend to identify, incorrectly, the general purchasing power gains and losses on monetary items with the overall impact of inflation and restatement. The proposed reconciliation reduces the tendency to make this misidentification by developing and highlighting the net impact of the general purchasing power restatement on results for the year.

The exhibits that follow illustrate the proposed supplementary reporting under model A. They are based on appendix E of the FASB exposure draft of December 31, 1974, modified as indicated above.

EXHIBIT A

Balance Sheets
December 31, 1976 and 1975
Condensed General Purchasing Power Information

	In $ (1976)	
	1976	1975
Current assets	$14,980,000	$17,170,000
Less current liabilities and deferred		
taxes	3,920,000	7,000,000
	11,060,000	10,170,000
Property, plant, and equipment	36,200,000	35,740,000
Less depreciation	28,510,000	25,890,000
	7,690,000	9,850,000
Long-term debt	(4,700,000)	(5,370,000)
Stockholders' equity	$14,050,000	$14,650,000

Balance Sheets
December 31, 1976 and 1975
Condensed General Purchasing Power Information
(Alternative Presentation)

	In $ (1976)	
	1976	1975
Net monetary assets (liabilities)		
Current and working items	$ 5,420,000	$ 1,820,000
Long-term debt	(4,700,000)	(5,370,000)
	720,000	(3,550,000)
Nonmonetary assets		
Marketable securities	—	1,920,000
Inventories	5,640,000	6,430,000
Property, plant, and equipment,		
net of depreciation	7,690,000	9,850,000
Stockholders' equity	$14,050,000	$14,650,000

EXHIBIT B

Income Statements
Years Ended December 31, 1976 and 1975
Condensed General Purchasing Power Information

	In $ (1976)	
	1976	1975
Sales	$27,810,000	$32,640,000
Operating profit, after depreciation of		
$2,770 and $3,150	480,000	1,720,000
(Loss) on sales of equipment and securities	(290,000)	(20,000)
Federal income taxes		
On general purchasing power net income	(170,000)	(900,000)
On taxable net income in excess of		
general purchasing power net income	(590,000)	(330,000)
Earnings (loss) from operating transactions	(570,000)	470,000
Net general purchasing power loss,		
exclusive of gain on long-term debt	(200,000)	(20,000)
General purchasing power gain on long-		
term debt	370,000	210,000
Net earnings (loss) for year	(400,000)	660,000
Dividends	(200,000)	(220,000)
Balance added to (deducted from)		
stockholders' equity	(600,000)	440,000
Stockholders' equity—beginning of year	14,650,000	14,210,000
Stockholders' equity—end of year	$14,050,000	$14,650,000
Per share		
Earnings (loss) from operating transactions	$ (x.xx)	$ x.xx
Net earnings (loss) for year	$ (x.xx)	$ x.xx
Dividends	x.xx	x.xx

EXHIBIT C

Reconciliation of Net Income in Units of Money

	1976	1975
Net income per income statement (in historical dollars)	883,000	1,243,000
Increase (decrease) from restatement in dollars of 1976 general purchasing power		
Sales	810,000	2,640,000
Cost of sales	(1,004,000)	(2,225,000)
Depreciation	(700,000)	(840,000)
Other costs and expenses, net	(108,000)	(328,000)
(Losses) on sales of securities and equipment	(451,000)	(20,000)
Net general purchasing power gains on monetary items, including long-term debt	170,000	190,000
Net impact of restatement on results for the year	(1,283,000)	(583,000)
Price-level–adjusted net income (loss) (in dollars of 1976 general purchasing power)	(400,000)	660,000

Exhibit D illustrates certain disclosures that would be made of general purchasing power information, but other disclosures would be required in actual situations, depending on the particular facts and circumstances—for example, see note 3 on page 68 of the FASB exposure draft of December 31, 1974.

EXHIBIT D

Explanatory Note to Supplementary General Purchasing Power Information

The accompanying general purchasing power information, expressed in units of the general purchasing power of the dollar at December 31, 1976, is based on the financial statements in units of money (historical dollars) and should be read in conjunction with them (including the notes). The historical dollar financial statements combine amounts expressed in dollars expended at various times in the past with amounts expressed in dollars expended more recently, regardless of changes in the general purchasing power of the dollar. Amortization of the expenditures of dollars in prior years is deducted from revenues received currently in determining net income. The result is a mixture of dollars that represent various amounts of general purchasing power. In the general purchasing power information, historical amounts have been restated to recognize the reductions that have occurred in the general purchasing power of the dollar (inflation). The amounts originally recorded are restated into units of the general purchasing power of the dollar at December 31, 1976, using the gross national product implicit price deflator (GNP deflator).

General purchasing power restatement does not change the underlying accounting principles; the same principles are used in both the historical dollar financial statements and the general purchasing power information. The latter retains the historical cost basis of accounting; only the unit of account is changed. That is, historical cost is expressed in amounts restated for changes in the general purchasing power of the dollar as measured by the GNP deflator. The restated amounts do not purport to be appraised value, replacement cost, or current value, nor do they purport to be based on prices at which transactions would take place currently. Establishing units of general purchasing power is a process of translation, not of valuation.

Changing to units of general purchasing power should not be confused with reporting the effects of changes in the prices of particular goods and services. Movements in specific prices are caused in part by changes in general purchasing power and in part by various other factors (for example, supply and demand and technological changes). Changes in the general price level may be more or less rapid than, and may even be counter to, changes in specific prices.

Inflation over a period of time has cumulative effects on historical dollar financial statements. The cumulative effect of inflation is particularly significant for long-lived nonmonetary assets such as property, plant, and equipment, shown by the restatement of these items in the supplementary balance sheet information and in the corresponding restatement of depreciation in the supplementary income statement information. Restatement of inventories significantly affects cost of sales. The resulting increases in the amounts at which nonmonetary assets are presented in the balance sheet are not included in income, since they are merely the results of changing the unit of account.

Holders of monetary assets, such as cash and receivables, lose general purchasing power during inflation because monetary assets buy fewer goods and services as the general level of prices rises. Conversely, those who owe monetary liabilities gain general purchasing power during inflation because the liabilities will be payable with dollars that have less general purchasing power than those received when the liabilities were incurred. Information about general purchasing power gain or loss is necessary to evaluate the overall impact of inflation on the results of business operations. The accompanying general purchasing power income statement reflects a general purchasing power loss of $200,000 in 1976 ($20,000 in 1975) due to holding net monetary assets (before deducting gain on long-term debt) and a general purchasing power gain of $370,000 in 1976 ($210,000 in 1975) due to owing long-term debt.

The cumulative effect of inflation disclosed by the restatement of historical units of money to units of general purchasing power includes all the elements discussed in the preceding two paragraphs. The net impact of restatement on results for the years 1976 and 1975 and the relative importance of the various elements of inflationary effect for the years are shown in the reconciliation of net income in units of money with net income in units of December 31, 1976, general purchasing power.

No deferred tax charge or credit has been provided with respect to the restatement of assets or liabilities, since the restatements do not affect income taxes.

Uncondensed Statements

Exhibits E and F present the uncondensed financial statements that served as the basis for exhibits A through D. Exhibits E and F are not part of the proposed supplementary reporting under model A. They are presented solely for guidance and information, to indicate differences in restatement methodology between model A and the FASB exposure draft.

EXHIBIT E

Balance Sheets
December 31, 1976 and 1975

	In $ (1976)	
	1976	1975
Assets		
Current assets		
Cash	$ 3,135,000	$ 3,352,000
Marketable securities		1,920,000
Receivables	6,170,000	5,424,000
Inventories	5,636,000	6,427,000
Prepaid expenses*	42,000	51,000
Total current assets	14,983,000	17,174,000
Property, plant, and equipment	36,197,000	35,738,000
Less depreciation	28,514,000	25,892,000
	7,683,000	9,846,000
Total assets	$22,666,000	$27,020,000
Liabilities and Capital		
Current liabilities		
Deferred income*	$ 50,000	$ 107,000
Accounts payable	2,521,000	5,123,000
Total current liabilities	2,571,000	5,230,000
Deferred income taxes*	1,342,000	1,768,000
Long-term debt	4,700,000	5,370,000
Total liabilities	8,613,000	12,368,000
Common stockholders' equity	$14,053,000	$14,652,000

*   Treated as monetary in model A, nonmonetary in the FASB exposure draft.

EXHIBIT F

Income Statements
Years Ended December 31, 1976 and 1975

	In $ (1976)	
	1976	1975
Sales*	$27,810,000	$32,639,000
Operating expenses		
Cost of sales	21,863,000	24,958,000
Depreciation	2,771,000	3,153,000
Selling and administrative*	2,699,000	2,804,000
	27,333,000	30,915,000
Operating profit	477,000	1,724,000
Gain (loss) on sale of equipment	28,000	(23,000)
Gain (loss) on sale of securities	(320,000)	
Net general purchasing power gain	174,000	193,000
Income before federal income taxes	359,000	1,894,000
Federal income taxes**		
On general net income	172,000	909,000
On taxable net income in excess of general price-level net income	582,000	326,000
	754,000	1,235,000
Net income (loss)	(395,000)	659,000
Stockholders' equity—beginning of year	14,652,000	14,210,000
Dividends	(204,000)	(217,000)
Stockholders' equity—end of year	$14,053,000	$14,652,000

* Deferred component treated as monetary in model A, nonmonetary in the FASB exposure draft.

** Treated as monetary in model A, nonmonetary in the FASB exposure draft.

Model B

Model B is a modification of historical cost to compensate for the most significant effects of inflation.

Features of the Model

The following outlines the features of the model:

- Historical cost remains the primary basis for accounting and financial reporting.
- LIFO is used for inventories.
- Depreciation charged in the income statement is computed on a current cost basis.
  - The current cost of depreciable fixed assets is determined by application of an appropriate index to the historical cost of the assets. The *Handbook of Basic*

Economic Statistics (Bureau of Labor Statistics) and *Engineering News Record Construction Cost Index* illustrate the types of indexes considered suitable.

- Depreciation is computed on the current cost of depreciable assets by using the same rates and lives as now used in computing historical cost depreciation.

- The objective of indexing depreciation should be to approximate current cost depreciation at the lesser of replacement cost or reproduction cost (as those terms are used in SEC replacement cost). Therefore, in approximating both replacement and reproduction cost, only gross capital asset cost should be considered (that is, future savings from labor, maintenance, and so forth, should be ignored).

- The asset side of the balance sheet is not affected except to reflect LIFO inventories.

- Current cost depreciation in excess of historical cost depreciation is credited to a special shareholders' equity account entitled "accumulated current cost depreciation."

- On sale or retirement of a depreciable fixed asset—
  - Gain or loss is computed on the basis of historical cost depreciation.
  - Any amount in the accumulated current cost depreciation account related to the asset sold is transferred to retained earnings.

- Model B is based on a model that was originally developed by proposers who believe that changes in financial accounting to reflect changing prices and inflation should be designed with the possibility of obtaining related changes in income taxes in mind. Although they continue to hold those views, the question of the likelihood of such a change in the tax laws is beyond the purview of this experimentation with financial accounting models. Model B therefore illustrates the treatment under present tax laws, and provides for the consequent tax differences.

- Deferred federal income tax benefits (credits) are provided based on the difference between current cost depreciation and depreciation claimed for tax purposes. After such time as depreciation (as determined at current cost) is equal to historical cost, current cost depreciation would then be charged to the statement of income without tax benefit.

Positions on General Choices

The positions of model B on the choices for a conceptual framework for accounting and reporting described in chapter 2 are the same as those reflected in present practice except for its positions on choices 8, 9, 10, and 12. The positions of model B on those choices are as follows.

Choice 8—Types of changes. The events and changes reported are those reported under present practice, which are mostly confined to changes in quantities of resources or obligations. Changes in the purchase prices of depreciable fixed assets are reflected, but only in determining the amounts of the depreciation charges.

Choice 9—Types of prices. The prices emphasized by model B are the same as those emphasized by present practice, except that current buying prices of depreciable fixed assets are used to determine the amounts of the depreciation charges.

Choice 10—Single measurement basis vs. multiple measurement basis. Model B, like present practice, essentially uses a single measurement basis, emphasizing historical cost. However, depreciation charges are based on current buying prices instead of historical cost.

Choice 12—Starting point to determine income (the "capital maintenance" question). Income should be measured starting with stockholders' equity previously reported, including accumulated current cost depreciation.

Concepts Underlying Model B

Model B incorporates the following views.

- The proposed response to inflation should not be so complex as to eliminate any reasonable chance of acceptance by diverse groups of financial statement users, such as institutional investors, small shareholders, creditors, taxing authorities, and the management and employees of the enterprise.
- Net income should continue to receive the highest priority and should be adjusted to recognize the most material effects of inflation on a company's costs (cost of sales and depreciation).
- Balance sheet valuation can reasonably continue to be based substantially on historical cost, which effectively presents current assets and liabilities as elements of a conservatively portrayed financial position.
- As a partial solution to the problem of inflation, LIFO has the effect of bringing the most recent costs incurred into cost of goods sold to be matched with current revenue dollars; the result is a more understandable net income figure than would otherwise be obtained during a period of inflation.
- During periods of inflation, depreciation on a historical cost basis understates the cost of replacing depreciable property consumed through operations. Furthermore, corporate net income should represent the increase in net assets that a company has obtained through operations and that it can distribute to its shareholders without reducing the company's ability to continue as a going concern at approximately the same scale of activity without obtaining additional capital. During an inflationary period, historical cost depreciation does not measure asset use in current cost terms, so historical cost net income overstates the amount that could be distributed to shareholders if the company is to replace its assets at current prices.

    The solution to those problems is to charge depreciation on a current cost basis. In this way, the depreciation charge more closely reflects the cost of replacing depreciable property and a net income amount more closely approximating the concept of net income described in the preceding paragraph is obtained.

    Model B is based on the assumption that indexes can be established following procedures that are similar to those which the Internal Revenue Service followed in establishing LIFO inventory procedures that are now used by many retail companies. Authorized indexes could be developed for adjustment of depreciation expense following the precedent that has already been established in gaining acceptance for LIFO inventories. Many of the implementation details, which are often quite troublesome in adapting to change, have already been carefully established for LIFO and they could be useful for depreciation.

Deferred Tax Accounting

In addition to deferred tax accounting required under present principles, model B requires deferred tax accounting for the difference between current cost depreciation charged to determine net income and historical cost depreciation charged to determine taxable income. Income tax attributable to the difference is accounted for as a deferred tax benefit (or reduction of deferred tax credit) that accumulates until accumulated current cost depreciation equals the historical cost of the asset. Current cost depreciation is then charged to determine net income without crediting net income for any income tax benefit of depreciation. That treatment reduces the deferred tax benefit related to the asset (or increases the deferred tax credit) until it is eliminated (or until the deferred tax credit for that asset is stated without regard for current cost depreciation).

For purposes of experimenting with model B, companies should determine deferred tax benefits (credits) based on asset groupings that are used for federal income tax purposes. For example, if tax depreciation is determined on an individual asset basis, deferred tax accounting should be similarly based. If composite asset groupings are used, deferred tax benefits (credits) should be based on total accumulated depreciation compared to historical cost of all assets in the groups. Therefore, it is possible that individual assets in a composite group may have deferred tax benefits provided in excess of historical cost, inasmuch as the tax accounting should be based on a comparison of accumulated depreciation and historical cost of all assets in the group. As necessary, experimenters should make reasonable approximations in determining appropriate deferred tax accounting.

The following illustrates deferred tax accounting for differences caused (1) by using straight-line depreciation to determine net income and accelerated depreciation to determine taxable income and (2) by charging current cost depreciation to determine net income and historical cost depreciation to determine taxable income.

Asset acquired for $10,000 and 6 percent annual price increase index at acquisition equals 100). Book depreciation is straight-line; tax depreciation is accelerated; 50 percent assumed tax rate.

Depreciation

Year	Straight-line	Current cost adjustment	Total	Tax depreciation	Difference	Average index
	Book depreciation					
	(1)	*(2) (note 1)*	*(1) + (2) = (3)*	*(4)*	*(3) − (4) = (5)*	
1	$2,000	$ 60	$ 2,060	$ 4,000	$(1,940)	103
2	2,000	180	2,180	2,400	(220)	109
3	2,000	300	2,300	1,440	860	115
4	2,000	420	2,420	1,080	1,340	121
5	2,000	540	2,540	1,080	1,460	127
	$10,000	$1,500	$11,500	$10,000	$ 1,500	

		Depreciation-related income tax expense			Net depreciation-related reduction in net income
Year	Total book depreciation	Currently payable	Deferred	Total	
	(6)	(50%) × (4) = (7)	(8) (note 2)	(7) + (8) = (9)	(3) − (9) = (10)
1	$ 2,060	$2,000	$(970)	$1,030	$1,030
2	2,180	1,200	(110)	1,090	1,090
3	2,300	720	430	1,150	1,150
4	2,420	540	670	1,210	1,210
5	2,540	540	(20)	520	2,020
	$11,500	$5,000	$ −0−	$5,000	$6,500

Note 1. [Book cost depreciation × average index ÷ index of acquisition] − book cost depreciation.

Note 2. Fifty percent of column 5 until such time as total depreciation equals historical cost. Accumulated depreciation through year 4 is $8,960. Remaining historical cost basis is therefore $1,040. Amortization of the deferred tax debit in year 5 is the difference between the tax benefit of allowable tax depreciation, or 50 percent × $1,080 and the tax benefit of remaining historical cost basis or 50 percent × $1,040.

Illustrative Statements

The following simplified illustration presents the essentials of current cost depreciation. It is unrelated to the illustration of deferred tax accounting in the preceding paragraphs. For this illustration, straight-line depreciation is used for both book and tax purposes. A company with the following balance sheet on December 31, 1976, keeps its accounts in accordance with generally accepted accounting principles.

Other assets	$400,000	Other liabilities	$285,000
Properties and		Taxes payable	15,000
equipment	500,000	Shareholders' equity	
Less depreciation	200,000	Capital stock	200,000
	300,000	Retained earnings	200,000
	$700,000		400,000
			$700,000

The company's income statement for 1976 includes the following:

Revenues	$1,000,000
Other costs	850,000
Depreciation	50,000
	900,000
	100,000
Federal income tax	50,000
Net income	$ 50,000

The properties and equipment are being depreciated for both book and tax purposes over ten years using straight-line depreciation, and the cost indices appropriate to those assets have gone up an average of 40 percent since the assets were acquired. The current cost of the assets, therefore, is $700,000, and depreciation at a 10 percent rate for the current year is $70,000.

An income statement for 1976 using current cost depreciation would appear as follows:

Revenues	$1,000,000
Other costs	850,000
Depreciation	70,000
	920,000
	80,000
Federal income tax	
Current payable	50,000
Deferred tax benefit	(10,000)
	40,000
Net income	$ 40,000

This company's year-end balance sheet for 1976 under current cost depreciation would appear as follows:

Other assets	$400,000	Other liabilities	$285,000
Deferred tax benefit	10,000	Taxes payable	15,000
Properties and		Shareholders' equity	
equipment	500,000	Capital stock	200,000
Less depreciation on		Retained earnings	190,000
an historical cost		Accumulated current	
basis	200,000	cost depreciation	20,000
	300,000		410,000
	$710,000		$710,000

4

Models C and D

Models C and D represent more radical departures from the conventional model than models A and B. Assets under model C and assets and liabilities under model D are stated principally at current value and changes in current value are explicitly recognized in the financial statements. Also, the financial statements presented under the two models incorporate concepts not incorporated in financial statements presented under the conventional model.

Model C

Model C is based partially on historical cost and partially on current costs and values to accommodate the impact of inflation and other value changes. It retains the dominance of the recognition and measurement of revenues and expenses over the recognition and measurement of resources and obligations and, for practical reasons, retains certain historical costs, for example, for intangibles and deferred items. The model introduces current costs (principally replacement costs) for items affecting operating results and market values for certain investment assets.

Model C departs from the traditional presentation format by classifying the elements of income determination into operating results and value changes ("holding gains and losses"), reporting the two categories separately, and clearly distinguishing between realized and unrealized value changes. Except for presentation, model C in many respects resembles the models proposed by U.K. Exposure Draft 18 and the Australian provisional standard.

Positions on General Choices

Model C incorporates the following positions on the choices for a conceptual framework for accounting and reporting in chapter 2.

Choice 1—Theory of the entity. The resources and obligations accounted for and income determinations are those of the entity, which is separate from its parties at interest.

Choice 2—Articulation. The financial statements interlock.

Choice 3—Controlling factors for recognition and measurement (revenues and expenses approach vs. resources and obligations approach). Measurement theory is based on the income determination approach, emphasizing the present concept of matching of costs and revenues. Thus, the values used for resources and obligations are those considered most appropriate for this matching. The balance sheet retains items that are not strictly definable as separable resources and obligations (for example, intangibles and deferred costs and credits). In essence, the balance sheet is a link between periodic income determinations and value changes, but nevertheless provides a current value view of liquidity, which is its primary purpose in this orientation.

Choice 4—Individual resources and obligations. The financial statements present aspects of individual resources and obligations of the entity and avoid trying to present the value or prospects of the entity as a whole.

Choice 5—Selection of resources. Balance sheets present (1) resources that are exchangeable separately from the business as a whole and from significant segments of the business and (2) resources that are not separately exchangeable but that are of value to the continuation of the business and significant segments of the business. Group 2 consists principally of intangibles such as purchased goodwill, patents, trademarks, and significant deferred charges.

Choice 6—History. The statements generally portray the history of the enterprise up to and including the balance sheet date and avoid what might have been or what may be estimated to be coming in the future. Current cost determinations may, however, require a certain amount of judgment about the likely future course of events.

Choice 7—Unit of account. The unit of account is defined in terms of units of money. General price level changes are not introduced.

Choice 8—Types of changes. In addition to changes in quantities, changes in prices and values of certain resources are recognized while they are held. However, fixed-dollar obligations are not changed unless actual liquidation takes place or is required at amounts other than historical cost values.

Choice 9—Types of prices. Current prices are emphasized for items that enter into income and determination of value changes. They may be buying or selling prices, depending on the type of resources and their intended use.

Choice 10—Single measurement basis vs. multiple measurement basis. The basis used is related to the present or contemplated use of the asset. That concept requires a multiple measurement basis.

Choice 11—Realized vs. unrealized gains or losses. Gains and losses are recognized when costs, prices, or values change and are reported separately as value changes, distinguishing value changes realized during the period through exchange or operations—for example, depreciation based on replacement cost—from unrealized value changes.

Choice 12—Starting point to determine income (the "capital maintenance" question). The starting point to determine operating income is the stockholders' equity at the beginning of the year adjusted by value changes of operating assets held during the year. The general purchasing power represented by stockholders' equity is ignored as a starting point because it is considered not relevant for determination of the current income of the entity. Valuation of owners' equity is not the objective. Model C has been prepared under the view that users need a better understanding of (1) an entity's current operating results—which can best be determined if the capital assets consumed thereby are maintained or replaced—and (2) the other value changes (realized and unrealized) that have occurred with respect to its resources. Because obligations are normally liquidated in terms of fixed amounts, and general price level changes and market influences infrequently accelerate this process, obligations are not revalued. However, the corporate equity valuations change from year to year as a result of certain asset value changes (as indicated by current prices), and these are recognized. General price level changes are not recognized.

Choice 13—Emphasis of net results. Net operating income, which includes separate presentation of extraordinary items and discontinued operations, is clearly distinguished from nonoperating value changes, realized and unrealized. Net results accordingly are presented in three statements plus a balance sheet and statement of changes in financial position.

Concepts Underlying the Model

The preceding section on choices defines the basic concepts underlying model C. They require elaboration, particularly since they influence the measurement of values that enter into the determination of operating results and nonoperating value changes.

Value to the Business and Deprival Value

Model C incorporates the view that the present use or management's intended use of resources in the business should have a bearing on the valuations assigned to the resources. The concept of "value to the business" (sometimes called "deprival value") is closely compatible with model C. This valuation concept is that the value ascribed to a resource in a balance sheet should be the amount by which the business would be poorer if it were suddenly deprived of the resource at the balance sheet date. (In the case of depreciable assets the "gross" deprival value is also the basis for calculating depreciation charges.) The emphasis is on current prices at the balance sheet date and on management's intentions concerning use of the assets.

If a resource is one that management would replace in the ordinary course of business, its deprival value is the net replacement cost. If the resource is one that management cannot or will not replace in the ordinary course of business, the value to the business is the higher of (a) discounted present value of cash flows—assuming that the resource will be used until it is exhausted and (b) current net realizable value in an orderly disposition. Since determination of discounted present value may be impracticable or impossible, the current net realizable value may be the only available information to use for valuing the resource.

Those general propositions about resource valuation can be further described in relation to specific categories, including related tax accounting considerations.

Assets Held for Use

Assets Representing Sources of Liquidity. Assets such as accounts receivable, notes receivable, and marketable securities are generally stated at current net realizable value at the balance sheet date. Notes receivable due after one year are valued at their discounted present value using the market interest rate at the balance sheet date; the value is an estimate of current net realizable value. If liquidation would result in a tax liability, for example, capital gains tax on sale of a marketable security, the tax is deducted.

Plant and Equipment. Problems of valuation of plant and equipment are reviewed in more detail in "Tangible Property" in this list and in chapter 5.

Intangible Assets. Assets such as deferred charges, patents, trademarks, licensing agreements, leaseholds, franchises, and goodwill should theoretically be valued at current cost under model C, preferably at appropriate replacement cost, because these assets presumably have value to the business as long as it is a going concern. However, current replacement costs for most intangible assets cannot be reasonably estimated. These assets arise out of unique circumstances of time and place, developmental effort, scientific expertise, specific negotiations, personal services, and economic conditions that can seldom be simulated in other times and contexts for the purpose of measuring current cost. Such assets generally cannot be purchased, replaced, reproduced, sold separately from the business as a whole or from significant segments of the business, or valued by identifiable cash flows.

For practical reasons and because full disclosure can minimize this measurement imperfection, a general rule of valuing intangible assets at historical cost is acceptable, except for circumstances in which replacement cost or current net realizable value can be reasonably determined.

Assets Held for Disposal

Inventories. Inventories, in the form of raw materials, work in process, and finished goods are normally stated at the lower of current replacement cost and current net realizable value.

Surplus Property. Property specifically designated by the company for sale may be in the form of marketable securities, land, building, whole plants, and so forth. Once property is so designated, it is carried at current net realizable value. Determination of the value of some property, such as securities or property for which an offer has been received, is not difficult. For other items, realizable values may be uncertain in an early stage of sales negotiations, and an estimate has to be made based on the best information available at the balance sheet date.

Noncurrent Investments

Noncurrent investments include certain types of property investments, investments in affiliates less than majority-owned, long-term notes and mortgages, as well as securities. Assets in the noncurrent category rarely include assets that could readily serve as sources of the firm's liquidity (that is, are readily marketable at realistically determinable prices).

Fixed Return Securities. Securities with fixed returns, terms, and maturity values, for example, bonds, long-term receivables, and most mortgages, are stated at net realizable value (excluding latent taxes); unrealized gains and losses and any subsequent unrealized value changes are not recognized in current operating income. Such value changes, if any, are presented in a separate statement of value changes. This treatment restricts the income measurement to the cash return. However, all securities that are readily marketable are carried as current assets representing sources of liquidity.

Securities Having Significant Equity Characteristics. Securities having significant equity characteristics or otherwise outside fixed return securities are stated at realizable values (excluding latent taxes) on the balance sheet date. Gains and losses from one measurement date to another are recognized in the separate statement of value changes.

Securities Providing Significant Influence Over Another Entity. Securities providing significant influence over another entity (for example, 20% interest or more) are valued by using the equity method of accounting. This may be the best way to cope with the fact that securities may or may not have a quoted price and, even if they do, that the quoted price might not represent one obtainable by the enterprise. The investee's financial statements should be prepared in accordance with model C.

Tangible Property. Property such as real estate may be operated for current income or held for price appreciation or both. To be consistent with the treatment of other noncurrent investments discussed above, such properties should also be stated at market value, that is, current net realizable value (excluding latent taxes). However, tangible properties may also have operating characteristics for which valuation at replacement cost, like plant and equipment, might be appropriate.

For property operated for current returns, the operating characteristics viewpoint appears to be more consistent with the classification of tangible property as a noncurrent investment. Therefore, current cost is determined using appropriate replacement cost, subject to the same value to the business consideration of net present value and current net realizable value as for assets in general. The appropriate valuation for tangible property that does not produce current rents, royalties, and so forth, is current net realizable value (excluding latent taxes).

Accounting for Income Taxes

Interperiod income tax allocations are provided in model C, but the nature of the allocations differs from that presently found in conventional financial statements.

Presenting Assets at Current Net Realizable Value. The concept of asset valuation provides the rationale for recognizing income tax effects. For assets that purport to be sources of liquidity, financial statements should disclose the dollar amounts that might be realized at the balance sheet date should those assets be converted in a taxable exchange. Since the goal is to present liquidity position, there must be a presumption that the conversion of assets such as marketable securities and property held for disposition will occur in a taxable exchange, in other words, that the assets will be converted into cash.

The implied tax effect is incorporated in the valuation of the asset, since it is an integral element of current net realizable value. There is no "deferred credit" because creation of such a credit might suggest a liability that does not exist at the balance sheet date. A consistent treatment for assets held in a tax loss position ("deferred debits") would be appropriate, provided that there is reason to believe that a tax benefit could be realized.

Reversible Timing Differences. Reversible timing differences may arise with respect to accounting for depreciable assets. The problems of accounting for timing differences will persist, regardless of the cost measurement used for financial accounting purposes, as long as tax accounting adheres to historical cost or as long as allocation methods used for financial and tax purposes, for example, straight-line or accelerated methods, may differ.

Current cost accounting, however, introduces the feature of a different asset base, for example, replacement cost, which compounds the problems of income tax accounting. If the current cost of an asset differs from historical cost, the difference between depreciation for taxes and for financial accounting may include elements of difference in both valuation and allocation methods.

Current replacement costs may rise and fall unpredictably in different periods, causing depreciation charges for financial statements to be more or less than allowable tax deductions. A systematic allocation of the tax benefit (somewhat along the lines presently used in historical cost accounting) is used to accomplish a better matching of income tax expense with income before taxes.

To illustrate how this method of tax allocation differs from model B, assume the same set of facts given in that model in chapter 3. The depreciation tax benefits are accounted for as follows.

Year	Current (replacement) cost depreciation per statement*	Tax depreciation taken (accelerated)	Tax benefit derived 50% × (2)	Tax benefit deferred [$1000 − (3)]	Cumulative deferred taxes [(4) cumulative]	Net depreciation charge (net effect) to operating income
	(1)	(2)	(3)	(4)	(5)	(6)
1	$ 2,060	$ 4,000	$2,000	($1,000)	($1,000)	$1,060
2	2,180	2,400	1,200	(200)	(1,200)	1,180
3	2,300	1,440	720	280	(920)	1,300
4	2,420	1,080	540	460	(460)	1,420
5	2,540	1,080	540	460	–0–	1,540
	$11,500	$10,000	$5,000	–0–	–0–	$6,500

* This column is the same as column 3 on the first schedule of the illustration in model B.

Deferred credits and charges arising from the allocations are preferably reflected as allowances related to the balance sheet measurements of the assets rather than deferred credits or charges. However, whether deferred income taxes are shown "net" against the related asset or "broad" is not central to model C concepts.

Differences That May or May Not Reverse. Model C creates some unique differences between tax methods and financial accounting methods. Some may reverse and some may not, depending on current costs to be determined in the future.

Cost of goods sold based on replacement cost may be different from that based on historical cost, and this relationship may be perpetual as long as prices continue to change in the same direction. Each annual difference may eventually reverse, but only if future prices reverse. Predictions of future price changes should not be used to justify treating a current difference as a reversible timing difference; thus, differences relating to cost of goods sold are considered permanent and not subject to income tax allocation accounting.

Latent Tax Effects.   Asset valuations in the statement of financial position may differ from both the historical cost and the tax basis as a result of accounting for the current costs of the assets. The implied tax effect is recognized in the cost of assets held as sources of liquidity for reasons explained under "Presenting Assets at Net Realizable Value" above and in other cases in which the valuations purport to present current net realizable value. However, no other latent tax effects are accounted for in the statement of financial position. For example, the tax effect of the difference between current replacement cost of a plant and the tax basis is not accounted for as a valuation adjustment to the asset because the valuation does not purport to be a current net realizable value; nor is there a deferred tax credit, because there exists no liability-like amount.

The only tax effect adjustments that might be accounted for related to assets are (1) those that arise from predictable reversible depreciation deduction differences, (2) those relating to presentation of current net realizable value, and (3) other reversible timing differences as they would be treated under present accounting practice.

Financial Statements

The financial statements presented for model C, exhibits A through E, consist of a statement of operating income, a statement of value changes, a statement of realized value changes, a statement of financial position (balance sheet), and a statement of changes in financial position.

Statement of Operating Income.   The statement of operating income is limited to the usual commercial operations of a company, segmented by product lines if necessary. It follows the traditional format, except that current replacement costs are used for calculating cost of goods sold and depreciation (straight-line method) to match costs with current revenue and thereby provide an estimate of income available for distribution—dividends after allowance for interest and taxes—without impairment of the capital asset base. Dividends are deducted from the equivalent of distributable income, assuming no other losses, and the statement concludes with a presentation of retained operating income. Nonrecurring, nonoperating types of gains and losses other than those presently known as "extraordinary items" appear in the other statements. Extraordinary items, including charges or credits resulting from discontinued operations and accounting changes, are deducted from net operating income —continuing operations (before extraordinary items) to arrive at net operating income.

EXHIBIT A

Current Cost Company
Statement of Operating Income
Year Ended December 31, 1976

Sales		$8,000
Operating costs		
Cost of goods sold (replacement cost)		4,180
General and administrative expenses		3,086
Depreciation (replacement cost)		320
		7,586
Operating income before interest and income taxes		414
Interest on debt—$96, less investment income—$26		70
Income taxes		
On current cost income	$165	
On taxable income in excess of current cost income	125	290
		360
Net operating income—continuing operations (before extraordinary items)*		54
Retained operating income		
Balance January 1, 1976		4,200
		4,254
Dividends*		154
Balance December 31, 1976		$4,100

*   These figures are also expressed on a per-share basis.

Statement of Value Changes.   The statement of value changes presents changes in the value of specific assets other than those that result from transactions reported in the statement of operating income. Changes in the buying or selling prices of an entity's resources result from one or both of the following: (1) changes in the general purchasing power of the unit of money and (2) changes caused by changes in supply or demand for specific resources.

The model is based on the view that it is difficult, if not impossible in some cases, to unscramble the mix of these two causes of price changes; therefore, no such attempt is made. For each type of resource, the measure of value considered appropriate is used, principally current replacement cost or current net realizable value, although for pragmatic reasons some historical costs are retained.

Value changes, sometimes referred to as "holding gains and losses" (not in model C), may be either realized or unrealized and have varying characteristics and impacts. For example, the change in the replacement value of a plant that is not intended to be sold but consumed through operations creates a value change (which recognizes backlog depreciation) that is different from the value change of a marketable security, which is unrealized unless a sale has taken place, and which may occur for a variety of reasons. The statement specifies value changes that are realized and those that are not; the accumulations of the various classes of unrealized and realized value changes are carried forward into two separate capital accounts.

EXHIBIT B

Current Cost Company
Statement of Value Changes
Year Ended December 31, 1976

	Marketable securities	Long-term investments	Inventory	Plant and equipment	Land	Total
Balance, unrealized value changes, January 1, 1976	$ 7	$ 180	$ 30	$1,100	$1,000	$2,317
Net value increases (decreases) for the year	49	(100)	130	420	328	827
Realized during the year (exhibit C)	56	80	160	1,520	1,328	3,144
Net (gains) losses realized through sale	11	(40)	—	0	0	(29)
Capital maintenance allowances recovered through operations*	0	0	(142)	(120)	0	(262)
	11	(40)	(142)	(120)	0	(291)
Balance, unrealized value changes, December 31, 1976	$67	$ 40	$ 18	$1,400	$1,328	$2,853

* Capital maintenance allowances recovered through operations are the differences between deductions for cost of sales and depreciation based on current costs (for example, replacement costs) and what the deductions would have been had they been based on historical cost.

Note: Marketable securities are carried at net realizable values; unrealized value changes related to them are shown net of income taxes that would become due on realization of those values. All other changes are *not* net of latent taxes, which would be approximately $693 and $836 at December 31, 1975, and 1976, respectively, if the assets were realized in exchanges taxable at a capital gains rate of 30 percent.

Statement of Realized Value Changes. Value changes that are realized through exchange transactions or operations are also shown in a separate statement of realized value changes and accumulated in a separate capital account. Ordinarily, an investor would not look to this accumulation as a source of dividends, except to the extent that the value changes resulted from gains caused by changes in the supply or demand for specific resources and were not needed for reinvestment.

EXHIBIT C

Current Cost Company
Statement of Retained Realized Value Changes
Year Ended December 31, 1976

Balance January 1, 1976*		$ 0
Capital maintenance allowances recovered from operations		262
Capital gains (losses) on exchanges of marketable securities (net of tax)		(11)
Capital gains (losses) on exchanges of other assets	$40	
Less related income taxes	12	28
		279
Balance December 31, 1976		$279

* Assumed starting point for new concept—hence a zero balance.

Statement of Financial Position (Balance Sheet). Because, among other reasons, accounting under model C emphasizes the matching of current costs with current revenues and because diverse measurement methods including historical costs and some incomplete allocations are applied to assets and liabilities in that determination, balance sheets cannot be used to determine the current net worth of a business. They do, however, provide information considered adequate and values considered relevant for all items carried forward so that an investor can assess liquidity, viability, continuity, and prospects for future development. In essence, balance sheets become connecting links between periodic business income statements.

EXHIBIT D

Current Cost Company
Statement of Financial Position
December 31, 1976

Assets and Deferred Costs

Current assets

Cash		$ 1,033
Accounts receivable (net)		1,020
Marketable securities, at cost	$ 564	
Valuation adjustments to market (net of taxes)	67	631
Inventories, at cost (FIFO)	1,362	
Valuation adjustment to replacement cost	18	1,380
Total current assets		4,064
Long-term investment securities, at cost	1,200	
Valuation adjustment to current cost estimate	40	1,240

Plant and equipment

Land, at cost	1,980	
Valuation adjustment to current cost estimate	1,300	3,280
Plant and equipment, at cost	4,000	
Accumulated depreciation on cost	(2,000)	
Valuation adjustment to net replacement cost	1,400	3,400
Total plant and equipment		6,680

Other assets and deferred costs

Land held for disposition, at cost	20	
Valuation adjustment to net realizable value estimate	28	48
Prepaid expenses, at cost		44
Patents, at cost—less amortization		66
Goodwill, at cost—less amortization		290
Total other assets and deferred costs		448
Total assets and deferred costs		$12,432

Liabilities, Deferred Income, and Equity

Current liabilities	$ 1,000
Long-term debt, 8% due 1989	1,200
Total liabilities	2,200

Corporate equity

Contributed capital, common stock	3,000
Retained operating income (exhibit A)	4,100
Retained realized value changes since January 1, 1976 (exhibit C)	279
Unrealized value changes (exhibit B)	2,853
	10,232
Total liabilities, deferred income, and equity	$12,432

Statement of Changes in Financial Position.   The statement of changes in financial position traces the sources and uses of financial resources (working capital), indicating in detail the causes of the increase or decrease in net current assets. It is based on present concepts.

EXHIBIT E

Current Cost Company
Statement of Changes in Financial Position
Year Ended December 31, 1976

Sources of Current Financial Resources
Revenues

Sales	$8,000
Investment income	26
Proceeds from sale of long-term investments and other property	640
Increase in net realizable value of marketable securities	44
Increase in replacement cost valuation of inventories	130
	8,840

Uses of Current Financial Resources

Current cost of goods sold	4,180
General and administrative expenses	3,086
Interest	96
Income taxes	297
Dividends	154
	7,813
Increase (decrease) in net current financial resources	$1,027

Model D

Model D represents a financial accounting model of completely new design rather than a modification of the model inherent in present practice. Its main features are the dominance of the recognition and measurement of resources and obligations over the recognition and measurement of revenues and expenses and its use of current values.

Positions on General Choices

Model D incorporates the following positions on the choices for a conceptual framework for accounting and reporting discussed in chapter 2.

Choice 1—Theory of the entity.   The resources and obligations accounted for are those of the entity, which is separate from its parties at interest. The perspective of the shareholders and users is reflected in the treatment of shareholders' equity.

Choice 2—Articulation.   The financial statements interlock.

Choice 3—Controlling factors for recognition and measurement (revenues and expenses approach vs. resources and obligations approach).   Measurement theory starts by determining the resources and obligations that should be recognized and determining their measurement, and those determinations dominate the recognition and measurement of revenues and expenses.

Choice 4—Individual resources and obligations.   The financial statements present aspects of individual resources and obligations of the entity and avoid trying to present the value or prospects of the entity as a whole.

Choice 5—Selection of resources.   The balance sheet presents only those resources that are exchangeable separately from the business as a whole and from significant segments of the business.

Choice 6—History.   The financial statements generally portray the history of the enterprise up to and including the balance sheet date and avoid what might have been or what may be estimated to be coming in the future. Current valuations may require a certain amount of judgment about the likely future course of events.

Choice 7—Unit of account.   Except for a few items, the unit of account is defined in terms of units of money.

Choice 8—Types of changes.   In addition to changes in quantities, changes in prices of both resources and obligations are recognized while the resources are held and the obligations are owed.

Choice 9—Types of prices.   Current prices are emphasized. They should be buying or selling prices, depending on the type of resource and its intended use.

Choice 10—Single measurement basis vs. multiple measurement basis.   The basic measurement concept relates the basis used to the value of the asset in its present or contemplated use. That concept requires a multiple measurement basis.

Choice 11—Realized vs. unrealized gains or losses.   Gains and losses are recognized when prices change and are reported as value changes, with supplementary disclosure of value changes realized during the period.

Choice 12—Starting point to determine income (the "capital maintenance" question).   The starting point for determining the change in stockholders' equity exclusive of dealings with owners is stockholders' equity at the beginning of the year as reported (in dollars) adjusted for changes in the general purchasing power of the dollar during the year, exclusive of transactions with owners. (To exclude transactions with owners, those transactions must be restated for changes in the general purchasing power of the dollar from their dates to the year-end.)

Choice 13—Emphasis of net results.   Changes in stockholders' equity are all presented in a single statement to avoid emphasizing or playing down specific types of changes. Related types of change are presented together. A subtotal is presented of all changes other than those resulting from transactions with owners.

Concepts Underlying the Model

The preceding section on choices provides some of the concepts that underlie model D. Other concepts involve the respective roles of the preparers and users of the information and valuation of resources and obligations.

Respective Roles of Preparers and Users.   The present historical cost financial accounting system has developed a certain balance between the presentation of information and the presentation of preparers' interpretations and evaluations, both of which are considered useful by users of the financial statements in making decisions. Preparers' interpretations and evaluations include, for example, the expected lives of long-lived assets, the salability of inventories, the collectibility of receivables, the composition of the items of change that should be collectively identified as net income, and the calculations of earnings per share amounts based on various assumptions.

Model D shifts the balance to entrust the users with more responsibility to interpret and evaluate the information provided and to require less interpretation and evaluation by the preparers. To help the users make their interpretations and evaluations, model D tends to provide more data, for example, the amounts spent on discretionary items such as research and development costs. Various kinds of changes in resources and obligations are listed and described separately, and the users rather than the preparers are expected to judge their implications for the prospects of the enterprise. One interpretation by preparers is added, however. Operating income is derived and presented, which is intended to be an index to the enterprise's long-term earning capacity.

Valuation of Resources and Obligations.   Model D is based on the view that the measurements included in financial statements of economic resources and obligations, results of operations, and changes in net resources should be based on current values. Accordingly, an objective of model D is to present the current value of each separable economic resource and economic obligation of the entity. However, the model is not based on acceptance of any one of the rationales that have been presented in support of specific approaches to current value, such as current reproduction cost, current replacement cost, or exit value. Model D has been designed to encourage experimentation in the practical application of the varying approaches to current value to obtain insights that will contribute to the formulation of a current value concept that is both useful and practical in the preparation of financial statements.

Model D is also based on the view that the particular method of valuation used for each individual resource and obligation depends on the nature of the business, management's intentions, and practicality of application. Accordingly, all of the principal approaches to current value—present value of future cash flows, current replacement costs, and net realizable value—can be considered in making the valuations. The table in the following section sets forth as bases for assigning amounts to specific types of resources and obligations the approaches that in the design of model D appeared most likely to be useful at the present time. However, experimentation could well indicate that variations in valuation of specific resources and obligations from those indicated in the table would be appropriate. The discussion of replacement cost in chapter 5 is not an essential part of model D, but insofar as the concepts relate to the valuation of productive capacity, they are generally compatible with the objectives of model D.

Bases for Assigning Amounts to Specific Types of Resources and Obligations

Model D incorporates the following bases for assigning amounts to resources and obligations:

Cash
Amount.

Current accounts and notes receivable
Collectible amounts.

Marketable securities
Current net realizable value.

Inventories
Lower of current replacement cost and net realizable value.

Prepaid expenses
Replacement cost (usually at historical cost for convenience).

Investments in affiliates
Equity method applied to financial statements on the basis of the model.

Noncurrent accounts and notes receivable
Discounted present value of collectible amounts.

Idle land and facilities
Current net realizable value.

Land in use
Current net realizable value.

Buildings and structures, machinery and equipment
Current replacement cost (computed net of discounted cost savings) for items the enterprise would replace; current net realizable value for items the enterprise would not replace.

Capitalized lease rights
Same valuation basis as for owned resources of same type.

Accumulated depreciation
Allocated portion of current replacement cost using straight-line method over estimated life in years or units of production.

Patents, copyrights, and so forth
Current net realizable value if the rights are transferable and have a market; otherwise at zero.

Goodwill
Zero.

Deferred tax debits or credits; latent tax debits or credits
The tax effect of the difference between the amount of a resource or obligation as carried in the balance sheet and its tax basis is treated as an element in valuation; the tax effect is deducted from or added to the gross amount of the resource or obligation as a valuation account on the face of the balance sheet; the changes in the valuation accounts are included in the valuation portion of the statement of changes in stockholders' equity.

Deferred charges
Zero unless the item clearly fits into another caption in this list.

Current and accrued payables
Amounts.

Long-term debt
Balance sheet obligations at the amounts that would be required to liquidate the obligations currently. The change during the period in the amounts required to liquidate the obligations currently should be analyzed in the statement of changes

in shareholders' equity into (1) the amounts attributable to a change in the market rate of interest based on the change in the market interest rate on obligations of the rating at which the obligations were rated at the beginning of the period and (2) the amounts attributable to changes in ratings of the obligations during the period. The interest expense component of operating income is computed at the average market rate for the year applied to the average carrying amount.

Capitalized lease obligations
Discounted.

Future service obligations (warranties)
Estimated amounts required, discounted only if dates incurred can be estimated and are more than one year after balance sheet date.

Pension obligations
See discussion below.

Pension Obligations

Under model D, unfunded accrued pension obligations are shown on the balance sheet as an obligation (liability). Accordingly, a determination of the "accrued pension obligation" and of the "value of the pension trust fund," if any, is necessary at each balance sheet date. The differences between those two amounts is the unfunded accrued pension obligation.

The pension fund should be valued at current values at the balance sheet date, which involves using quoted market value for all marketable securities and the best approximation of market value for securities for which no quoted market is available.

Accrued pension obligations should include the actuarial determination of the present value of all vested benefits as well as the present value of earned but unvested benefits of all covered persons employed at the balance sheet date. Under the concepts employed in model D, accrued benefits should be based on the employee's pay and service history at the date of the balance sheet and should not include any projection as to future service or advancement nor should it take into account future cost of living adjustments. Assumptions as to mortality, turnover, and so forth, and an appropriate interest rate used to discount all amounts to the balance sheet date, would of course have to be made. The objective should be to determine the present value of accrued benefits at the balance sheet date without making forecasts as to future changes in the composition of the work force or in compensation levels.

The task force recognizes that the actuarial determinations that most companies have available are based on funding considerations and may not necessarily be, in concept, fully in accord with the above requirements. It is not intended that new actuarial determinations be made for the purpose of applying model D unless a company desires to do so. It would be appropriate to use whatever data are available making, where possible, approximate adjustments to bring them into line with the above concepts.

In the statement of changes in stockholders' equity, the change in the unfunded accrued pension obligation should be presented as follows:

1. The net increase in the excess of accrued pension obligations over the value of the pension fund, from the beginning to the end of the year, excluding (a) the effect of plan amendments, (b) changes in actuarial assumptions, (c) changes in aggregate value of the pension fund (excluding administrative expenses), and

(d) the employer contribution, should be shown as a change in results of operations.
2. The changes due to plan amendments should be shown in unusual events and transactions.
3. The effects of changes in actuarial assumptions and the changes in value of the pension fund should be shown in value changes (separately identified).

Under the above approach, administrative expenses paid by the trust fund and expenses paid directly by the company should be included in results of operations.

All earnings on trust fund assets (interest, dividends, and so forth) as well as both realized and unrealized gains and losses on investments flow through value changes.

In unusual cases in which the value of the trust fund exceeds the accrued pension obligation, the net excess should be shown as an asset in the balance sheet but should be carefully labeled to indicate that it is restricted to the payment of pension obligations.

Illustrative Financial Statements

Model D provides that all changes during the year that affected shareholders' equity appear in a single statement of changes in shareholders' equity. The statement consists of sections on results of ordinary operations, unusual transactions and events, value changes, and transactions with shareholders. Exhibit A illustrates a statement of shareholders' equity, with typical items included, exhibit B illustrates a statement of financial position, and exhibit C illustrates a statement of cash flows.

EXHIBIT A

Current Value Company
Statement of Changes in Shareholders' Equity
Year Ended December 31, 1976

Results of ordinary operations			
Sales		$ 6,500	
Cost of sales (at current cost at date of sale)		(3,200)	
Depreciation (at average current cost, straight-line method, no catch-up depreciation)		(207)	
Operating expenses (at amounts paid or accrued)		(2,591)	
Pensions (normal cost)		(76)	
Interest expense (at current market rate)		(47)	
Research and development costs		(115)	
Interest and dividends earned		10	
Equity in result of ordinary operations of affiliates		78	
Income taxes related to operations			
On current cost results	$112		
On taxable results in excess of current cost results	191	(303)	49

Continued on next page

Current Value Company
Statement of Changes in Shareholders' Equity
Year Ended December 31, 1976

Unusual transactions and events		
Discontinued operations	(130)	
Cost of acquiring goodwill	(85)	
Casualty losses	(20)	
Gain on sale of affiliate	33	
Equity in unusual items of affiliates (net)	13	
Change in prior service pension obligation due to plan amendment	19	
Income taxes related to unusual items	(42)	(212)
Value changes (net of income taxes)		
Change in market value of marketable securities while held	10	
Change in current cost of inventories while held	300	
Change in current cost of depreciable resources and land while held	146	
Equity in value changes of affiliates	34	
Changes in obligations due to interest rate changes while owed		
General market change element	(46)	
Risk change element	14	
Change in market value of pension fund portfolio	(89)	
Adjustment of pension obligation because of changes in actuarial assumptions	15	
Foreign currency translation adjustments	(29)	355
Amount required to recognize effect on shareholders' equity of increase in the general price level during the year		(82)
		110
Shareholders' equity at beginning of year		880
Capital stock issued		105
Dividends paid		(53)
Shareholders' equity at end of year		$1,042

EXHIBIT B

Current Value Company
Statement of Financial Position
December 31, 1976

Resources

Current assets

Cash		$ 35
Marketable securities		100
Accounts receivable		125
Inventories		950
		1,210
Investment in affiliates at equity		430
Depreciable property and land at current value	$1,591	
Less accumulated depreciation and imputed income tax	(671)	920
		$2,560

Obligations

Current liabilities

Bank loans	$ 155
Accounts payable and accruals	200
Accrued income taxes	185
Current portion of debt	210
	750
Long-term debt	560
Pension commitments	124
Finance-lease commitments	84
Stockholders' equity	1,042
	$2,560

EXHIBIT C

Current Value Company
Statement of Cash Flows
Year Ended December 31, 1976

Recurring Operations

Cash provided by recurring operations

Collections from customers	$5,950
Interest and investment income	15
	5,965

Cash used in recurring operations

Payments for materials and supplies	1,396
Wages, salaries, and fringe benefits	2,073
Payments for purchased services	2,023
Interest expense	12
Income taxes	75
	5,579
Net cash provided (used) by recurring operations	386

Other Sources and Uses of Cash

Cash provided by

Marketable securities sold, less purchases	100
Sale of depreciable property and land	438
Sale of interest in affiliate	224
Increase in short-term borrowing	75
Proceeds of long-term borrowing	106
Sale of capital stock	100
	1,043

Cash used for

Purchase of property, plant, and equipment	575
Repayment of long-term debt	50
Dividends to shareholders	50
Purchase of goodwill	85
	760
Total cash provided	$ 669

5

Replacement Cost Under Models C and D

Calculation of the replacement cost of assets—particularly property, plant, and equipment—is an important feature of models C and D. This chapter elaborates on the concepts underlying that calculation, which were briefly described in chapter 4. A comparison is made between calculation of replacement cost under models C and D and calculation of replacement cost under SEC Accounting Series Release no. 190 and the SEC Staff Accounting Bulletins that interpret ASR 190.

Productive Capacity as the General Rule

Replacement cost concepts generally rely on the premise that there is a need to maintain, and ultimately replace, the productive capacity presently in operation. No clear and unambiguous definition of productive capacity exists, but a good starting point is in terms of units of output (or throughput) per year for a number of years of useful life. Whether theoretical (maximum) capacity or practical capacity should be used is explored in this experimentation with financial statement models, and it particularly explores the question of whether one definition produces valuations different from the other.

Productive capacity may be replaceable with physical assets virtually identical to the ones presently held. If so, the gross replacement cost is the current buying and installing cost of the physical assets, provided the cost of obtaining and installing a modern asset is not lower. The replacement cost is thus the same as the reproduction or repurchase cost, but this equality holds only for replacement with virtually identical assets that are economically viable. The economic viability criterion is that replacement with the older technology would be profitable (though not necessarily optimally so) and that the new technology is not clearly preferable, for example, because it is largely untried. If, however, the old technology becomes unavailable or uneconomic, current replacement cost should be determined by reference to modern assets that would provide equivalent productive capacity.

Some productive capacity may not be replaceable in any way—neither by reproduction of existing assets nor by replacement of assets with similar capabilities. Also, management may decide to discontinue a line of business or a productive operation causing concepts of replacement of productive capacity to be irrelevant in the circumstances. Replacement cost cannot in either case be said to exist. The value to the business of the asset held becomes the higher of discounted present value or current net realizable value, as discussed in chapter 4.

Productive capacity may be replaceable with physical assets that have technological characteristics different from those presently held. Improved machines may perform the same operations but more rapidly, with less maintenance, more efficiently with respect to operating costs or scale of production, or with a useful life longer than previously available (or a combination of those changes). Improved machines may have prices equal to, greater than, or less than the older machines.

In applying the new prices, therefore, consideration must be given to differences in capacity, asset lives, and operating costs.

Capacity

If replacement assets have significantly greater capacity, adjustment for the difference in capacity is accomplished by applying the fraction of existing capacity divided by the reference capacity (that is, the capacity of the replacement assets). For example, the replacement asset package may be capable of producing 10,000 units a year and current capacity is 5,000 units a year. However, the reference capacity used in the denominator should not exceed output quantities that could profitably be used by the enterprise.

Asset Lives

The replacement asset may have a useful life of thirty years whereas the older technology still in use has a total expected life of twenty years. Total capacity is a function of both output per year and useful life in years. Thus, if replacement assets have useful lives that differ materially from the existing assets, an adjustment somewhat similar to that discussed above is necessary.[1]

Operating Costs

Technological change may change not only the specifications of equipment, but may modify the production process as well and thus change the material, labor, or overhead costs of using the equipment. An extreme example of such a change is the transformation of a production process from labor intensive to capital intensive. The capital expenditure to obtain a nonidentical, modern replacement asset may then exceed the capital expenditure to obtain an identical asset, but the total unit cost of production over its life may be lower.

In general, improved technology gives rise to expectations of future cost savings that could be realized on replacement of productive capacity with the technologi-

---

1.   The relative utility to a company of two assets that have different useful lives may not be proportional to their useful lives. The relative utility may be measured by the ratio of an annuity of one for a period equal to the useful life of one asset to an annuity of one for a period equal to the useful life of the other asset.

cally superior asset. Significant problems arise in connection with accounting for the future cost savings expected from replacement with improved technology.

There are at least four possible ways of accounting for expected cost savings.

1. *Ignore them.* Account for the replacement cost of the new assets for balance sheet presentation and as a basis for calculating depreciation. The thought underlying this alternative is to obtain a measure of the equipment cost alone, thus providing depreciation charges approximately equivalent to amounts required for future asset replacements.

2. *Take cost savings into account directly.* A depreciation charge is determined on the same basis as in alternative 1. The difference is that the other costs (for example, direct labor, overhead, material usage) are determined as if the new equipment had been used during the period. This amounts to a pro forma accounting for many kinds of production costs and pro forma net results of operations as if the new technology had been used rather than the old.

3. *Take cost savings into account through adjustment of the replacement cost of the asset(s).* Under this method the gross buying and installing price of the replacement assets is reduced by the discounted present value of the expected future cost savings. This net amount is the gross replacement cost on the balance sheet and the basis for calculating depreciation. The actual cost of labor, materials, and overhead for the current period is used.

4. *Account for the old technology.* The lower of the equipment replacement cost of (*a*) the old technology still in use, so long as it is available, ignoring the expected cost savings, and (*b*) the new technology is accounted for according to alternative 1 described above. Accounting for the old technology produces a matching of current cost of the technology in use, but ignores expectations or plans, if any, about actual future replacement. Accounting for the lower equipment cost of new technology takes cost savings into account to the extent that they are reflected in lower prices of assets.

Cost savings as described in alternative 3 above may be a composite of many cost differences, and in some extreme cases may even be net increases (usually offset by greater capacity). Some elements of cost difference may be increases, for example, property taxes and other overhead, as well as decreases, for example, labor. One element of difference that may be considered is the cost of capital for the difference in capital expenditure required to obtain a nonidentical replacement as opposed to an identical replacement. Opinions vary on this subject since capital costs are not yet included in present accounting although their inclusion has been proposed.

The elements of cost difference should be extended at prices prevailing at the valuation date. An argument can be made that estimated future prices should be used, but this introduces additional forecasting uncertainties as well as some conceptual problems, and that basis has been rejected for model C and D purposes.

Several possibilities exist for selecting a discount rate, including an enterprise's marginal long-term borrowing rate, an enterprise's internal rate of expected return on new capital investments, and an arbitrary rate that could be applied by all companies, such as the prime rate. Some may believe that the net differences should not be discounted at all. For model C and D purposes, the rate of return expected on new assets should be used.

Adjustment Formula

The various adjustments that may be required in calculating current replacement cost as described above may be expressed in a formula, as follows:

$$\text{CRC} = (\text{CRA} - \text{PVOC}) \times \frac{\text{EC}}{\text{RC}} \times \frac{\text{EUL}}{\text{RUL}} \text{, in which}$$

CRC = current replacement cost
CRA = cost of a reference asset (modern replacement asset)
PVOC = present value of operating cost differentials
EC   = capacity of existing assets
RC   = capacity of reference assets
EUL = useful life of existing assets when new
RUL = useful life of reference assets[2]

Comparison With SEC Concepts

For purposes of calculating the value of plant and equipment under models C and D, information developed for compliance with the replacement cost disclosure rules of the SEC may be used. Because of conceptual differences, however, it may not be appropriate simply to insert in the models the amounts computed for SEC purposes.

In the models, the objective is to determine an appropriate current cost (value) of existing assets. In this context, depreciation is a measure of the current cost (value) used up during a period. In contrast, the SEC requirements, as stated in its staff accounting bulletins, are designed to measure the current cost of acquiring assets that would (among other things) replace the capacity of existing assets. In this context, *depreciation* may be said to measure the average annual cash requirements for acquiring replacement assets. Because of this basic difference, a number of computational differences emerge.

For SEC purposes, management intent regarding the style of replacement is a factor since the cost of replacement assets that management intends to acquire is used. For models C and D, precise intent is much less important. For example, if assets essentially identical to those held are available and economical, their cost would be used even if management intends eventually to convert to newer technology.

SEC staff interpretations indicate that future capital requirements for assets such as environmental protection equipment should be comprehended in present replacement costs. Since such assets are not part of existing assets, they would be excluded in the models.

One SEC staff interpretation indicates that if management can reasonably assume it will replace existing asset capacity with assets having twice that capacity and such additional capacity can be used, it "may not be appropriate" to use one-half the cost of the replacement assets. They explain, in essence, that a plant with one-half the capacity could probably not be acquired for one-half the cost. Under the concepts of

---

2.   See note 1.

the models, it would be considered appropriate to use the simple fraction in the circumstances described.

In general, differences in useful lives are ignored in the required SEC disclosures.

Under the SEC rules, the computation of cost of sales may be affected by operating cost differentials or it may be disclosed, but the computation of replacement cost and related depreciation is not to be adjusted.

SEC Interpretations

The SEC interpretations of ASR 190 are published as staff accounting bulletins (SABs). Those interpretations provide guidance in calculating replacement cost under models C and D as well as for purposes of complying with SEC requirements.

The most comprehensive interpretation regarding the types of measurement techniques available for determination of replacement cost is contained in SAB 11:

Four types of replacement cost measurement techniques are most generally applicable: (1) *indexing*, (2) *direct pricing*, (3) *unit pricing*, and (4) *functional pricing*.

Indexing provides a valid measurement of replacement cost provided the index is adjusted for technological change or if the asset type has not had technological change. Indexing should be applied to homogeneous asset groups on a vintaged basis and should not be applied to used asset purchases or assets acquired in business combinations accounted for as purchases.

Direct pricing applies to assets or groups of assets whereby direct labor and material prices are determined from purchase orders, invoices, engineering estimates, price lists, manufacturers' quotes, internally published labor and material prices, and other direct price sources.

Unit pricing is a structured variation of direct pricing whereby a building, inventory lot, or other type of asset is directly priced based upon labor, material, and overhead estimates, then divided into a unit measure (e.g., replacement cost per square foot of building, replacement cost per unit of inventory, etc.).

Functional pricing is generally used to determine the replacement cost for a processing function rather than for a specific asset or asset group. Functional pricing can be applied to a heterogeneous group of assets. Functional pricing often combines the techniques of indexing, direct pricing, and unit pricing. It measures the cost of productive capacity based on the number of units which can be produced within a particular time period. For example, a meat packing plant with a replacement cost of $5,000,000 has the capacity to process 500 head of cattle per day, resulting in the functional replacement cost of $10,000 per head of cattle per day. Functional pricing may involve the usage of information such as:

- Engineering studies
- Recently built processing facilities
- Design specification for processing plants
- Major equipment suppliers
- Manufacturers' quotes
- Internal estimates for installation and/or modifications
- Trade association studies

Functional pricing takes into consideration and adjusts for technological change, but one major consideration is additional adjustments for economies of scale.

While these are the most common approaches, other techniques may be appropriate under various factual circumstances.

The SEC further commented on the use of indices as an acceptable approach to determination of replacement cost in SAB 12 as follows:

Any logical approach to the estimation of replacement cost is acceptable provided it results in a conclusion which reasonably approximates the replacement cost of productive capacity.

The estimation of the replacement cost of productive capacity is basically a two-step process. Management must first decide if existing capacity would be replaced with assets similar to those presently owned or if different assets would be required because of technology advances, new governmental regulations, or other current economic and operating considerations. The second step is the selection of appropriate methods to price the replacement assets. In many cases, a combination of direct pricing methods and indexing will be required.

Typically, indices do not reflect technological changes to any appreciable extent. Adjusting the original cost of presently owned assets by appropriate indices results in the current cost to reproduce those assets. Reproduction cost may be equivalent to replacement cost if existing productive capacity would be replaced using assets similar to those presently owned. However, if replacement cost is to be estimated on the basis of using assets different from those presently owned, because of technological changes or other factors, measurement techniques other than indexing are usually required.

For those assets which would not be replaced through reproduction, normally some repricing will be required to reflect the replacement cost of productive capacity.

For structures which will be replaced in a different form, unit pricing is one acceptable method of estimating replacement cost. If the structures are an integral part of the manufacturing process, as in a brewery or chemical facility, the functional pricing method may be appropriate.

As with structures, machinery and equipment which has been affected by technological change usually requires specific identification of the replacement of substitute facilities to serve as a basis for estimating replacement costs using a direct, unit, or functional pricing technique. However, because a large number of assets may be involved, this procedure may be costly and time consuming. Sampling techniques may be used in these situations to minimize the number of items requiring direct pricing. The cost of estimating replacement costs of property, plant, and equipment which have undergone technological change can be reduced accordingly.

Using one sampling technique, the estimated replacement cost, based on direct pricing, of the items in the sample divided by the items' indexed original cost results in a factor which approximates the effect of the technological change. If the sample is representative of the total group of assets from which it is taken, the technological change factor computed for the sample may be applied to the indexed historical costs of other items in the group to adjust for the effects of technological change for the entire group.

The SEC issued the following interpretation in SAB 10 regarding the appropriateness of used asset prices as a measure of replacement cost:

The replacement cost disclosures should not be made on the basis of the current selling value of the company's assets in the used market. However, the objectives of Rule 3-17 could be achieved in certain situations by assuming replacement with used equipment and facilities.

This approach could be justified by a managerial policy of replacing productive capacity with used items considering current economic circumstances. The following conditions would appear to be necessary for basing replacement cost on the current prices of used items:

1. Used facilities and equipment are available and, in management's judgment, will continue to be available during the remaining life of its existing productive capacity.

2. Under current economic conditions, management would replace its productive capacity with used facilities and equipment.

The cost of the used facilities and equipment would become the gross replacement cost for purposes of Rule 3-17. Disclosure should be made if used facilities and equipment provide the basis for replacement of a significant portion of productive capacity.

The question of whether operating cost savings expected as a result of technological improvements from the assumed replacement of productive capacity should be considered in replacement cost of sales and inventories was answered in SAB 11:

In general, the staff believes that prospective cost savings from new productive capacity should only be considered in calculating replacement cost data relative to inventory and cost of sales *when the savings are reasonably assured and quantifiable within reasonable limits.* In such cases, where cost savings are explicitly considered, Rule 3-17(e) requires disclosure of the amount and elements of the cost savings used in the calculation.

An alternative approach to disclosure of such cost savings would be to not reflect such savings directly in the replacement cost of sales number, but to disclose supplementally the nature and magnitude of such savings. When cost savings are not reasonably assured and quantifiable, registrants are encouraged to disclose the general nature and magnitude of savings in such fashion as they believe will be most meaningful to investors.

For inventories and cost of sales, the SEC noted that frequently the FIFO method of pricing year-end inventories approximates the replacement cost of such inventories, and the LIFO method of computing cost of sales approximates replacement cost of sales. In response to the question if such methods are acceptable substitutes for replacement cost, SAB 7 states:

Any method will be acceptable if it results in amounts which do not materially differ from amounts computed using replacement cost. However, it will not be acceptable to simply use FIFO and LIFO amounts without assuring that they do not differ materially from replacement cost amounts.

6

Comparison of the Models

The four models discussed in the preceding chapters span the spectrum from the historical cost (present) framework to substantially different approaches using current values extensively. The models incorporate the various available alternatives of concept, measurement, and presentation.

Models A, B, and C generally follow the revenues and expenses (income statement) approach to measurement recognition while model D follows the resources and obligations (balance sheet) approach. Some other similarities and differences among the models are the following:

- Model D accounts for the difference between replacement cost and historical cost of plant and equipment as a "latent" tax but model C does not.
- Models A and B retain the concept of net income but models C and D substitute other concepts under which value changes and operating results are separated.
- Models A and D incorporate general purchasing power accounting in varying degrees but models B and C do not.

The major differences among the four models are highlighted in the following summary in which the manner of accounting for the various types of assets and liabilities is described for each model. Details are given in the separate sections for each of the models.

SUMMARY

Bases for Assigning Financial Statement Amounts

(All items in model A are the same as in present GAAP but stated in units of general purchasing power rather than in units of money)

Item	Model B	Model C	Model D
Cash	*	*	*
Current accounts and notes receivable	*	*	*
Marketable securities	*	Current net realizable value	Current net realizable value
Inventories	Lower of LIFO historical cost and market	Lower of current replacement cost and net realizable value	Lower of current replacement cost and net realizable value
Prepaid expenses	*	Replacement cost (historical cost for convenience)	Replacement cost (historical cost for convenience)
Investments in affiliates	Equity method using financial statements based on the model	Equity method using financial statements based on the model	Equity method using financial statements based on the model
Noncurrent accounts and notes receivable	*	Net realizable value	Discounted present value of collectible amounts
Idle land and facilities	*	Current selling price	Current selling price
Buildings and structures; machinery and equipment	*	Lower of (a) current replacement cost (net of discounted future cost savings) and (b) higher of net realizable value and net present value	Current replacement cost (net of discounted future cost savings) for items to be replaced; current net realizable value for others
Capitalized lease rights	Same basis as for owned resources of same type	Same basis as for owned resources of same type	Same basis as for owned resources of same type

Accumulated depreciation	Allocated amount of historical cost deducted from asset on balance sheet; allocated amount of excess of historical cost adjusted by specific indexes over historical cost included in shareholders' equity	Allocated amount of current replacement cost	Allocated amount of current replacement cost
Patents, copyrights, and other identifiable intangibles	*	Allocated amount of historical cost or replacement cost	Current selling price if rights are transferable, otherwise zero
Goodwill	*	*	Zero
Deferred taxes	*	*	Latent tax effects of difference between balance sheet and tax basis treated as element in valuation (applies to Deferred taxes and Latent tax debits or credits)
Latent tax debits or credits	*	No latent tax effects recognized except for marketable securities	
Deferred charges and credits	*	*	Zero unless item fits another category
Current and accrued payables	*	*	*
Long-term debt	*	*	Amounts required to liquidate currently
Capitalized lease obligation	*	*	*
Payments for future services and service obligations	*	*	*
Pension obligations	*	*	Excess of amount earned by employees (accrued benefits) over amount funded
Executory contracts	*	*	*
Realized vs. unrealized gains and losses	*	Report both, separately	Report both, separately

* Same basis as in present generally accepted accounting principles.

7

Illustration of the Application of the Models

This chapter illustrates the different results obtained by a hypothetical company under each of the four models discussed in the preceding chapters, derived from a common data base. It also provides instructions for calculating key amounts in the financial statements called for under the models.

The chapter contains five sections. The first contains financial statements prepared under present generally accepted accounting principles and a summary of the data from which they were prepared. The other four sections contain financial statements prepared under the principles that pertain to each of the four models and the explanations needed to understand the calculation of the statements. Explanation of calculations for each model is provided only for financial statement amounts that differ from those contained in the statements presented in the first section and whose calculation cannot be readily inferred from reading the description of the model in the preceding chapters. The statement of changes in financial position is not illustrated because its preparation depends on and can be inferred from the preparation of the statement of financial position and the income statement, which are illustrated.

The preceding chapters do not specify all the accounting principles involved in preparing financial statements under the four models, but limit specification to those principles that differ from presently accepted practice. If accounting for a particular type of transaction is not specified under a model, the accounting is the same as that called for under present practice. For example, the investment tax credit is accounted for under each model the same way it is accounted for in the conventional financial statements of the company applying the models.

All amounts in the financial statements are stated in thousands of dollars.

Section 1
Present Generally Accepted Accounting Principles

	Statement of Financial Position December 31, 1976 and 1975	
	1976	*1975*
Assets		
Current assets		
Cash	$ 3,135	$ 3,121
Receivables	6,170	5,050
Securities, at cost	—	1,500
Inventories, at FIFO	5,542	5,940
Prepaid expense	42	48
	14,889	15,659
Investments	600	600
Fixed assets		
Land	1,000	1,000
Buildings, equipment	25,400	24,900
Less depreciation	(20,210)	(18,260)
	6,190	7,640
Patents	33	35
Goodwill	145	150
Total assets	$ 21,857	$ 24,084
Liabilities and Equity		
Current liabilities		
Accounts, notes, accruals	$ 2,521	$ 4,770
Deferred income	50	100
	2,571	4,870
Long-term debt, 8%	4,700	5,000
Deferred income taxes	1,342	1,646
Total liabilities	8,613	11,516
Stockholders' equity		
Contributed capital	10,000	10,000
Retained earnings	3,244	2,568
	13,244	12,568
Total liabilities and equity	$ 21,857	$ 24,084

Statement of Results of Operations
Year Ended December 31, 1976

	1976
Sales	$27,000
Investment income	40
	27,040
Operating expenses	
Cost of goods sold	20,856
Depreciation	2,070
General and administrative expense	2,010
Pensions	150
Research and development cost	100
Amortization of intangibles	7
	25,193
Operating income before interest and taxes	1,847
Interest on debt	(400)
Income taxes	(684)
Operating income after taxes	763
Gain from sale of equipment and securities, less related income taxes of $48	113
Net income	876
Retained earnings, December 31, 1975	2,568
Dividends	(200)
Retained earnings, December 31, 1976	$ 3,244

Building and Equipment				
	Year acquired	Cost December 31, 1975	Purchases	Retirements	Cost December 31, 1976
---	---	---	---	---	---
A building	1962	$15,000			$15,000
B machine	1969	300		$300	—
C machine	1962	4,500			4,500
D machine	1962	5,000			5,000
E machine	1976	—	$800		800
F autos	1972	100			100
		$24,900	$800	$300	$25,400

Cash Transactions

		1976
Cash receipts		
Current sales	$26,880	
Accounts receivable, December 31, 1975	5,050	
Accounts receivable, December 31, 1976	(6,170)	
Investment income	40	$25,800
Additions to deferred income		70
Proceeds—sale of equipment		241
Proceeds—sale of marketable securities		1,600
		27,711
Cash payments		
Inventory purchases	20,458	
General and administrative expenses	1,970	
Payables, December 31, 1975	4,770	
Payables, December 31, 1976	(2,521)	24,677
Pensions		150
Research and development costs		100
Interest (.08 × 5,000)		400
Income taxes (per tax return)		1,036
Dividends		200
Expenses classified prepaid		34
Plant and equipment additions		800
Payment of long-term debt		300
		27,697
Net receipts		14
Cash balance, January 1, 1976		3,121
Cash balance, December 31, 1976		$ 3,135

Accumulated Depreciation (Books)

	Balance December 31, 1975	Depreciation expense	Retirements	Balance December 31, 1976
A building	$ 9,750	$ 760		$10,510
B machine	120	—	$120	—
C machine	3,815	685		4,500
D machine	4,500	500		5,000
E machine	—	100		100
F autos	75	25		100
Total	$18,260	$2,070	$120	$20,210

Deferred Income Tax Credit

	Balance December 31, 1975	Increase (decrease)	Balance December 31, 1976
A building	$1,224	$ 106	$1,330
B machine	38	(38)	—
C machine	233	(233)	—
D machine	144	(144)	—
E machine	—	12	12
F autos	7	(7)	—
	$1,646	$(304)	$1,342

Deferred Income

	1976
Balance, December 31, 1975	$ 100
Increase	70
Decrease	(120)
Balance, December 31, 1976	$ 50

Inventories and Cost of Goods Sold

	Units	Unit price	Amount
Inventory, December 31, 1975	1,188	$5	$ 5,940
Purchases	3,720	$5.50*	20,458
	4,908		26,398
Inventory, December 31, 1976	(1,012)	(at FIFO)	(5,542)
Cost of goods sold	3,896		$20,856

* Average price during the year.

Accumulated Depreciation (Tax)

	Balance December 31, 1975	Depreciation expense	Retirements	Balance December 31, 1976
A building	$12,300	$ 980		$13,280
B machine	200	—	$200	—
C machine	4,300	200		4,500
D machine	4,800	200		5,000
E machine	—	125		125
F autos	90	10		100
	$21,690	$1,515	$200	$23,005

Income Tax Expense

Income tax paid in 1976	$1,036
Decrease in deferred income tax credit	(304)
Income tax expense	$ 732*

* $684 is included in operating income and $48 in capital gains.

Section 2
Model A

Statement of Financial Position
December 31, 1976 and 1975

	In $ (1976)	
	1976	*1975*
Assets		
Current assets		
Cash	$ 3,135	$ 3,352
Receivables	6,170	5,424
Securities	—	1,932
Inventories	5,640	6,422
Prepaid expense	43	53
	14,988	17,183
Investments	720	720
Fixed assets		
Land	1,470	1,470
Buildings, equipment	37,290	36,806
Less depreciation	(29,964)	(27,076)
	8,796	11,200
Patents	46	37
Goodwill	203	209
Total assets	$24,753	$29,349
Liabilities and Equity		
Current liabilities		
Accounts, notes, accruals	$ 2,521	$ 5,123
Deferred income	50	107
	2,571	5,230
Long-term debt, 8%	4,700	5,370
Deferred income taxes	1,342	1,768
Total liabilities	8,613	12,368
Stockholders' equity		
Contributed capital	14,700	14,700
Retained earnings	1,440	2,281
	16,140	16,981
Total liabilities and equity	$24,753	$29,349

Statement of Results of Operations
Year Ended December 31, 1976

	In $ (1976)
Sales	$27,810
Investment income	41
	27,851
Operating expenses	
Cost of goods sold	21,860
Depreciation	3,025
General and administrative expense	2,071
Pensions	155
Research and development cost	103
Amortization of intangibles	9
	27,223
Operating income before interest and taxes	628
Interest on debt	(412)
Income taxes	(710)
Operating income after taxes	(494)
Losses from sale of equipment and securities, after related income taxes of (76) $50	(340)
General purchasing power loss on monetary items, excluding long-term debt	(170)
General purchasing power gain on long-term debt	370
Net loss	(634)
Retained earnings, December 31, 1975	2,281
Dividends	(207)
Retained earnings, December 31, 1976	$ 1,440

The same basic techniques are used to calculate the amounts in the financial statements called for under model A as are used to calculate the statement amounts called for under the FASB exposure draft on general purchasing power accounting. Those techniques are explained and illustrated fully in the exposure draft. Their application in preparing the preceding financial statements is therefore not explained in this chapter.

The only modification of techniques of calculation that is needed for model A concerns the classification of certain items as monetary or nonmonetary. As discussed in chapter 3, the FASB exposure draft treats prepaid and deferred items and deferred income tax credits or debits as nonmonetary, but model A usually treats those items as monetary. The exposure draft treats foreign currency items as nonmonetary, but model A treats them as monetary.

The index numbers used in the preceding illustration are the same as those used in the FASB exposure draft example. Those index numbers, which apply to 1972 and 1973 rather than to 1975 and 1976, were used in the preceding illustration to make it conform more closely with the exposure draft example.

Section 3
Model B

Statement of Financial Position
December 31, 1976 and 1975

	1976	1975
Assets		
Current assets		
Cash	$ 3,135	$ 3,121
Receivables	6,170	5,050
Securities	—	1,500
Inventories, at LIFO	4,554	5,346
Prepaid expense	42	48
	13,901	15,065
Investments	600	600
Fixed assets		
Land	1,000	1,000
Buildings, equipment	25,400	24,900
Less depreciation	(20,210)	(18,260)
	6,190	7,640
Patents	33	35
Goodwill	145	150
Total assets	$20,869	$23,490
Liabilities and Equity		
Current liabilities		
Accounts, notes, accruals	$ 2,343	$ 4,770
Deferred income	50	100
	2,393	4,870
Long-term debt, 8%	4,700	5,000
Deferred income taxes	892	1,646
Total liabilities	7,985	11,516
Stockholders' equity		
Contributed capital	10,000	10,000
Retained earnings	1,227	1,974
Accumulated current cost depreciation	1,657	—
	12,884	11,974
Total liabilities and equity	$20,869	$23,490

Statement of Results of Operations
Year Ended December 31, 1976

	1976
Sales	$27,000
Investment income	40
	27,040
Operating expenses	
Cost of goods sold	21,250
Depreciation	3,727
General and administrative expense	2,010
Pensions	150
Research and development cost	100
Amortization of intangibles	7
	27,244
Operating income before interest and taxes	(204)
Interest on debt	(400)
Income taxes	(56)
Operating income after taxes	(660)
Gain from sale of equipment and securities, less related income taxes of $48	113
Net loss	(547)
Retained earnings, December 31, 1975	1,974
Dividends	(200)
Retained earnings, December 31, 1976	$ 1,227

Depreciation Expense

	Year acquired	Price index* at acqui-sition date	Price index* at June 30, 1976	Historical cost expense	Multi-plier	Current cost expense
A building	1962	80	178	$ 760	178/80	$1,692
C machine	1962	98	154	685	154/98	1,076
D machine	1962	97	160	500	160/97	825
E machine	1976	154	160	100	160/54	104
F autos	1972	120	145	25	145/120	30
				$2,070		$3,727

*   These numbers were devised for illustrative purposes only and were not used by experimenters in applying model B.

Accumulated Current Cost Depreciation

	Balance December 31, 1975	Current cost expense	Historical cost expense	Balance December 31, 1976
A building	—	$1,692	$ (760)	$ 932
C machine	—	1,076	(685)	391
D machine	—	825	(500)	325
E machine	—	104	(100)	4
F autos	—	30	(25)	5
		$3,727	$(2,070)	$1,657

Deferred Income Tax Credit

	Depreciation expense Tax	Depreciation expense Books	Books over (under) tax	Increase (decrease) in deferred income tax credit	Balance December 31, 1975	Balance December 31, 1976
A building	$ 980	$1,692	$ 712	$(342)[1]	$1,224	$882
B machine	—	—	—	(38)[2]	38	—
C machine	200	1,076	876	(233)[2]	233	—
D machine	200	825	625	(144)[2]	144	—
E machine	125	104	(21)	10 [1]	—	10
F autos	10	30	20	(7)[2]	7	—
	$1,515	$3,727	$2,212	$(754)	$1,646	$892

1. 48% of the difference between book and tax depreciation expenses.

2. Since asset is fully depreciated for book purposes on a historical cost basis, the balance in the deferred income tax credit account at December 31, 1975, is removed from the account.

Income Tax Expense*

Income tax paid in 1976	$858
Decrease in deferred income tax credit	(754)
Income tax expense	$104

* $56 is included in operating income and $48 in capital gains.

Section 4
Model C

Statement of Financial Position
December 31, 1976 and 1975

	1976	1975
Assets		
Current assets		
Cash	$ 3,135	$ 3,121
Receivables	6,170	5,050
Securities	—	1,710
Inventories	5,819	6,118
Prepaid expense	42	48
	15,166	16,047
Investments	760	750
Fixed assets		
Land	1,650	1,500
Buildings, equipment	46,776	43,717
Less depreciation	(37,818)	(33,495)
	10,608	11,722
Patents	33	35
Goodwill	145	150
Total assets	$26,712	$28,704
Liabilities and Equity		
Current liabilities		
Accounts, notes, accruals	$ 2,521	$ 4,770
Deferred income	50	100
	2,571	4,870
Long-term debt, 8%	4,700	5,000
Total liabilities	7,271	9,870
Stockholders' equity		
Contributed capital	10,000	10,000
Retained realized value changes	1,287	—
Unrealized value changes	6,197	6,266
Retained operating income	1,957	2,568
	19,441	18,834
Total liabilities and equity	$26,712	$28,704

Statement of Operating Income
Year Ended December 31, 1976

	1976
Sales	$27,000
Investment income	40
	27,040
Operating expenses	
Cost of goods sold	21,426
Depreciation	2,674
General and administrative expense	2,010
Pensions	150
Research and development cost	100
Amortization of intangibles	7
	26,367
Operating income before interest and taxes	673
Interest on debt	(400)
Income taxes	(684)
Net loss	(411)
Retained operating income, December 31, 1975	2,568
Dividends	(200)
Retained operating income, December 31, 1976	$ 1,957

Statement of Value Changes
Year Ended December 31, 1976

	Marketable securities	Inventories	Noncurrent investments	Land	Building and equipment	Total
Balance, unrealized value changes, December 31, 1975	$210	$178	$150	$500	$5,228	$6,266
Net value increases (decreases)	(140)	669	10	150	547	1,236
	70	847	160	650	5,775	7,502
Realized						
Net (gains) losses realized through sale	(70)	—	0	0	(61)	(131)
Capital maintenance allowance charged to operations	0	(570)	0	0	(604)	(1,174)
	(70)	(570)	0	0	(665)	(1,305)
Balance, unrealized value changes, December 31, 1976	$ 0	$277	$160	$650	$5,110	$6,197

Statement of Retained Realized Value Changes
Year Ended December 31, 1976

Balance, December 31, 1975		
(date of change in accounting)		$ 0
Capital maintenance allowances charged to operations		1,174
Capital gains (losses) on exchanges of marketable securities (net of tax)		70
Capital gains (losses) on sale of equipment, less related income taxes	$61	
	(18)	43
Balance, December 31, 1976		$1,287

Investments

Investments, December 31, 1975 (market value)	$750
Increase in market value	10
Investments, December 31, 1976	$760

Land

Land, December 31, 1975 (appraised value)	$1,500
Increase in appraised value	150
Land, December 31, 1976	$1,650

Marketable Securities

	Total	Cost	Unrealized value change	Tax at 30% of unrealized value change
Securities amount, December 31, 1975	$1,710	$1,500	$300	$(90)
Unrealized value change from December 31, 1975, to date of sale	(140)		(200)	60
Securities amount at date of sale	$1,570	$1,500	$100	$(30)

$1,600 is received from the sale of the securities, of which $1,570 is credited to the asset account and $30 is credited to income tax expense to offset the capital gains tax of $30 (30% of $1,600–$1,500).

The capital gain of $70 reported on the statement of value changes is the difference between the proceeds of sale ($1,600) and historical cost ($1,500) reduced by $30 for the income tax on the gain of $100.

Inventories and Cost of Goods Sold

	Units	Price	Market value
Inventories, December 31, 1975	1,188	$5.15	$ 6,118
Unrealized value change			416
	1,188	$5.50*	6,534
Purchases	3,720	$5.50	20,458
	4,908		26,992
Cost of goods sold	(3,896)	$5.50	(21,426)
	1,012		5,566
Unrealized value change			253
Inventories, December 31, 1976	1,012	$5.75	$ 5,819

* The average purchase price during the year.

Unrealized value changes total $669 (416 + 253).

Capital maintenance allowance charged to operations:

Cost of goods sold, current value	$21,426
Cost of goods sold, historical cost	(20,856)
Allowance	$ 570

Depreciation Expense

	1976

A building

The A building space is replaceable with a similar structure. Although some modern design changes would be involved, they are considered minor. Management is planning to replace the present structure by erecting a larger building nearby and moving the entire operation. Cost to replace existing space:

December 31, 1975, $30,500
December 31, 1976, $32,000
Useful life—20 years
Replacement cost depreciation expense
$(30,500 + 32,000) \times \frac{1}{2} \times \frac{1}{20}$ $1,563

C machine

The C machine represents a tried technology. It can be replaced basically in kind, and management plans to do so in 1978. Cost of the replacement:

December 31, 1975, $6,500
December 31, 1976, $7,000
Useful life—15 years
Replacement cost depreciation expense
$(6,500 + 7,000) \times \frac{1}{2} \times \frac{1}{15}$ 450

D machine

> The *D* machine cannot be replaced in kind. Technology of its type is no longer available. The new technology promises future operating cost savings (chiefly lower maintenance costs) of approximately $50 per year in each of the 15 years of expected usefulness. The company's internal rate of return target for new projects is 14 percent. Savings discounted at this rate amount to $307. The new technology became available in 1975. Cost of replacement:
>
> > December 31, 1975, $8,200 − $307 = $7,893
> > December 31, 1976, $8,500 − $307 = $8,193
> > Useful life—15 years
> > Replacement cost depreciation expense
> > $(7{,}893 + 8{,}193) \times \frac{1}{2} \times \frac{1}{15}$ 536

E machine

> The *B* machine, a standard production model that was about worn out in 1975, was replaced in 1976 with the *E* machine, which differs only by being of stronger construction. The *B* machine could be expected to operate efficiently for 7 years, the *E* machine for 8. The *E* machine also has twice the productive capacity of the *B* machine. Cost of replacement:
>
> > December 31, 1975, $800
> > December 31, 1976, $800
> > Useful life—8 years
> > Replacement cost depreciation expense
> > $(800 + 800) \times \frac{1}{2} \times \frac{1}{8}$ 100

F automobiles

> The *F* automobiles represent 20 vehicles purchased at a fleet price of $5 each in 1972. Essentially similar vehicles will be purchased as replacements. Cost of replacement:
>
> > December 31, 1975, $120
> > December 31, 1976, $125
> > Useful life—5 years
> > Replacement cost depreciation expense
> > $(120 + 125) \times \frac{1}{2} \times \frac{1}{5}$ 25
> >   Total depreciation expense $2,674

	Value at December 31, 1975	Purchases	Retirements	Gross increase in value	Value at December 31, 1976
A building	$30,500	—	—	$1,500	$32,000
B machine	350	—	$350	—	—
C machine	6,500	—	—	500	7,000
D machine	7,893	—	—	300	8,193
E machine	—	$800	—	—	800
F autos	120	—	—	5	125
Total	$45,363	$800	$350	$2,305	$48,118

Accumulated Depreciation at December 31, 1976

	Value of asset at December 31, 1976	Years of life expired over total life in years	Accumulated depreciation at December 31, 1976
A building	$32,000	14/20	$22,400
C machine	7,000	15/15	7,000
D machine	8,193	15/15	8,193
E machine	800	1/8	100
F autos	125	5/5	125
			$37,818

Change in Accumulated Depreciation

	Balance December 31, 1975	Depreciation expense	Adjust B machine reserve[2]	Retirements	"Backlog" depreciation[1]	Balance December 31, 1976
A building	$19,825	$1,563			$1,012	$22,400
B machine	140	—	$210	$(350)	—	—
C machine	6,067	450			483	7,000
D machine	7,367	536			290	8,193
E machine	—	100			—	100
F autos	96	25			4	125
	$33,495	$2,674	$210	$(350)	$1,789	$37,818

1. "Backlog" depreciation is calculated by adding depreciation expense to and subtracting retirements from accumulated depreciation at December 31, 1975, and subtracting that amount from accumulated depreciation at December 31, 1976. "Backlog" depreciation could be calculated independently of those variables, but independent calculation is more complicated and is unnecessary if the other variables are all calculated independently.

2. See section on value changes pertaining to building and equipment.

Income Tax Allocation for Depreciation

As explained in the program under model C, income tax benefits resulting from deducting depreciation expense in the tax return are allocated to operating income over the life of the property on a straight-line basis. The difference between accumulated tax benefits allocated on a straight-line basis and accumulated tax benefits obtained in tax returns is subtracted from the current cost of the asset on the balance sheet.

The result called for under model C can be obtained by following all the procedures required for accounting for depreciation timing differences under present generally accepted accounting principles except for deducting the deferred tax credit from the asset value instead of reporting it in the liability section of the balance sheet. In this illustration, building and equipment at December 31, 1975, are stated at $43,717 (45,363 − 1,646), and at December 31, 1976, are stated at $46,776 (48,118 − 1,342). The decrease in the deferred credit of $304 (1,646 — 1,342) is deducted from income tax expense in the Statement of Operating Income.

Value Changes in 1976 Pertaining to Building and Equipment	
Net value increase	
Gross increase in value	$ 2,305
"Backlog" depreciation	(1,789)
Proceeds of sale of equipment	241
Increase in depreciation reserve of equipment sold to make item fully depreciated at date of sale	(210)
	$ 547
Gain from sale of equipment	
Proceeds of sale	$ 241
Unamortized historical cost ($300 − $120)	(180)
Gain	$ 61
Capital maintenance allowance charged to operations	
Depreciation expense on a current cost basis	$ 2,674
Depreciation expense on a historical cost basis	(2,070)
	$ 604
Balance, unrealized value changes, December 31, 1975	
Unamortized current cost ($45,363 − $33,495)	$11,868
Unamortized historical cost ($24,900 − $18,260)	(6,640)
Total	$ 5,228
Balance, unrealized value changes, December 31, 1976	
Unamortized current cost ($48,118 − $37,818)	$10,300
Unamortized historical cost ($25,400 − $20,210)	(5,190)
Total	$ 5,110

Income tax per tax return			
Tax on "ordinary" income			
22% of $ 25	$ 6		
26% of 25	7		
48% of 1,952	937		
$2,002	$950		$950
Tax on sale of securities: ($1,600 − $1,500) × 30%			30
Tax on sale of equipment			
Depreciation "recapture": ($180 − $100) × 48%		$38	
Capital gains tax: ($241 − $180) × 30%		18	56
Total			$1,036

	Tax per return	Other sources	Total income tax expense
Section of financial statements reported in			
Statement of operating income—			
Income tax expense	$ 988[2]	$(304)[1]	$684
Statement of retained realized value changes—sale of equipment	18		18
Statement of operating income—			
Income tax expense	. 30	(30)[3]	—
Total	$1,036	$(334)	$702

1. Change in the deferred income tax account.
2. $950 + $38.
3. Credit from entry made on sale of marketable securities.

Statement of Financial Position
December 31, 1976 and 1975

	1976	1975
Assets		
Current assets		
Cash	$ 3,135	$ 3,121
Receivables	6,170	5,050
Securities	—	1,710
Inventories	5,686	6,033
Prepaid expense	42	48
	15,033	15,962
Investments	680	673
Fixed assets		
Land	1,455	1,350
Buildings, equipment	48,118	45,363
Less depreciation and imputed income tax	(41,612)	(37,650)
	7,961	9,063
Total assets	$23,674	$25,698
Liabilities and Equity		
Current liabilities	$ 2,571	$ 4,870
Long-term debt, 8%	4,648	5,000
Unfunded accrued pension obligation, less		
imputed income tax	317	312
Total liabilities	7,536	10,182
Stockholders' equity	16,138	15,516
Total liabilities and equity	$23,674	$25,698

Statement of Changes in Stockholders' Equity
Year Ended December 31, 1976

		1976
Results of ordinary operations		
Sales	$27,000	
Investment income	40	
Cost of goods sold	(21,426)	
Depreciation	(2,674)	
General and administrative expenses	(2,010)	
Pensions	(170)	
Research and development	(100)	
Interest on debt	(410)	
Income taxes related to operations	(950)	$ (700)
Unusual transactions and events		
Pension plan amendment		(52)
Value changes		
Marketable securities	(140)	
Investments	7	
Inventories	621	
Land	105	
Building and equipment	852	
Long-term debt		
General market element	95	
Risk change element	(43)	
Interest expense differential	10	
Pensions	67	1,574
Amount required to recognize impact on stockholders' equity of increase in the general price level during the year		(1,141)
		(319)
Stockholders' equity, December 31, 1975		16,664
Dividends paid		(207)
Stockholders' equity, December 31, 1976		$16,138

Investments

	Appraised value	Imputed taxes (30%)	Net
Investments, December 31, 1975 (cost, $600)	$705[1]	$32	$673
Value change	9	2	7
Investments, December 31, 1976	$714[2]	$34	$680

1. After estimated disposal costs of $45.
2. After estimated disposal costs of $46.

Marketable Securities

	Market value	Imputed taxes (30%)	Net
Securities, December 31, 1975 (cost, $1,500)	$1,800	$90	$1,710
Value change	(200)	(60)	(140)
Securities at date of sale (December 1976)	$1,600	$30	$1,570

$1,600 is received from the sale of the securities, of which $1,570 is credited to the asset account and $30 is credited to income tax expense to offset the capital gains tax of $30 (30% of $1,600–$1,500).

Land

	Appraised value	Imputed tax (30%)	Net
Land, December 31, 1975	$1,500	$150	$1,350
Value change	150	45	105
Land, December 31, 1976	$1,650	$195	$1,455

Long-Term Debt

	Amount
Debt, December 31, 1975	$5,000
Retirement	(300)
	4,700
Value change (interest rate)	(95)
	4,605
Value change (risk element)	43
Debt, December 31, 1976	$4,648

Gain from interest rate change:

From the beginning to the end of the year, the long-term interest rate rose from 8% to 9%. The bonds have a remaining life of 5 years, hence the discounted value at December 31, 1976 is

Principal $4,700 × 0.6449	$3,055
Interest $376 × 3.89	1,463
	$4,518
Book value after retirement	$4,700
Discounted value	(4,518)
Gain before tax	182
Imputed tax at 48%	(87)
Gain after tax	$ 95

Loss from risk change element

Market price of debt at 12/31/76	$4,600
Tax on $100 gain ($4,700–$4,600) at 48%	48
Total	4,648
Book value after value change (interest rate)	4,605
Loss	$ 43

Interest expense would have been $410 if interest on the debt had been restructured in the middle of the year to reflect the change in rate and risk.

$(9\% + 8\%)/2 \times (\$5,000 + \$4,648)/2 = 410$

The company actually paid $400 interest in 1976; hence a gain of $10 on the interest differential was reported as a value change, less imputed income tax of $5.

The following journal entry is made to record the payment of interest.

Interest expense	$410	
Cash		$400
Value change		10

Inventories and Cost of Goods Sold

Inventories, cost of goods sold, and market value changes in inventories are calculated under model D the same way they are calculated under model C. The only difference between models C and D for those items is that model D incorporates imputed income taxes on value changes but model C does not.

	Market value	Imputed tax (48%)	Net
Inventories, December 31, 1975			
(cost, $5,940)	$ 6,118	$ 85	$ 6,033
Purchases	20,458		20,458
	26,576	85	26,491
Value change	669	321	348
	27,245	406	26,839
Cost of goods sold	(21,426)	(273)*	(21,153)
Inventories, December 31, 1976			
(cost, $5,542)	$ 5,819	$133	$ 5,686

* Forty-eight percent of the difference between the current cost and historical cost of goods sold [($21,426 − $20,856) × 48%]. This amount plus the $348 net value change during the year (a total of $621) is shown as an addition to "stockholders' equity" in the "value change" section.

Imputed Income Tax on Building and Equipment

The gross current cost of building and equipment, accumulated depreciation, gross value change in current cost, and "backlog" depreciation are calculated under model D the same way they are under model C. Another similarity between models D and C is the calculation of imputed income tax on the difference between unamortized cost for tax purposes and unamortized cost on a straight-line historical cost basis. Model D goes one step further than model C in calling for the calculation of imputed income tax on the difference between unamortized cost on a straight-line historical cost basis and unamortized cost on a current cost basis.

Imputed income tax on building and equipment and the changes in that amount during the year are calculated most simply at the difference between unamortized current cost and unamortized cost for tax purposes. The two components of imputed income taxes described in the preceding paragraph need not be calculated separately except as noted below.

Imputed income tax, December 31, 1975		
Unamortized current cost ($45,363 − $33,495)	$11,868	
Unamortized cost for tax purposes		
($24,900 − $21,690)	(3,210)	
Difference	$ 8,658	
Tax at 48%		$4,155
Depreciation expense difference		
Current cost basis	$ 2,674	
Tax basis	(1,515)	
Difference	$ 1,159	
Tax at 48%		(556)
Value change		
Gross increase in value	$ 2,305	
"Backlog" depreciation	(1,789)	
Net increase in value	$ 516	
Tax at 48%		248
Sale of equipment		
Unamortized current cost ($350 − $140)	$ 210	
Unamortized cost for tax purposes (300 − 200)	(100)	
Difference	$ 110	
Tax at 48%		(53)
Imputed income tax, December 31, 1976		$3,794
Unamortized current cost ($48,118 − $37,818)	$10,300	
Unamortized cost for tax purposes		
($25,400 − $23,005)	(2,395)	
Difference	$ 7,905	
Tax at 48%	$ 3,794	

The $53 imputed income tax expense on equipment sold includes $38 that pertains to 48 percent of the difference between accumulated depreciation for tax purposes of $200 and for straight-line historical cost purposes of $120. This amount was "recaptured" by the U.S. government and $38 was paid as part of 1976 taxes. Therefore, $38 is debited to the imputed income tax account and credited to income taxes payable. The remaining $15 is deducted from the book value of the equipment sold in calculating the gain on sale.

Proceeds of sale		$241
Unamortized current cost ($350 − $140)	$210	
Less imputed income tax	(15)	
Book value of equipment		195
Gain on sale		$ 46

Income Tax Paid

Income tax on operating income	$ 950
Income tax on sale of equipment: ($241 − $180) × 30%	18
Income tax on sale of securities	30
Income tax on "recaptured" depreciation	38
	$1,036

Value Change Pertaining to Building and Equipment

Tax effect on depreciation expense difference		$556
Value change	$516	
Less imputed income tax	(248)	268
Gain on sale of equipment		
Gross	46	
Income tax	(18)	28
Total		$852

Stockholders' Equity

	Unrestated	Restatement factor	Restated
Stockholders' equity, December 31, 1975	$15,516	155/144.32	$16,664
Dividends paid	200	155/149.76	207
Index of general price level:*			
December 31, 1976 155			
June 30, 1976 149.76			
December 31, 1975 144.32			

* These numbers were devised for illustrative purposes only and should not be used by experimenters in applying model D.

Amount required to recognize impact of increase in general price level:

Restated stockholders' equity	$16,664	
Unrestated stockholders' equity	(15,516)	$1,148
Unrestated dividends	200	
Restated dividends	(207)	(7)
Total		$1,141

Pensions

	Accrued pension obligation	Value of trust fund	Unfunded obligation	Financial statement classification (see below)
Balance, December 31, 1975	$1,000	$400	$600	
Accrual of discount on beginning balance	60		60	O
Interest and dividends earned by trust fund		20	(20)	VC
Benefits earned by employees	110		110	O
Actuarial gain or loss	(5)		(5)	O
Change in actuarial assumption	(50)		(50)	VC
Gains and losses on trust fund investments (realized and unrealized)		40	(40)	VC
Benefits paid to retired persons	(100)	(100)	—	
Employer's contribution		150	(150)	BS
Administrative costs		(5)	5	O
Effect of plan amendment	100		100	U
Balance at end of period	$1,115	$505	$610	

	Unfunded pension obligation
Balance, December 31, 1975	$600
Increase (O = ordinary operations)	170
Increase (U = unusual transactions)	100
Decrease (VC = value changes)	(110)
Decrease (BS = cash payment to fund)	(150)
Balance, December 31, 1976	$610
Imputed income tax on unfunded obligation (48%)	
Balance, December 31, 1975	$288
Unusual transactions	48
Value changes	(43)*
Balance, December 31, 1976	$293

* The imputed income tax on value changes is calculated at the amount required to make the imputed tax balance at December 31, 1976 equal 48 percent of $610.

Pension cost charged to ordinary operations is $170. Pension cost charged to unusual transactions is $52 (100 − 48). Pension cost credited to value changes is $67 (110 − 43).

8

Implementation of the Experiment

Preparation Time

In implementing the experiment, the participants differed significantly in the time spent on the project. They used various estimation procedures to save time, and also saved time by using the replacement cost information submitted under ASR 190. Some participants modified the models in applying them.

Model A

Comparison of the time spent by the participants on model A financial statements is complicated in that fifteen participants had previously prepared financial statements in units of general purchasing power for the years 1972, 1973, and 1974 in connection with the experiment conducted by the FASB, the results of which were published in 1977. Participation in the FASB experiment presumably shortened the time needed to prepare model A financial statements because much of the work done on the FASB experiment could be used in preparing the model A statements.

Participants in the FASB experiment spent the following number of hours on that experiment, classified by the number of employees in the segment for which financial statements were prepared.

Participants	Employees	Hours
4	Over 100,000	750–1,274**
4	50,000–100,000	90–1,100
2	25,000–50,000	200–500
1	10,000–25,000	4,100
2	Under 10,000	340–1,540
13*		

*　Two participants did not report time.

**　One participant spent 9,000 hours.

The time shown above pertains to staff accountants and their supervision. Two participants also reported computer programming times of 8 and 200 hours, and one participant reported computer running time of 2 hours.

The participants in the FASB experiment spent the following number of hours preparing model A financial statements.

Participants	Employees	Hours
4	Over 100,000	391–517
4	50,000–100,000	64–396
2	25,000–50,000	260–550
2	10,000–25,000	20–720
3	Under 10,000	60–280
15		

The time shown above pertains to staff accountants and their supervision. Two participants also reported computer programming times of 6 and 8 hours and computer running times of 2 hours. Several participants reported that they had carried forward the FASB experiment and had prepared financial statements for 1975 and 1976 under the principles set forth in the FASB exposure draft of December, 1974; the time spent on the work is included in the time summary above for model A statements.

The nonparticipants in the FASB experiment spent the following number of hours in staff accounting and supervision preparing model A financial statements.

Participants	Employees	Hours
2	25,000–50,000	246–450
2	10,000–25,000	100–176
4	Under 10,000	250–466
8		

Three participants also reported computer programming times of 6 to 170 hours, and five participants reported computer running times of 1 to 10 hours.

The participants in the FASB experiment were asked to estimate the time that would be needed each year in the future to prepare financial statements alternatively under the principles set forth in the FASB exposure draft or under the principles set forth for model A. No participant estimated less time under the exposure draft than under model A, and the following schedule shows the percent amount by which time under the exposure draft was estimated to exceed time under model A.

Participants	% of time in excess
5	Under 10
2	10–20
3	20–70
2	70–90
12*	

* Three participants did not report time.

Two participants estimated that from 50 percent to 300 percent more computer programming hours would be needed under the exposure draft than under model A, and one participant estimated that 100 percent more computer running hours would be needed.

Model B

The participants spent the following number of hours in staff accounting and supervision preparing model B financial statements.

Participants	Employees	Hours
4	Over 100,000	40–495
4	50,000–100,000	16–132
4	25,000–50,000	49,154
4	10,000–25,000	12–115
7	Under 10,000	56–300
23		

Three participants reported computer programming times from 8 to 100 hours, and four participants reported computer running times from 1 to 10 hours.

Models C and D

Most of the time spent by the participants on preparing financial statements under models C and D went into calculation of the replacement cost of inventories and plant and equipment in accordance with the requirements of ASR 190.

The participants spent the following number of hours in accounting, engineering, and computer programming on that (ASR 190) calculation, which was used in both models C and D.

Participants	Employees	Hours
4	Over 100,000	1,913–58,973
4	50,000–100,000	1,700–16,600
4	25,000–50,000	725–29,980
3	10,000–25,000	380–4,500
4	Under 10,000	200–1,000
19		

Nine participants reported computer running times ranging from 1 to 100 hours.

Four participants were not required to file replacement cost information under ASR 190. Those participants spent from 300 to 675 hours in accounting, engineering, and computer programming to calculate the replacement cost of inventories and plant and equipment for models C and D purposes. All four had under 25,000 employees.

All the participants spent the following number of hours in accounting and supervision preparing the financial statements called for under models C and D in addition to the time spent on calculating replacement price shown above.

		Hours	
Participants	Employees	Model C	Model D
4	Over 100,000	80–270	160–552
4	50,000–100,000	40–520	32–390
4	25,000–50,000	100–910	100–1,040
4	10,000–25,000	35–200	40–425
7	Under 10,000	20–150	47–235
23			

For model C two participants reported computer programming times of 45 and 50 hours, and three participants reported computer running times ranging from 1 to 10 hours. For model D two participants reported computer programming times of 21 and 50 hours, and three participants reported computer running times ranging from 1 to 10 hours.

Comparison of the Models

The time spent by the participants preparing financial statements for the four models is not very comparable because some participants had the advantage of having previously participated in the FASB experiment whereas others did not. Furthermore, the initial year in which a model is applied is not indicative of future time requirements. Time estimates for future years are likely to be more comparable.

Sixteen participants estimated that model B would require the least time to carry out in future years of any of the four models, and four participants estimated that model A would require the least. Three participants made no estimates.

The following schedule compares the time (excluding computer running time) estimated by the participants to be required each year in the future to carry out each model. In the schedule, the time estimated for models A, C, and D is expressed as a ratio of the time estimated for model B. In estimating the time needed for models C and D, the time estimated to be required to prepare replacement cost information for inventories and plant and equipment—for most participants, in connection with ASR 190—was added in total to the time estimates for each model even though that information is usable in each.

	Time for Models A, B, C, and D expressed as a ratio of time for Model B			
Participants	A	B	C	D
1	7.5	1	404.0	430.0
2	2.3	1	22.3	23.1
3	1.1	1	1.6	1.8
4	1.2	1	1.9	1.8
5	1.1	1	27.5	27.5
6	5.0	1	8.0	8.2
7	3.8	1	302.5	302.5
8	3.7	1	9.2	9.2
9	2.1	1	6.6	7.1
10	2.0	1	5.2	5.8
11	3.3	1	22.0	23.3
12	1.4	1	11.9	12.2
13	4.2	1	14.0	14.6
14	2.7	1	15.1	16.8
15	1.3	1	27.3	28.1
16	6.4	1	78.4	77.1
17	0.8	1	19.4	18.4
18	0.1	1	2.2	2.2
19	0.7	1	7.3	7.6
20	0.3	1	1.0	1.0

The estimates of lower preparation time for model B and secondarily for model A than for models C and D are consistent with the ranking for simplicity in application given each model by the participants. The following schedule shows the rankings of each model from 1 to 4, in which 1 means simplest and 4 means most complex.

	Participants			
	A	B	C	D
Rank 1 (simplest)	9	13	1	0
Rank 2	9	10	4	0
Rank 3	2	0	18	3
Rank 4 (most complex)	3	0	0	20
	23	23	23	23

The advantage of model B in preparation time is somewhat offset by the time that would have to be spent by companies not on LIFO to change to LIFO, as required by the model. Eight participants not on LIFO provided estimates of the hours or monetary cost that would be needed to make the change, and their estimates are shown in the following schedule.

Participants	Non-LIFO-inventory amount	Monetary cost	Hours Accounting and supervision	Computer programming	Computer running
1	$ 1,681,000	$ 14,100	210	40	132
2	1,657,000		700		
3	34,125,000	1,500	40		
4	483,600,000	400,000			
5	197,647,000	840,000	24,800	3,000	200
6	13,961,000		450	150	20
7	57,038,000	10,000	320	80	10
8	495,028,000	500,000	10,000	3,000	3,000

Use of ASR 190 Information

Nineteen participants filed replacement cost information under ASR 190. The task force permitted those participants to use that information as the basis for calculating the replacement cost of inventories and plant and equipment for models C and D purposes. The participants were permitted to use depreciation expense under ASR 190 as the depreciation expense reported for model B purposes unless the replacement cost of plant and equipment under ASR 190 significantly exceeded the reproduction cost of plant and equipment. Participants not on LIFO were permitted to use cost of goods sold under ASR 190 as the cost of goods sold for model B purposes and to charge the excess over historical cost as a LIFO reserve against inventory.

The participants were encouraged to reduce the replacement cost information for plant and equipment submitted under ASR 190 for operating cost savings for models C and D purposes, which none of them had done for SEC purposes. Only two participants made the reduction, however. The amount of the reduction made by one participant was not disclosed, and the reduction made by the other participant amounted to 11 percent of the gross replacement cost.

The participants that did not make a reduction for operating cost savings gave as reasons the belief that estimates would not be sufficiently accurate (thirteen participants) or that the savings would be immaterial (two participants).

One participant modified the ASR 190 information to omit a "product improvement factor." The omission resulted in increasing replacement price by 4 percent for models C and D purposes.

Deviations From the Models

Some participants modified one or more of the models before preparing financial statements, either because of expediency or because they strongly disagreed with certain of their features. The most common modification was the statement in all four models of the investment in investees accounted for by the equity method at the amount calculated under the conventional accounting model, instead of at the basis required by the respective model.

Model A

Two participants treated deferred income taxes as nonmonetary in applying model A instead of as monetary, as called for by the model. One participant gave the following reason for the deviation:

We feel the FASB procedure of treating deferred taxes as nonmonetary rather than monetary is appropriate. To say deferred taxes are monetary is to say they are equivalent to debt, which is not true. We concur with APB 11 which explicitly states deferred taxes are deferred credits. Additionally, to treat them as monetary exaggerates the current year impact on net income of inflationary "gains" and worsens the mismatch of inflationary accounting of long-term debt with accounting for plant.

Another participant preferred nonmonetary treatment but did not modify model A for that preference.

Model B

One participant applied model B retroactively by calculating the replacement cost of plant and equipment and related accumulated depreciation at January 1, 1975, and reporting the difference between accumulated depreciation at historical cost and at replacement cost at that date as an appropriation of retained earnings after reduction for income taxes. The participant explained the reason for retroactive application:

Due to the effect of rising prices during the year on the beginning balance in accumulated current cost depreciation, the amount charged to expense during the year as "current cost depreciation" will not be large enough to bring the accumulated current cost depreciation up to the proper level. The objective of this model is to demonstrate in the financial statements the amount of retained earnings which is not available for distribution to shareholders if the company is to maintain its productive capacity. Therefore, it is necessary to make a further entry to adjust the beginning balance for "catch-up" or "backlog" current cost depreciation.

That participant probably reported depreciation expense and deferred income taxes in 1975 and 1976 at amounts different from those that would have been reported without retroactive application.

Model D

For one participant, application of the pension accounting requirements of model D would have resulted in reporting an asset rather than a liability for pensions. The participant refused to do that, for the following reason:

Because pension funds are neither controllable or accessible, these funds cannot be associated as an asset. If overfunded pensions are referred to as an asset, then similar funds as Group Insurance ought to be treated equivalently. However, we do concur with the treatment of underfunded pensions in the model.

Shortcuts in Applying the Models

The task force encouraged the participants to approximate the procedures theoretically called for under the four models by following simplifying assumptions and using shortcut procedures to save time in applying the models. The shortcut procedures used are described below.

Model A

Shortcut procedures used for model A of the type that were used by the participants in the field test on general purchasing power accounting conducted by the FASB and that were described in the publication of the results of the test are omitted. Also omitted are shortcut procedures used to calculate replacement cost information that are described in the SEC staff accounting bulletins pertaining to ASR 190.

Model B

Model B calls for accruing deferred income taxes until accumulated depreciation on a current-cost basis exceeds the historical cost of the asset. To avoid a detailed investigation of individual asset records, some participants simply assumed that accrual of deferred taxes in total for all assets met that requirement of the model, at least for the two years for which accrual was made. As one put it,

> Analysis would probably disclose instances in which the assumption was not valid, but we doubt that the effect would be material for the two years reported since they represent a "transition period."

Another participant made the same simplifying assumption but verified it.

> The tax implication of model B (tax effect depreciation until historical cost basis is recovered) was not practical to apply on an individual asset basis because tax basis records are not computerized. Consequently, we used a concept of composite asset grouping by year of addition and found that all excess current cost depreciation would be tax affected in 1975 and 1976. This, however, would not have been true had the model been applied at an earlier date, i.e., backlog depreciation claimed.

Models C and D

Two participants did not directly calculate the minority interest in earnings and stockholders' equity for models C and D because the amount was believed to be immaterial. The minority equity reported under model A was used as a surrogate by one participant. The other participant used the ratio of minority–majority interest in the conventional financial statements to approximate the minority interest for the two models.

One participant used the following shortcut in the two models:

> Equity in earnings of the 50-percent-owned company was determined by restating their financial statements as best as possible using the ratio of our restated financial statement items to our original cost amount for each line item in their balance sheet. The appropriate equity pickup was then applied to the final net adjustment to their shareholders' equity.

Another participant used the amount of equity in unconsolidated investees reported under model A as a surrogate in models C and D for the amount of the same item.

Two participants used the GNP implicit price deflator to approximate the current value of land and construction in progress in the two models. One participant used the GNP implicit price deflator to approximate current value for all assets at January 1, 1975.

Model D

Two participants used shortcuts in calculating pension liabilities under model D:

The company has in excess of thirty separate pension plans. One plan, representing approximately 50 percent of annual pension costs and unfunded accrued pension benefits obligation, was analyzed in accordance with model D requirements. The results were then extrapolated as being representative of the company as a whole.

We didn't calculate unfunded past service liabilities for 1974. After checking with our actuaries, we determined it wouldn't be worthwhile to have them calculated both from a time and accuracy standpoint. So, in order to get to 1975 value changes, we used approximations from pension expense trends.

One participant used a shortcut procedure in calculating long-term debt:

Since publicly traded parent company long-term debt comprises approximately 70 percent of consolidated long-term debt and the vast majority of our debt is fairly recent (1974 to 1976), we determined the current value and effective rates for the parent company debt and extrapolated the results to consolidated indebtedness.

9

Opinions of the Participants

The participants expressed differing opinions on the usefulness of the experiment and each of the models. Some recommended improvements in one or more of the models.

Evaluations of the Usefulness of the Models

Acceptance of the Models

Sixteen participants were favorably disposed toward one or more of the models. Two participants recommended replacing the conventional accounting model with one of the four models; one participant favored model B and the other favored model C. Fourteen participants approved one or more of the models for use in supplementary financial statements, and the following tabulation shows their choices (multiple choice of models was expressed by four participants):

	Participants
Model A	6
Model B	3
Model C	7
Model D	5
	21

Seven participants rejected all the models for use in primary or supplementary financial statements. The rejection was made vehemently by one participant, who described construction of the models as "game playing":

This "game playing" can give as many answers as the theories and the assumptions advanced with inaccuracy compounded by permutations and combinations of such. In our opinion the inclusion of such data would do more to confuse the investor than enlighten him.

Another participant declared that "the shortcomings of historical financial statements are insignificant when compared to the implementation and conceptual problems inherent in the experimentation models."

Ranking of the Models

The participants ranked the four models on overall usefulness to outsiders in making decisions to buy or sell shares in the company or lend money to the company. They also ranked them on relevance, measurability, reliability, and comparability as those qualitative characteristics are described in paragraphs 329–365 of the FASB discussion memorandum.

Ranking was made numerically from 1 (most conforming to the characteristic) to 4 (least conforming) as follows (one participant refrained from ranking):

		Participants			
Overall usefulness		A	B	C	D
1		2	9	7	3
2		5	4	8	4
3		7	5	5	4
4		8	4	2	11
	Total	22	22	22	22
Relevance					
1		4	6	9	4
2		5	5	6	3
3		3	8	4	5
4		10	3	3	10
	Total	22	22	22	22
Measurability					
1		13	6	2	0
2		5	10	3	2
3		2	4	15	1
4		2	2	2	19
	Total	22	22	22	22
Reliability					
1		15	5	1	0
2		5	12	4	1
3		1	3	14	2
4		1	2	3	19
	Total	22	22	22	22
Comparability					
1		7	7	4	3
2		8	8	4	2
3		4	4	12	0
4		3	3	2	17
	Total	22	22	22	22

Comments on the Models

Some participants commented on the usefulness of the models for investment decisions. The comments are set forth below, except that comments on model A that are essentially the same as those made by participants in the field test on general purchasing power accounting conducted by the FASB and that were summarized in the publication of the results of the test are omitted. Comments by the one participant in the banking industry on the usefulness of the models in financial accounting for banks are set forth in a separate section.

Model B. One participant criticized model B as a whole:

> We believe that these statements, by emphasizing the income statement and not accounting for the changes in the values of assets and liabilities, do not present meaningful relationships between the income statement and the balance sheet. If depreciation charged to the income statement is determined on the basis of current costs, we feel that the related assets should also be stated at their current value . . . all amounts shown on the basic financial statements must be based upon the same concept.

Another participant stated:

> . . . this model does have the potential of usefulness *if* the IRS will accept a massive shift to LIFO and the use of indexed depreciation deductions (with the corresponding loss of revenue) for tax purposes. In such an unlikely event, we would have to rethink our position with regard to this model. Barring that, we continue to view this as a basically non-productive endeavor.

Specific aspects of model B were criticized by two participants. Operating cost savings were discussed by one:

> . . . our main objection to model B is the exclusion of operating costs savings from current cost depreciation. While we recognize the complexity of quantifying anticipated operating costs savings, ignoring this problem does not invalidate the fact that current cost depreciation expense, unadjusted, represents an overstatement of its effect on net income.

The other participant called for development of "some more rational basis for the allocation of the tax benefit of depreciation—if it should be allocated at all."

Replacement Cost Under Models C and D. Some participants criticized the use of replacement cost in models C and D, but their criticisms apply to its use in general in financial accounting. For example:

> Model C's and D's use of replacement cost and other current value concepts present financial statement amounts that are meaningless, and hence misleading, because of the subjectivity necessarily involved in making these estimates and because the replacement cost concept is based on the unrealistic premise of total replacement of productive capacity at one point in time. Current value financial statements do not explain how inflation *has* impacted an entity's costs of doing business but, rather, attempts to predict how inflation will, may, or might impact an entity's costs. More uncertainty is injected into the financial statements than is removed because of the subjective nature of current values. Increased uncertainty will further erode the credibility of financial reporting.

101

The value of individual assets is not expressed by the cost which would be incurred were we to replace them; such an expression indicates only the amount of capital that might have to be raised if the assets had been replaced at the balance sheet date—a contingency that didn't happen and for which different prices will apply if it ever does happen. We believe that the value of individual assets is dependent on the purpose for which the value representation is needed, and the interdependency of various assets may make their combined value substantially different from the sum of their individual values.

Model C. A unique feature of model C is the separation of unrealized and realized value changes and their presentation in a separate statement. That feature was strongly supported by one participant:

> We believe that the determination of net income should not include value changes in assets or liabilities until these changes are "realized" through an actual transaction or through the passage of time. To this end, we find that the statement of unrealized value changes included in model C is useful, although we are not enthusiastic about adding another statement to the standard financial package. It does allow the recording of changes in asset and liability values without impacting the income statement. This is a strong plus for model C. Model C also accounts for the amount of value changes which have been charged to operations (capital maintenance allowance charged to operations), which is an especially useful indicator of the ability or inability of management to raise selling prices to current replacement costs.

Other participants were not so enthusiastic, however. One participant could "only speculate how the investment community would react to the net change in realized and unrealized value changes." Another found the model "virtually incomprehensible to operating managers."

Model D. Model D received more vehement criticism than any of the other models. One participant found the model "so completely unrealistic and meaningless that it's difficult to comment on specific aspects." Another found the model "totally impractical" and containing "serious conceptual problems." And another stated the following judgment:

> Our opinion of the value of much of the information produced by model D can be summed up in the words of J. R. Hicks: "It has no more to its credit than its obedience to the laws of arithmetic."

The treatment of pension costs called for under model D was criticized by two participants:

> We found the pension obligation calculations confusing and do not have a satisfactory interpretation or explanation for the results produced. The preparer of the model D methodology seems satisfied to "force" the calculation into a balanced condition.
> The model calls for analyzing changes in the pension liability, treating changes due to plan amendments as an unusual item and splitting the other changes between operations and value changes. For an organization with numerous plans and trustees, this is difficult to do on a timely basis especially if plan years are the same as the company's fiscal year.

One participant had misgivings about the presentation of items in the statement of changes in stockholders' equity without highlighting specific items:

The concept of not highlighting specific line items (such as net income or EPS) and thereby requiring the reader to interpret and evaluate the information presented is an appealing one. Unfortunately, we believe there exists only a relatively small population of reasonably knowledgeable readers willing to make the effort needed to study such statements. Therefore, we believe it would be better for preparers of statements to evaluate and interpret in order to promote as wide dissemination of useful information as possible.

Comments by a Bank

The following comments were made by the banking participant in the experiment on the usefulness of the four models:

In general we concluded that none of the AICPA models was representative of the way a bank does its business. In addition, for reasons indicated below, we were unable to develop a theoretical model that would have incorporated the precision we believe the profession would require and reflected the way we manage our business.

One difficulty with any of the models described below relates to the fact that banks deal daily with large volumes of currency, be they U.S. or foreign. Transactions valued in the billions of dollars take place each day. While total assets may not change significantly, the individual assets or liabilities do. These rapid movements may result in a balance sheet as of any one date that is not representative of our business. As a result, most money center banks have expanded their reports to include average balance data. While we believe this is more representative of our asset and liability positions, it is impossible to ascribe accurately maturity and rate data to the average items. Of course, that can be done on some weighted average assumptions, but precision, auditability, and comparability are lacking.

A second difficulty is mechanically reflecting the way a bank manages its assets and liabilities. The models appeared to require separate account valuations, but a bank cannot consider assets and liabilities separately. In some situations, the assets and liabilities are matched as to maturity and rates so that changes in rates will be offset. As a result, the income of these transactions (the spread between the rate earned and the rate paid) will most likely remain the same even in a changing rate environment. In other cases, bank management may use a more flexible approach than matching specific assets with specific liabilities. For example, a bank may presume its investment portfolio is supported by stockholders' equity or demand deposits in order to evaluate its funds match at one point in time. Of course, these decisions will vary by bank, but bank management must, for profitability, be sure that it obtains funds more cheaply than it lends or invests them and, for liquidity, management must also consider maturities.

A third problem relates to stated versus actual maturities. For example, demand deposits have a theoretical immediate maturity but, in reality, for a going concern, core demand deposits have a consistent indefinite maturity. This is also true for many demand loans. To use the stated demand terms for reporting purposes would be to presume liquidation of assets and liabilities.

We encountered many other conceptual difficulties and will discuss some of them further in our comments on the individual models.

Model A—General Purchasing Power. Model A, the general purchasing power model, is useful to the extent that it places the balance sheet in constant dollars, thereby eliminating the impact of inflation in interperiod comparisons. However, the following problems limit the usefulness of the income statement:

1. The monetary/nonmonetary distinction, which fundamentally determines the size of the price level loss, is very difficult to make, especially in financial institutions, because many of the assets exhibit characteristics of both monetary and nonmonetary items. In a bank, the monetary/nonmonetary classification is questionable for a sufficient volume of assets to make the price level loss a number of limited value.

    For example, we classified all investment and trading securities as monetary, but it can be argued that trading securities are definitely nonmonetary.

2. Making the transaction-by-transaction analyses necessary for proper restatement was difficult. Since the volume of transactions occurring in a bank is large and individual or even groups of transactions are difficult to trace, average rates and restatement factors had to be used to complete the model. Our feeling is that the use of average factors could introduce an error factor.

3. Foreign currency items are difficult to deal with on a conceptual level. This problem can be significant for businesses with substantial foreign assets.

4. The equity method of accounting is almost impossible to apply for a corporation with a significant number of minority-owned subsidiaries because of the lack of data, particularly for foreign operations.

5. The historic data necessary for evaluating fixed assets are generally not readily available within a bank because fixed assets are not significant to operations. We would presume that in most financial institutions the records are maintained manually and that, while retrievable, would require a tremendous effort.

Overall, model A has many of the problems we encountered in the FASB price level study. Because of these problems, we do not believe the model should replace our current financial statements, and its presentation supplementally would probably not be beneficial. If the FASB believes that disclosure of some form of price level adjusted data is necessary for financial institutions, consideration should be given to a presentation limited to stockholders' equity. The trends are ascertainable without the detailed mechanics.

Model B—Adjusted Inventories and Fixed Assets. Model B with its adjustments for inventories and current cost depreciation is basically inappropriate to a bank. As mentioned for model A, the implementation was difficult because of fixed asset records. We were unable to adapt the philosophy here to our asset structure.

Model C—Asset Valuations and Value Changes. Model C with its impact on current values of investment securities and replacement cost of fixed assets also is not appropriate for a financial institution. The fixed asset problem remains the same as models A and B even though the valuation method changes.

The investment securities valuation is questionable because of the amount of long-term bonds in our portfolio. Short-term valuation swings are only significant in a liquidity crisis. Mechanically, the model can be implemented, but the use of market values will not reflect the true nature of a bank's investment portfolio—long-term yield. When a bank sells an investment security, it effectively does not realize a gain or loss but adjusts the yield on its portfolio. This may or may not be done in conjunction with a tax planning strategy. (Tax-exempt state and municipal securities are not beneficial if a bank is not in a taxable income position.)

Model D—Current Value. Model D's adjustments for current values were the most difficult to implement conceptually because of the lack of logical guidelines for arriving at "current values" for financial transactions. One-day-market-values for the individual assets and liabilities not only conflict with the averaging and matching nature of our business but imply some type of discounted cash flows that deal with stated maturities. The use of market values may attempt to cope with the problem of inflation but is more closely allied with liquidation concepts.

Most of our assets are not for sale or trade, so that short-term fluctuations in market values are seldom realized. We may choose to borrow in the short-term market in order to finance a long-term asset because we feel this strategy would produce the best net yield. The market value of the short-term liabilities will probably be close to historical cost, while the market value of the long-term asset may vary significantly from cost. However, this sort of fluctuation will not affect the net yield on the transaction. There is, therefore, no reason for recording it in the financial statements.

Summary. After examining these models and considering alternatives, we have come to the conclusion that current accounting practices reflect the economic value of a financial institution more accurately than any of the suggested models.

It will be difficult to devise a method of accounting for inflation that will make conceptual sense to all or even a majority of the interested parties even if the problems of implementation could be overcome. As regards financial institutions, we feel that it would be much more meaningful to supply the users of financial statements with information as to the rate sensitivity and maturity of assets and liabilities than to restate the financials themselves. It seems preferable to give each user the ability to assess the impact of inflation on a business using assumptions and concepts that make sense to him rather than to provide an assessment of inflation's impact using assumptions and concepts with which many users may disagree. In a financial institution, a knowledge of rate sensitivity and maturity is sufficient to make such an assessment.

Improvements Recommended for the Models

Some participants recommended improvements for the models to make them more suitable for primary or supplementary financial statements. The improvements recommended are described below. Improvements recommended for model A of the type that were also recommended by participants in the field test of general purchasing power accounting conducted by the FASB and that were summarized in the publication of the results of the test are omitted.

Model B

One participant recommended that model B should state inventory at FIFO, calculate cost-of-goods-sold at LIFO, and include the difference in a stockholders' equity account similar to that used for the difference between historical-cost and current-cost depreciation. Another participant recommended the same procedure except that cost-of-goods-sold would be calculated at current cost instead of LIFO.

Elimination of the accrual of deferred income taxes on the difference between historical-cost and current-cost depreciation was recommended by several participants. Two participants stated the following:

> In our view, current-cost depreciation should be construed as giving rise to a permanent difference between book and tax income, rather than a timing difference on which deferred tax is taken. We believe the concept of timing differences should be restricted to cases where the *same amount* is being depreciated over different time periods for book and tax purposes.
>
> This type of rule would produce drastic differences in income statements between companies for which accumulated depreciation on a replacement basis falls below historical cost and for companies for which accumulated depreciation on a replacement basis exceeds

historical costs. In addition proponents of this model desired to show that businesses were being penalized unduly from lack of sufficient tax incentives to encourage capital investment; therefore, the allowance of a tax benefit cancels one major effect which the statements were intended to portray.

Another participant would continue the accrual procedure but in a different form:

The model calls for taking tax benefit on current cost depreciation as long as benefit remains, or until the accumulated current-cost depreciation equals the tax basis in the assets. The effect of this is to front-end the tax benefit and distort earlier operations by taking more of the tax benefit associated with a given asset in the earlier years than in the later years. A more proper theoretical answer would be to spread the tax benefit over the useful life of the assets and thereby achieve a proper matching of revenues and expenses. This would be accomplished by taking the tax benefit associated with straight-line depreciation on the tax basis of the asset over the useful life of the asset.

One participant made the following recommendation:

. . . depreciation should include a provision for still productive, but fully depreciated assets. This could be accomplished by indexing the gross basis of plant and equipment to arrive at current replacement value and calculating depreciation using appropriate useful lives.

Replacement Cost Under Models C and D

Some participants preferred the approach taken in model B to determining replacement cost rather than that in models C and D. One participant made the following statement:

Our major concern with model C is the way in which depreciation and the replacement cost of property, plant, and equipment are determined. We feel that the determination of replacement cost of property, plant, and equipment as described in the "Replacement Cost—Concepts and Implementation" section of the Experimental Program booklet is subjective and not workable in a practical situation. Although it is possible to determine reproductive costs, attempting to include factors for future technological change and making other "as if" assumptions for differences in asset lives and capacity is too subjective to be useful to management. We understand the theoretical considerations which have caused the framers of models C and D to attempt to identify the present value of future cost savings when determining these values. However, the determination of these cost reductions is also extremely difficult to estimate and necessarily subjective. Therefore, from a practical standpoint, we recommend specific indices, as used in model B, be used when computing these costs. Using specific price indices that are approved by the FASB or other central authority will also help to establish credibility for "inflation" adjustments made to a company's historical cost records. One criticism often made of financial statements is that management is allowed too much flexibility in deciding what they should show. The introduction of replacement cost concepts would lead to additional flexibility in the preparation of financial statements, which in turn would certainly cause users to have less confidence in financial statements.

Another participant, who also would not recognize operating cost savings in the two models, would disclose them supplementally:

. . . provision should be made for *supplemental* disclosure of anticipated cost savings from the replacement of productive capacity. We believe this data is of importance to investors in gauging the profit and loss impact of current cost accounting. We suggest supplemental disclosure of this item rather than integration into the calculation in order to highlight the subjectivity of this item and also to avoid jeopardizing any possible income tax deductibility of current cost depreciation.

Elimination of the "deprival value" concept was recommended by one participant:

Replacement cost of plant and equipment has been estimated under the "deprival value" concept, which requires that the value to be ascribed to an asset should be the amount by which the business would be poorer if it were suddenly deprived of the resource at the balance sheet date. It is unrealistic to think that a business would replace all its assets at one time; replacement in the ordinary course of business is a more reasonable approach.

One participant recommended a treatment of "backlog" depreciation different from that specified under the models:

Backlog depreciation should not be charged against the value change statements, but should be charged to the operating statement in order to shelter from taxes and dividends enough resources to replace the fixed assets at current prices. Under model C as presented, as replacement costs increase from year to year the portion of the increase that should have been recovered from prior years' operation is never charged to operations. Since the current year's operating earnings are not charged for this consideration, the incremental resources achieved are subject to depletion by income taxes and dividend payouts.

Elimination of the use of replacement cost for land was called for by one participant:

Land is not normally consumed in the production process, hence variations in land replacement costs are not relevant to measurement of annual earnings. If required, land replacement costs would be difficult to estimate within reasonable limits and might well require appraisal expenditures that would benefit only those with a stake in the appraisal industry. (Useful land cost indexes are not available.)

Model C

Some participants would incorporate certain features of model D in model C, including the treatment of deferred income taxes, pension liabilities, long-term debt, and the elimination of intangibles as assets.

Two participants recommended changing the manner in which realized and unrealized gains and losses are reported under model C. One participant would eliminate the distinction altogether and report unrealized value changes in the statement of changes in stockholders' equity. Another would retain the distinction but would combine realized gains and losses with operating income:

Eliminate distinction between "retained operating income" and "retained realized value changes." We know of no way to ascertain which of those captions should be charged for dividend payments. While one might think dividends would normally be paid from "operating income," obviously cases do exist where investment gains have been realized and used as the source of dividend payments. If the distinction in equity captions is retained, statement preparers would be faced, typically, with an arbitrary allocation requirement.

Several participants would eliminate the accrual of deferred income taxes on the difference between historical cost and net realizable value called for under model C. One stated the following:

> The model calls for assets representing sources of liquidity to be booked net of tax. The categorization of assets representing sources of liquidity is extremely arbitrary. Any asset can become a source of liquidity if the company decides to dispose of it. The disposition of an asset not previously categorized as a source of liquidity will result in net proceeds less than the carrying value of the asset. The reason for this is the taxes that must be paid out of the proceeds.

Other participants would retain the accrual procedure but would report the accrued taxes separately from the income statement and balance sheet items to which they pertain.

Model D

Elimination of the procedure under model D of recognizing the effect on stockholders' equity of the increase in the general price level during the year was recommended by one participant:

> The indexing forward of beginning shareholders' equity is confusing to the reader and of little value. If the point is to measure physical capital in units of purchasing power, then the 1975 assets and liabilities as well as results of operations should have been indexed forward.

Another participant would retain the procedure and extend it to the comparative balance sheet for the previous year:

> Some confusion is created in model D by the price level restatement of current year beginning stockholder equity with the offsetting charge to current year's activity. When comparative years are shown, this treatment results in a beginning balance for the current year different from the ending balance in the comparative year. While this discrepancy is valid in the model D treatment, it could be avoided by restating the entire comparative balance sheet by the current year's general price level change. The offsetting charge would be to the comparative year's "value change" statement. This balance sheet treatment is similar to that used in the price level adjusted statements (model A) and has the added benefit of restating the previous year's current values by a general index of inflation so that they might more closely approximate the current year's current values and, therefore, be more comparable. Unlike model A, the existing line items on the comparative year's operating statement and "value change" statement would not be restated for the price level change, but an additional line item would be added to the "value change" statement and the effect of restating the balance sheet charged to it.

Alterations in the manner of reporting changes in stockholders' equity under model D were recommended by several participants. Two participants would continue to report all changes in a single statement but would label the subtotals in the statement. One participant would go further and report value changes and results of operations in separate statements and would separate stockholders' equity in the balance sheet into amounts for capital stock, capital surplus, accumulated operating results, and accumulated value changes.

108

One participant would eliminate the procedure of stating long-term debt at current value:

> This treatment can be confusing because in many cases debt agreements do not allow the company to refund the debt until sometime in the future. These restrictions make the current valuation of debt less meaningful since there may be nothing that management can do to these changes in debt.

Several participants would eliminate the accrual of deferred income taxes on the difference between the historical cost and the current value of assets and liabilities called for under model D, but others would retain the accrual procedure and report the accrued taxes separately from the income statement and balance sheet items to which they pertain. Two participants would report intangibles as assets.

Usefulness of the Experiment

The eleven participants that commented on the usefulness of the experiment were divided in their opinions: six commented favorably on the usefulness, four commented unfavorably, and one was ambivalent. The favorable comments were as follows:

> The individuals who were involved gained significant new knowledge and insight about the company. In addition, these individuals are now at the forefront of accounting theory.
>
> The accounting staff working directly on the project gained valuable insights into the issues and practical implementation possibilities of the conceptual framework for accounting. Working with our numbers caused us to focus on the implications of various alternatives more than was the case when reading the FASB material and "conceptualizing"— practical application has been extremely valuable . . . Hopefully, the compiled results of this experiment will be of benefit to the accounting profession in determining a course for the future.
>
> The experiment provided the opportunity, as well as a frame of reference and technical guideline, for an in-depth view of the questions and considerations at issue in the FASB's current examination of a conceptual framework. Since the decisions that will be made on these issues could have profound effects, the experiment provided some needed insight that wouldn't have been achieved without our participation.
>
> The benefits derived from this program result mainly from the application of theory to practice. We believe that the nature of accounting dictates that accounting rules are not set solely based on the theoretical consideration but rather through "general acceptance." "General acceptance" can be achieved only when companies understand alternative methods designed to account for inflation and have decided on a preference. This understanding comes from working with various alternatives and attempting to apply them in practice.
>
> Application of the four models to actual corporate financial data has provided a comprehensive exposure to the conceptual framework project and the alternatives currently being considered for financial reporting in an inflationary environment. We feel that the experiment will demonstrate empirically the difficulties and far-reaching consequences likely to be encountered by any departure from the existing historical cost framework for financial accounting and reporting.
>
> We believe that the experiment was very meaningful and beneficial in that one can determine the feasibility and value of various measurements and presentations of financial information that differ from present practice. Much experimentation is needed before any deviations from present practice are instituted because such changes would involve every user of financial statements.

The unfavorable comments were these:

The original price level study gave us some perspective; this experiment did not add much other than to emphasize the implementation problems.

Based on the public hearing of the FASB on the conceptual framework project, it appears that the board is considering a much more limited alteration of accounting statements and accounting practices than was previously expected. This experiment appears to go far beyond what the board now envisages. To that end, a considerable amount of extra time preparing fruitless statements may have resulted from this particular project.

Our general feeling on completing our participation in the experiment was one of mild disappointment. We did not feel that we gained any particularly meaningful new insights for ourselves, nor did we unearth any new or startling evidence by which we could convince others of the correctness of the views we have publicly expressed to the FASB.

The experiment was of limited meaningfulness and produced no benefits except to confirm previously held views.

None of the participants who had submitted opinions to the FASB on the objectives of financial statements and part 1 of the FASB discussion memorandum stated that they had undergone a change in their opinions as a result of the experiment. Four participants stated that the experiment had helped them form an opinion on the issues raised in parts 2 and 3 of the discussion memorandum.

Eight participants believed that experimentation in financial accounting models should continue in the future after the completion of this experiment. Two participants recommended that companies individually experiment with various models. Two recommended that the models in this experiment be applied to a larger number of companies, and two foresaw a need to concentrate on different types of industries. One recommended that surveys be conducted of investors and lenders to determine their desires for information, and another would submit the results of this experiment to them to determine their reaction:

We suggest that the task force attempt to utilize the submitted data, in some form that would preserve the anonymity of individual submissions, in an experiment with selected financial analysts and other statement users to see what use they might make of the data, particularly the kinds of value change data presented in models C and D. We have seen many assertions that such data would be "useful to investors" but have seen no data, experimental or otherwise, in support of those assertions.

10

Information From the Participants' Financial Statements

Information from the participants' financial statements submitted for the conventional accounting model and the four experimental models is presented in this chapter in matrix schedules in which the columns describe the types of information and the rows identify the participants according to assigned number and type of industry. In keeping with the task force's promise to provide the utmost confidentiality of the data submitted, the matrices present percentages rather than absolute numbers. Also, some companies requested that their data be omitted, and this has been done. However, two participants consented to publication of their entire financial statements, which are presented in chapter 11.

Schedule I presents changes, expressed as percentages, in important financial statement items from 1975 to 1976. Schedule II presents ratios, expressed as percentages, between various items in the financial statements for both 1975 and 1976. Schedule III presents important financial statement items under the conventional model expressed as percentages of similar items under the four experimental models for both 1975 and 1976.

In some places, letters are inserted in the schedules rather than numbers. The letters have the following meanings:

a   Information necessary for calculation was not furnished by participant.

b   No income statement for 1975 was prepared by participant.

c   Increase or gain in one year, decrease or loss in other year; or zero amount for 1975.

d   Net interest income.

e   Loss instead of income.

f   Assets and liabilities stated at historical cost at January 1, 1975.

g   Dividends not paid.

h   Income tax credit.

i Information omitted at the request of participant.

j Model apparently was applied incorrectly.

NA Not applicable.

All balance sheet items used in the ratios reported in schedules II and III are amounts in effect at the end of the year to which the schedule refers. In interpreting the information presented for manufacturing company 4, it should be kept in mind that investments accounted for under the equity method were not restated in preparing the financial statements for the four experimental models, and that 61 percent and 49 percent of the company's net income under the conventional model in 1976 and 1975, respectively, came from those investments.

SCHEDULE I
Financial Statement Items Under the Four Experimental Models
Expressed as a Percent of Similar Items Under the Conventional Model
(Conventional (Historical Cost) Model = 100%)
1975

	Net income				Depreciation expense			
	Net income (Model A)	Net income (Model B)	Net operating income and unrealized value increases (Model C)	Increase in stockholders' equity from all items except capital transactions (Model D)	Model A	Model B	Model C	Model D
Transportation company	108.2	e	584.8	e	211.0	313.5	313.5	211.4
Retailer	23.3	68.2	118.8	21.9	122.5	127.9	127.9	127.9
Manufacturers								
1	26.6	37.0	157.0	48.0	147.3	155.8	i	i
2	90.9	b	b	b	118.5	b	b	b
3	68.3	86.8	185.5	71.9	143.3	126.4	146.6	91.4
4	74.5	72.5	132.8	50.3	155.3	168.4	168.4	168.4
5	96.0	88.7	110.4	67.4	136.4	125.5	174.5	170.9
6	j	52.4	e	36.6	j	159.2	159.2	159.2
7	47.5	86.3	f	f	138.9	152.7	152.7	152.7
8	60.2	73.6	108.9	26.6	128.5	125.9	125.9	125.9
9	46.5	83.5	f	f	146.4	144.1	196.9	196.9
10	e	35.7	231.5	e	140.1	140.1	189.0	189.0
11	97.6	55.9	f	f	125.2	187.3	187.3	172.1
12	68.3	87.1	116.8	37.6	136.2	126.9	117.1	117.1
13	85.1	98.1	114.8	60.9	160.5	113.4	113.4	113.4
14	79.2	75.6	145.8	70.9	143.5	173.6	133.5	133.5
15	j	66.3	f	f	j	143.9	143.9	136.4
16	126.6	86.8	141.0	104.1	134.2	131.6	107.9	107.9
17	40.2	30.8	f	f	141.2	134.2	134.2	134.2
18	72.4	70.4	f	f	149.5	155.3	155.3	155.3

SCHEDULE I (Continued)

Financial Statement Items Under the Four Experimental Models
Expressed as a Percent of Similar Items Under the Conventional Model
(Conventional (Historical Cost) Model = 100%)

1976

	Net income				Depreciation expense			
	Net income (Model A)	Net income (Model B)	Net operating income and unrealized value increases (Model C)	Increase in stockholders' equity from all items except capital transactions (Model D)	Model A	Model B	Model C	Model D
Transportation company	77.0	e	367.6	e	204.1	327.9	327.9	218.8
Retailer	74.9	82.6	107.1	84.1	123.8	131.4	131.4	131.4
Manufacturers								
1	56.5	63.1	116.8	63.7	138.1	148.6	i	i
2	83.7	75.0	124.4	84.6	113.9	159.2	141.6	141.6
3	75.6	86.1	143.5	92.1	137.9	126.6	165.0	90.5
4	41.0	63.8	63.3	3.5	153.4	174.8	174.8	174.8
5	87.6	102.2	112.1	76.6	126.3	131.1	169.5	166.1
6	j	95.0	65.1	39.7	j	147.1	147.1	147.1
7	48.5	85.5	117.8	73.4	142.6	142.0	142.0	142.0
8	77.6	80.1	100.5	78.1	122.4	125.9	125.9	125.9
9	70.8	90.0	133.3	131.4	138.9	146.2	200.0	200.0
10	52.7	78.7	131.9	36.5	134.0	134.0	186.6	186.6
11	87.6	66.7	82.7	75.0	125.8	187.3	187.3	173.0
12	78.0	92.1	114.4	77.3	125.8	131.9	121.2	121.2
13	81.7	97.9	104.3	69.0	152.9	119.2	119.2	119.2
14	80.0	69.3	142.9	93.1	131.2	179.5	115.2	115.2
15	j	59.2	70.9	2.9	j	153.4	153.4	160.3
16	101.5	88.4	172.1	104.1	124.8	128.2	153.4	108.0
17	23.5	100.0	106.0	e	142.0	136.2	108.0	136.2
18	79.2	78.6	153.6	93.3	138.1	155.3	136.2	155.3

SCHEDULE I (Continued)

Financial Statement Items Under the Four Experimental Models
Expressed as a Percent of Similar Items Under the Conventional Model
(Conventional (Historical Cost) Model = 100%)

1975

	Cost of goods sold				Income tax expense			
	Model A	Model B	Model C	Model D	Model A	Model B	Model C	Model D
Transportation company	NA	NA	NA	NA	108.1	h	83.8	136.4
Retailer	112.9	101.9	101.9	101.9	108.5	70.4	100.0	104.3
Manufacturers								
1	108.1	100.0	i	i	101.3	13.7	100.0	86.0
2	110.1	b	b	b	107.1	b	b	b
3	109.9	101.9	103.0	97.4	106.7	86.4	100.2	93.7
4	109.4	100.6	102.6	102.6	107.1	86.9	100.9	91.2
5	108.6	99.9	99.8	99.8	110.1	86.7	102.4	92.6
6	j	102.7	102.7	102.5	j	73.9	91.9	79.2
7	120.2	100.8	100.0	100.8	114.8	84.1	100.0	100.0
8	108.7	102.2	102.2	102.2	107.1	84.2	100.0	100.0
9	111.7	100.3	100.6	100.6	107.1	88.0	98.2	81.7
10	103.6	94.8	94.4	94.7	107.5	66.5	100.0	h
11	a	a	a	a	106.6	96.1	100.0	76.2
12	112.7	101.4	101.4	99.8	107.6	82.4	100.6	90.3
13	107.0	100.0	101.4	101.4	107.2	97.8	100.0	99.2
14	111.2	107.5	95.0	91.0	107.1	85.8	100.5	95.5
15	j	99.8	100.2	100.0	j	70.6	100.0	100.0
16	107.5	100.0	100.0	93.3	107.1	90.3	100.0	96.3
17	107.5	101.7	101.7	101.7	106.7	14.4	100.0	9.2
18	a	a	a	a	107.0	69.0	102.7	101.6

SCHEDULE I (Continued)
Financial Statement Items Under the Four Experimental Models
Expressed as a Percent of Similar Items Under the Conventional Model
(Conventional (Historical Cost) Model = 100%)

1976

	Cost of goods sold				Income tax expense			
	Model A	Model B	Model C	Model D	Model A	Model B	Model C	Model D
Transportation company	NA	NA	NA	NA	101.9	h	85.9	65.4
Retailer	103.6	101.8	101.8	101.8	101.7	83.5	100.0	101.5
Manufacturers								
1	102.5	100.0	i	i	99.2	61.7	100.0	65.4
2	103.3	101.2	98.8	98.8	101.9	70.3	100.0	96.7
3	104.3	102.6	104.7	98.4	101.7	86.4	99.9	97.7
4	104.4	100.2	102.4	102.4	101.9	79.6	98.4	82.7
5	102.1	99.4	99.4	99.4	102.0	102.2	101.2	100.2
6	j	100.2	102.7	102.4	j	102.1	99.2	97.0
7	107.4	101.0	100.0	100.6	105.2	83.8	100.0	100.0
8	103.1	101.9	101.9	101.9	101.9	93.5	100.0	100.0
9	104.4	100.2	100.2	100.2	102.0	91.6	100.0	87.7
10	97.8	94.8	94.9	95.6	101.7	85.3	100.0	66.4
11	a	a	a	a	101.7	97.8	100.0	81.0
12	104.8	100.7	100.0	99.0	101.8	88.5	100.8	94.9
13	101.9	100.0	100.7	100.7	101.9	97.2	100.0	99.2
14	105.5	108.8	93.6	89.6	101.9	83.1	98.9	96.0
15	j	99.8	100.1	100.0	j	52.1	100.0	100.0
16	102.6	100.0	100.1	93.9	101.9	88.6	100.0	91.9
17	103.2	98.6	98.3	98.3	99.6	100.1	100.0	75.4
18	a	a	a	a	101.4	78.9	100.7	101.9

SCHEDULE I (Continued)
Financial Statement Items Under the Four Experimental Models
Expressed as a Percent of Similar Items Under the Conventional Model
(Conventional (Historical Cost) Model = 100%)
1975

	Net property, plant, and equipment			Net assets			
	Model A	Model C	Model D	Model A	Model B	Model C	Model D
Transportation company	271.7	434.8	332.2	456.6	103.5	781.3	602.4
Retailer	133.3	129.2	114.9	120.0	98.0	111.9	100.5
Manufacturers							
1	123.2	138.5	121.5	126.1	104.0	154.1	111.0
2	122.5	143.3	120.2	138.3	93.9	139.7	106.2
3	138.1	145.3	114.8	132.5	100.5	170.6	131.9
4	152.2	158.7	124.5	159.2	99.9	159.7	125.5
5	129.7	135.9	112.4	126.9	99.7	141.2	120.5
6	j	180.2	138.3	j	100.5	162.1	119.9
7	137.0	123.8	114.5	126.6	100.2	109.9	105.2
8	128.0	134.6	117.9	115.7	100.0	117.6	112.1
9	138.1	177.9	132.1	144.1	100.9	163.9	125.2
10	146.0	244.5	182.5	141.2	101.3	218.3	165.0
11	167.8	222.7	155.8	159.7	110.1	156.5	71.2
12	130.5	112.9	104.4	126.3	100.4	114.8	105.7
13	161.3	176.7	138.9	118.1	100.2	121.5	111.2
14	134.6	186.2	149.5	126.9	100.6	167.5	141.6
15	j	216.0	214.1	j	107.1	225.7	208.8
16	128.9	135.7	117.5	172.4	102.6	162.1	135.5
17	145.1	109.1	100.1	132.5	99.8	116.6	111.7
18	132.3	193.1	146.6	151.7	101.8	193.4	140.3

SCHEDULE I (Continued)

Financial Statement Items Under the Four Experimental Models
Expressed as a Percent of Similar Items Under the Conventional Model
(Conventional (Historical Cost) Model = 100%)

1976

	Net property, plant, and equipment			Net assets			
	Model A	*Model C*	*Model D*	*Model A*	*Model B*	*Model C*	*Model D*
Transportation company	257.7	425.5	326.8	434.8	106.0	769.2	588.2
Retailer	125.0	129.7	113.1	112.5	96.4	111.5	101.6
Manufacturers							
1	115.9	133.5	119.3	119.8	107.2	153.4	111.4
2	117.8	138.1	116.7	129.7	93.2	138.5	106.5
3	132.8	151.3	116.7	125.3	100.5	169.5	132.8
4	149.9	163.1	125.9	152.4	100.3	154.8	122.1
5	123.5	133.3	111.1	118.8	102.2	135.7	116.8
6	j	169.2	133.7	j	99.3	151.3	113.6
7	129.4	128.4	117.0	116.2	100.0	111.4	105.5
8	121.2	127.2	114.2	110.6	100.5	115.7	112.0
9	133.0	179.5	132.6	133.5	99.8	160.8	126.9
10	138.1	243.3	183.8	132.8	102.5	212.3	160.5
11	163.9	216.0	156.0	169.5	108.7	164.5	82.4
12	125.6	115.1	105.2	119.2	101.3	115.9	105.7
13	145.3	169.5	135.0	111.4	100.5	120.3	109.6
14	128.0	185.5	148.1	121.4	101.3	168.9	143.1
15	j	185.5	185.2	j	114.0	206.6	188.7
16	120.0	136.1	116.8	163.4	104.6	172.7	137.2
17	140.6	107.9	96.9	126.6	101.9	116.7	109.6
18	126.3	192.3	146.2	142.9	103.6	192.3	141.6

SCHEDULE II
Ratios (Expressed as Percents) of Financial Statement Items
1975

| | Net income to stockholders' equity | | | Model C | | | Model D | |
| | | | | Net o/i | | | | |
	Conventional model	Model A	Model B	To s/e	To s/e less accumulated u/v/i	Net o/i and u/v/i to s/e	r/o/o and e/i to s/e	Increase in s/e from all items* to s/e
Transportation company	i	2.0	e	e	e	6.4	0.1	e
Retailer	10.5	2.0	7.3	4.3	4.8	11.2	3.3	2.3
Manufacturers								
1	i	1.5	2.5	2.1	3.0	7.2	e	3.1
2	17.2	11.3	b	b	b	b	b	b
3	11.2	5.7	9.6	4.0	6.9	12.1	3.7	6.1
4	11.1	5.2	8.1	3.1	5.0	9.3	3.1	4.5
5	21.6	16.4	19.2	10.9	15.3	16.9	14.1	12.1
6	7.7	j	4.0	0.2	0.3	e	e	2.4
7	13.5	5.1	9.2	9.1	10.0	f	9.5	f
8	10.6	5.5	7.8	6.1	7.2	9.8	6.1	2.5
9	11.2	3.6	9.3	2.7	4.4	f	4.6	f
10	4.4	e	1.6	e	e	4.7	1.3	e
11	9.7	8.5	4.9	2.9	4.6	f	10.9	f
12	12.7	6.9	11.0	8.6	9.9	12.9	10.7	4.5
13	11.6	8.4	11.4	8.0	9.3	11.0	8.8	6.4
14	16.5	10.3	12.4	7.7	12.9	14.4	9.6	8.3
15	20.7	j	12.8	2.1	4.6	f	3.5	f
16	26.1	19.1	22.1	15.2	24.6	22.7	18.2	20.0
17	3.3	1.0	1.0	e	e	f	0.7	f
18	14.2	6.8	9.8	2.6	5.0	f	e	f

* Except capital transactions

(s/e = stockholders' equity; o/i = operating income; u/v/i = unrealized value increases; r/o/o = results of ordinary operations; e/i = extraordinary items)

SCHEDULE II (Continued)
Ratios (Expressed as Percents) of Financial Statement Items
1976

| | Net income to stockholders' equity | | | Model C | | | | Model D |
| | | | | Net o/i | | | | |
	Conventional model	Model A	Model B	To s/e	To s/e less accumulated u/v/i	Net o/i and u/v/i to s/e	r/o/o and e/i to s/e	Increase in s/e from all items* to s/e
Transportation company	i	1.6	e	e	e	4.3	0.4	e
Retailer	18.5	12.3	15.8	11.2	12.4	17.7	13.0	15.3
Manufacturers								
1	i	5.4	6.7	4.7	6.4	8.7	3.3	6.5
2	18.6	12.0	14.9	9.9	13.8	16.7	13.7	14.8
3	14.7	8.8	12.6	4.6	7.8	12.4	6.7	10.2
4	8.4	2.2	5.3	1.1	1.8	3.4	0.3	0.2
5	21.4	15.8	21.4	15.4	20.7	17.7	18.0	14.0
6	13.6	j	13.0	4.1	6.2	5.8	5.0	4.7
7	14.4	6.0	12.3	10.1	11.3	15.2	10.8	10.0
8	14.8	10.4	11.8	9.4	10.8	12.8	9.7	10.3
9	16.1	8.5	14.5	6.1	9.8	13.3	6.6	16.7
10	10.8	4.3	8.3	0.6	1.3	6.7	1.5	2.5
11	15.5	8.0	8.5	4.9	7.2	7.8	14.4	23.2
12	17.9	11.7	16.2	13.5	15.7	17.7	15.3	13.1
13	14.5	10.7	14.2	11.1	12.6	12.6	12.2	9.1
14	16.2	10.6	11.1	7.9	13.3	13.7	9.6	10.5
15	18.1	j	4.2	1.5	3.0	6.2	0.6	0.2
16	27.3	16.9	23.0	15.1	26.0	27.2	19.3	20.7
17	6.7	1.2	6.5	6.2	7.3	6.1	7.7	e
18	16.6	9.2	12.6	4.7	9.1	13.3	9.1	11.0

* Except capital transactions

(s/e = stockholders' equity; o/i = operating income; u/v/i = unrealized value increases; r/o/o = results of ordinary operations; e/i = extraordinary items)

SCHEDULE II (Continued)
Ratios (Expressed as Percents) of Financial Statement Items
1975

	Dividends to net income			Model C Dividends		Model D Dividends	
	Conventional model	Model A	Model B	To net o/i	To net o/i and u/v/i	To r/o/o and e/i	To increase in s/e from all items*
Transportation company	i	42.3	e	e	7.3	1619.9	e
Retailer	51.7	240.7	75.7	112.8	43.5	170.7	242.9
Manufacturers							
1	i	318.3	213.7	170.2	50.4	e	160.8
2	25.8	30.4	b	b	b	b	b
3	44.6	69.7	51.4	72.1	24.0	104.2	63.2
4	47.4	68.2	65.5	105.6	35.7	139.0	96.7
5	g	g	g	g	g	g	g
6	68.9	j	131.5	1587.9	e	e	193.1
7	27.0	62.0	31.3	36.3	f	39.7	f
8	36.9	62.7	50.1	54.2	33.9	59.1	141.8
9	23.1	53.8	27.7	58.7	f	45.0	f
10	90.8	e	254.2	e	39.3	184.2	e
11	28.3	31.1	50.6	60.2	f	a	f
12	108.0	170.0	124.0	138.5	92.4	124.5	293.7
13	22.8	28.7	23.3	27.3	19.9	27.7	38.4
14	54.2	72.9	71.6	69.6	37.2	67.1	77.7
15	68.5	j	103.2	305.1	f	192.9	f
16	44.8	37.9	51.6	47.6	31.8	48.6	44.1
17	130.8	348.8	424.2	e	f	592.6	f
18	56.0	82.0	79.0	157.0	f	e	f

* Except capital transactions

(o/i = operating income; u/v/i = unrealized value increases; r/o/o = results of ordinary operations; e/i = extraordinary items; s/e = stockholders' equity)

SCHEDULE II (Continued)
Ratios (Expressed as Percents) of Financial Statement Items
1976

	Conventional model	Dividends to net income		Model C — Dividends		Model D — Dividends	
		Model A	Model B	To net o/i	To net o/i and u/v/i	To r/o/o and e/i	To increase in s/e from all items*
Transportation company	i	52.7	e	e	10.8	155.4	e
Retailer	26.9	36.5	32.5	39.8	25.1	38.1	32.5
Manufacturers							
1	i	103.3	90.9	90.6	49.2	175.4	88.1
2	25.8	31.4	34.4	34.8	20.7	33.7	31.2
3	29.2	39.3	33.9	54.8	20.3	48.8	32.3
4	61.1	151.9	95.7	290.3	96.5	1368.8	1774.7
5	6.1	7.0	5.9	6.2	5.4	6.3	8.0
6	36.7	j	38.7	79.9	56.4	89.1	94.3
7	29.0	62.7	33.9	36.9	24.6	38.6	41.5
8	25.4	33.3	31.7	34.4	25.3	35.3	33.1
9	22.5	32.5	25.0	36.9	16.9	43.6	17.2
10	33.3	64.3	42.3	286.6	25.3	149.8	92.5
11	20.7	24.0	30.9	39.8	25.0	27.5	17.0
12	73.6	96.1	80.0	83.9	64.4	83.2	96.9
13	21.1	26.3	21.5	23.0	20.2	23.3	31.1
14	51.3	65.2	74.0	62.4	36.0	61.4	55.9
15	40.1	j	67.7	240.0	56.6	594.2	1394.7
16	47.4	47.6	53.6	49.7	27.6	49.7	46.4
17	76.0	329.4	76.0	69.6	71.6	60.8	e
18	45.0	58.0	58.0	83.0	29.5	1467.5	52.6

* Except capital transactions

(o/i = operating income; u/v/i = unrealized value increases; r/o/o = results of ordinary operations; e/i = extraordinary items; s/e = stockholders' equity)

SCHEDULE II (Continued)
Ratios (Expressed as Percents) of Financial Statement Items
1975

	Net income to sales			Model C		Model D		Model A
	Conventional model	Model A	Model B	Net oli to sales	Net oli and u/v/i to sales	r/o/o and e/i to sales	Increase in s/e from all items* to sales	Net monetary gain (loss) to net interest expense
Transportation company	i	7.2	e	e	41.4	0.2	e	239.2
Retailer	2.7	0.6	1.8	1.2	3.2	0.8	0.6	70.0
Manufacturers								
1	i	0.9	1.4	1.7	5.9	e	1.8	56.8
2	5.8	4.9	b	b	b	b	b	80.0
3	5.9	3.8	5.1	3.7	11.0	2.6	4.3	(5.9)
4	6.8	4.7	4.9	3.1	9.0	2.4	3.4	56.0
5	1.3	1.1	1.1	0.9	1.4	1.0	0.9	32.5
6	3.0	j	1.6	0.1	e	e	1.1	j
7	5.6	2.3	4.9	4.2	f	4.2	f	63.1
8	4.5	2.6	3.3	3.1	5.0	2.9	1.2	(67.3)
9	4.7	2.0	3.9	1.8	f	2.4	f	62.6
10	2.0	e	0.7	e	4.7	1.0	e	68.3
11	5.5	5.0	3.1	2.6	f	4.4	f	104.2
12	8.2	5.2	7.1	6.4	9.6	7.3	3.1	88.9
13	7.3	5.8	7.1	6.1	8.4	6.1	4.4	(38.7)
14	12.4	9.1	9.4	9.6	18.0	10.2	8.8	d
15	7.5	j	5.0	1.7	f	2.7	f	j
16	11.0	13.0	9.6	10.4	15.6	10.4	11.5	176.4
17	1.6	0.6	0.5	e	f	0.4	f	42.7
18	3.9	2.6	2.8	1.4	f	e	f	1.0

* Except capital transactions

(o/i = operating income; u/v/i = unrealized value increases; r/o/o = results of ordinary operations; e/i = extraordinary items; s/e = stockholders' equity)

SCHEDULE II (Continued)

Ratios (Expressed as Percents) of Financial Statement Items

1976

	Net income to sales			Model C		Model D		Model A
	Conventional model	Model A	Model B	Net o/i to sales	Net o/i and u/v/i to sales	r/o/o and e/i to sales	Increase in s/e from all items* to sales	Net monetary gain (loss) to net interest expense
Transportation company	i	5.5	e	e	26.6	1.9	e	120.5
Retailer	4.6	3.4	3.8	3.1	5.0	3.3	3.9	56.7
Manufacturers								
1	i	3.0	3.5	3.5	6.4	1.8	3.5	29.1
2	6.2	5.1	4.6	4.6	7.7	4.8	5.2	49.2
3	7.2	5.3	6.2	3.8	10.3	4.4	6.6	(43.0)
4	5.2	2.1	3.3	1.1	3.3	0.2	0.2	20.1
5	1.4	1.2	1.4	1.3	1.6	1.4	1.1	17.1
6	5.0	j	4.8	2.3	3.3	2.1	2.0	j
7	5.2	2.4	4.4	4.0	6.1	4.1	3.8	55.2
8	5.9	4.5	4.7	4.3	5.9	4.3	4.6	(96.6)
9	5.9	4.1	5.3	3.6	7.9	3.1	7.8	43.3
10	4.6	2.4	3.6	0.5	6.1	1.0	1.7	26.7
11	7.7	6.6	5.2	4.0	6.4	5.9	9.6	d
12	10.7	8.2	9.8	9.3	12.2	9.6	8.2	22.8
13	9.8	7.9	9.6	9.0	10.3	9.1	6.8	(86.8)
14	10.0	9.4	8.3	9.8	17.1	10.2	11.1	d
15	7.0	j	4.2	1.2	5.0	0.5	0.2	j
16	11.3	11.3	10.0	10.8	19.5	11.0	11.8	76.9
17	3.2	0.7	3.2	3.5	3.4	4.0	e	(7.4)
18	4.7	3.6	3.7	2.6	7.2	0.2	4.4	(13.9)

* Except capital transactions

(o/i = operating income; u/v/i = unrealized value increases; r/o/o = results of ordinary operations; e/i = extraordinary items; s/e = stockholders' equity)

SCHEDULE II (Continued)
Ratios (Expressed as Percents) of Financial Statement Items
1975

	Income tax expense to pretax income					Gross margin to sales				
	Conventional model	Model A	Model B	Model C	Model D	Conventional model	Model A	Model B	Model C	Model D
Transportation company	i	8.0	e	e	122.6	NA	NA	NA	NA	NA
Retailer	47.2	76.5	47.3	64.5	72.5	34.3	31.7	33.1	33.1	33.1
Manufacturers										
1	i	69.8	18.7	57.4	51.0	i	24.2	25.1	25.1	25.1
2	41.3	45.4	b	b	b	54.5	53.2	b	b	b
3	46.6	57.6	46.5	58.6	56.7	31.2*	29.4	29.9	29.1	33.0
4	32.7	50.5	36.8	52.2	53.2	21.1*	19.4	20.6	19.1	19.1
5	46.0	48.6	45.4	55.1	50.0	3.9	4.1	4.0	4.1	4.0
6	51.7	j	60.2	95.8	109.4	24.5	j	22.5	22.5	22.6
7	44.4	65.9	43.8	51.8	51.8	24.4	20.8	23.8	24.4	23.8
8	46.4	60.6	49.7	56.0	57.5	26.6*	25.5	24.9	24.9	24.9
9	51.8	71.2	53.1	72.8	63.0	33.9*	31.0	33.7	33.7	33.7
10	46.7	99.5	61.9	e	h	13.4*	16.1	17.9	18.2	18.0
11	51.1	53.0	64.8	69.3	49.8	a	a	a	a	a
12	44.0	55.3	42.6	50.3	42.8	36.5	33.5	35.7	35.6	36.7
13	48.4	54.9	48.4	49.5	53.0	38.1*	38.1	38.1	37.2	37.2
14	44.5	52.1	47.7	41.2	48.3	41.0*	38.8	36.5	43.9	43.3
15	52.5	j	54.1	83.1	75.7	33.2	j	33.4	33.1	33.2
16	50.7	46.5	51.7	52.2	51.2	34.8*	34.6	34.8	34.8	39.2
17	45.5	69.3	28.3	214.8	25.6	22.6	22.4	21.3	21.3	21.3
18	39.9	49.3	39.4	65.5	113.9	a	a	a	a	a

* Part or all of the inventories were on LIFO.

SCHEDULE II (Continued)
Ratios (Expressed as Percents) of Financial Statement Items
1976

	Income tax expense to pretax income					Gross margin to sales				
	Conventional model	Model A	Model B	Model C	Model D	Conventional model	Model A	Model B	Model C	Model D
Transportation company	i	16.9	e	e	27.6	NA	NA	NA	NA	NA
Retailer	48.7	56.4	49.0	58.5	60.5	35.9	34.7	34.7	34.7	34.7
Manufacturers										
1	i	57.3	42.8	54.7	36.8	i	27.5	27.9	25.1	25.1
2	43.7	48.6	42.1	51.2	49.0	54.2	53.6	53.6	54.7	54.7
3	46.1	53.0	46.1	61.6	57.6	34.4*	32.8	32.7	31.3	35.4
4	27.9	55.6	32.5	64.4	80.7	18.0*	16.1	17.9	16.1	16.1
5	51.2	53.8	51.2	52.1	51.7	4.2	4.5	4.7	4.8	4.8
6	50.6	j	52.4	68.9	66.7	26.6	j	26.4	24.6	24.8
7	45.2	64.1	44.7	51.3	51.1	23.0	21.2	22.2	23.0	22.5
8	45.3	52.1	49.2	52.9	53.0	28.5*	27.7	27.2	27.2	27.2
9	51.9	60.9	52.3	63.9	58.8	34.0*	32.4	33.9	33.9	33.9
10	44.7	39.1	46.7	87.2	70.5	17.0*	20.0	21.3	21.2	20.6
11	50.7	53.5	61.4	64.4	50.1	a	a	a	a	a
12	44.5	51.1	43.5	47.9	43.9	39.2	37.5	38.8	38.9	39.8
13	43.6	49.1	43.4	45.8	45.4	43.4*	43.4	43.4	43.0	43.0
14	44.3	50.4	48.8	48.9	47.4	39.8*	37.8	34.5	43.7	43.1
15	46.0	j	42.8	83.6	92.7	30.7	j	30.9	30.7	30.7
16	42.9	43.0	43.0	44.1	41.6	32.0*	31.5	32.0	31.9	36.1
17	45.7	82.4	45.9	43.6	33.1	23.4	22.3	24.4	24.7	24.7
18	43.0	49.0	43.1	58.0	84.0	a	a	a	a	a

* Part or all of the inventories were on LIFO.

SCHEDULE II (Continued)

Ratios (Expressed as Percents) of Financial Statement Items

1975

	Long-term debt to stockholders' equity					Current assets to current liabilities				
	Conventional model	Model A	Model B	Model C	Model D	Conventional model	Model A	Model B	Model C	Model D
Transportation company	i	17.4	73.5	9.7	11.4	i	111.8	111.4	111.4	111.4
Retailer	50.1	44.1	51.1	44.8	46.8	298.5	299.4	303.0	298.5	298.7
Manufacturers										
1	i	19.2	22.3	15.0	21.0	i	210.6	198.3	229.9	223.3
2	74.8	56.6	79.6	53.5	69.9	199.3	211.9	190.9	207.8	203.7
3	9.1	7.2	9.1	5.4	6.3	231.0	233.3	231.3	239.0	239.2
4	42.7	28.1	42.8	26.7	33.9	217.2	266.0	214.6	289.6	254.9
5	57.0	47.4	57.1	40.3	45.4	255.3	255.3	256.9	258.9	258.9
6	55.1	j	54.8	34.0	45.5	314.1	j	315.4	316.5	315.3
7	22.1	18.3	22.0	20.1	20.9	391.0	416.9	395.9	392.3	391.7
8	8.1	7.3	8.1	6.9	6.6	219.5	221.5	218.0	224.8	223.2
9	25.2	18.3	24.9	15.3	17.6	208.8	229.0	207.6	226.1	217.2
10	45.4	33.7	44.8	20.8	27.0	360.3	375.7	360.3	381.3	364.1
11	12.9	8.5	11.8	8.3	18.2	171.0	170.3	170.5	171.9	174.8
12	28.6	23.8	28.5	24.9	27.5	326.9	328.7	330.4	328.8	327.8
13	22.4	19.8	22.3	18.4	20.3	532.6	535.7	532.5	559.9	558.9
14	3.8	3.3	3.8	2.3	2.9	243.3	252.7	244.0	272.9	267.2
15	28.5	j	26.7	12.7	13.7	174.6	j	177.1	179.9	173.1
16	141.2	85.6	137.7	87.2	102.0	147.4	154.6	147.4	165.9	157.0
17	27.7	21.9	27.8	23.8	23.0	436.7	436.2	455.2	439.6	438.0
18	25.5	17.7	25.0	13.2	17.2	142.5	165.7	141.4	168.2	157.6

SCHEDULE II (Continued)
Ratios (Expressed as Percents) of Financial Statement Items
1976

	Long-term debt to stockholders' equity					Current assets to current liabilities				
	Conventional model	Model A	Model B	Model C	Model D	Conventional model	Model A	Model B	Model C	Model D
Transportation company	i	18.6	76.2	10.6	13.0	i	110.1	109.9	109.9	109.9
Retailer	38.5	34.2	39.9	34.5	36.1	266.1	266.7	270.9	266.1	266.3
Manufacturers										
1	i	26.5	29.6	20.7	29.7	i	258.5	241.7	282.5	283.5
2	87.3	67.3	93.6	63.0	81.2	249.6	260.5	241.9	263.1	256.7
3	8.0	6.4	8.0	4.7	5.6	231.3	233.6	232.2	238.2	237.3
4	39.2	25.8	39.1	25.4	31.6	101.4	123.8	99.6	137.6	120.2
5	41.5	34.9	40.6	30.6	34.6	272.2	272.2	271.5	279.6	279.6
6	57.8	j	58.3	38.2	50.2	286.9	j	285.4	289.0	288.0
7	32.8	28.3	32.8	29.5	31.7	432.9	443.8	439.2	432.9	432.9
8	5.8	5.2	5.8	5.0	4.9	187.2	188.6	186.5	192.2	190.4
9	23.7	17.8	23.7	14.7	16.3	191.9	203.4	186.9	205.2	204.0
10	38.6	29.1	37.7	18.2	24.4	283.2	295.9	283.2	300.1	287.0
11	4.3	2.9	3.4	2.9	5.9	179.9	179.9	179.2	181.7	183.2
12	25.3	21.2	24.9	21.8	24.9	312.5	314.0	316.1	314.4	313.5
13	19.4	17.4	19.3	16.1	17.8	494.6	499.0	494.5	521.4	520.9
14	3.8	3.3	3.8	2.2	2.5	241.3	252.4	252.4	277.2	270.6
15	46.8	j	41.0	22.6	24.8	170.4	j	172.1	173.7	162.5
16	137.7	84.3	131.6	79.8	100.8	130.4	137.5	130.4	154.0	142.7
17	20.1	15.9	19.7	17.3	17.7	313.3	313.3	314.0	314.9	314.0
18	23.9	16.7	23.1	12.4	16.9	150.4	174.8	148.8	180.0	169.7

SCHEDULE III
Change in Earnings From 1975–1976 Under the Four Experimental Models Expressed as a Percent of the Change in Net Income Under the Conventional Model

	Net income		Model C			Model D	
	Model A	Model B	Net operating income (o/i)	Net o/i and unrealized v/c	r/o/o and e/i	r/o/o, e/i, and v/c	r/o/o, e/i, v/c, and p/l
Transportation company	i 534.1*	e* 141.4*	e* 192.5*	i 80.6*	i 355.3*	i 105.5*	e 657.5*
Retailer							
Manufacturers							
1	375.8	272.9	189.0	37.1	c*	22.9*	180.4*
2	61.2	b	b	b	b	b	b
3	134.0	97.5	56.3	29.1	224.6*	59.4*	187.5*
4	(257.0)	(141.7)	(285.2)	(282.5)	(403.1)*	(252.9)*	(424.2)*
5	54.6	179.4	292.9	108.4	229.0	98.7	170.6
6	j	268.5	2088.0	c	c	I	117.5*
7	113.3	94.1	135.6	f	139.9	f	f
8	179.9	124.3	123.2	78.5	140.8	146.8	633.5
9	232.9	119.7	239.8	f	101.4*	f	f
10	c	293.9	c	30.8	11.4	14.1	c
11	72.6*	151.5*	127.8*	f	88.3	f	f
12	138.6	115.5	134.1	94.5	104.3*	80.5*	385.7*
13	86.7*	99.3*	130.8*	69.6*	130.1*	48.5*	143.4*
14	118.3	I	201.7	63.3	160.0	155.0	653.3
15	j	(850.0)	(1900.0)	f	(5800.0)	f	f
16	I	111.6	108.1	233.3	118.2	52.5	100.5
17	18.8*	551.5*	c*	f	1016.6*	f	f
18	139.9	150.0	334.3	f	c	f	f

Parentheses denote loss for both the conventional model and the experimental model.

* Includes extraordinary items

I Income (loss) for the experimental model was accompanied by loss (income) for the conventional model.

(r/o/o = results of ordinary operations; e/i = extraordinary items; v/c = value changes; p/l = impact of general price level; o/i = operating income)

SCHEDULE III (Continued)
Percent Increase (Decrease) in Earnings From 1975–1976

| | Net income | | | Model C | | | Model D | |
	Conventional model	Model A	Model B	Net operating income (o/i)	Net o/i and unrealized value changes	r/o/o and e/i	r/o/o, e/i, and v/c	r/o/o, e/i, v/c, and p/l
Transportation company	i	(20.5)*	e*	e*	(29.5)*	981.9*	(30.8)*	e
Retailer	104.1*	556.0*	147.2*	200.4*	83.9*	369.9*	109.8*	684.5*
Manufacturers								
1	i	259.3	188.3	130.4	25.6	c*	15.8*	124.5*
2	25.5	15.6	b	b	b	b	b	b
3	47.1	63.1	45.9	26.5	13.7	105.8*	28.0*	88.3*
4	(22.3)	(57.3)	(31.6)	(63.6)	(63.0)	(89.9)*	(56.4)*	(94.6)*
5	23.8	13.0	42.7	69.7	25.8	54.5	23.5	40.6
6	93.1	j	250.0	1943.9	c	c	(23.6)*	109.4*
7	18.8	21.3	17.7	25.5	f	26.3	f	f
8	56.8	102.2	70.6	70.0	44.6	80.0	83.4	359.8
9	65.1	151.6	77.9	156.1	f	66.0*	f	f
10	163.8	c	481.4	c	50.4	18.6	23.1	c
11	59.8*	43.4*	90.6*	76.4*	f	52.8*	f	f
12	58.6	81.2	67.7	78.6	55.4	61.1*	47.2*	226.0*
13	43.5*	37.7*	43.2*	56.9*	30.3*	56.6*	21.1*	62.4*
14	6.0	7.1	(2.8)	12.1	3.8	9.6	9.3	39.2
15	(1.4)	j	(11.9)	(26.6)	f	(81.2)	f	f
16	19.8	(3.9)	22.1	21.4	46.2	23.4	10.4	19.9
17	102.6*	19.3*	565.8*	c*	f	1043.0*	f	f
18	30.6	42.8	45.9	102.3	f	c	f	f

* Includes extraordinary items. Percent changes in earnings before extraordinary items are shown on next schedule.

(r/o/o = results of ordinary operations; e/i = extraordinary items; v/c = value changes; p/l = impact of general price level; o/i = operating income)

SCHEDULE III (Continued)
Percent Increase (Decrease) in Financial Statement Items From 1975–1976

	Earnings before extraordinary items					Sales	
	Conventional model	Model A	Model B	Model C	Model D	Conventional models and models B, C, and D	Model A
Transportation company	i	(14.9)*	e	e	c	i	4.4
Retailer	104.1*	556.0*	125.2*	162.3*	241.0*	16.7	9.5
Manufacturers							
1	i	259.3	188.3	130.4	176.0*	i	10.5
2	25.5	15.6	b	b	b	17.9	12.1
3	47.1	63.1	45.9	26.5	44.4*	20.7	14.7
4	(22.3)	(57.3)	(31.6)	(63.6)	(84.8)*	1.2	(3.7)
5	23.8	13.0	42.7	69.7	54.5	15.1	8.2
6	93.1	j	250.0	1943.9	c	16.0	j
7	18.8	21.3	17.7	25.5	26.3	29.9	18.9
8	56.8	102.2	70.6	70.0	80.0	15.4	21.3
9	65.1	151.6	77.9	156.1	112.8*	29.9	23.7
10	163.8	c	481.4	c	18.6	16.7	10.7
11	50.5*	39.9*	75.8*	83.8*	56.1*	14.2	8.7
12	58.6	81.2	67.7	78.6	62.8	22.2	15.7
13	61.5*	59.6*	61.5*	80.9*	80.3*	5.9	0.8
14	6.0	7.1	(2.8)	12.1	9.6	9.7	4.3
15	(1.4)	j	(11.9)	26.6	(81.2)	5.9	j
16	19.8	(3.9)	22.1	21.4	23.4	16.7	11.0
17	89.8*	(14.0)*	524.5*	c	986.2*	5.5	0.3
18	30.6	42.8	45.9	102.3	c	9.7	3.6

* Extraordinary items were reported under the model. Percent changes in earnings including extraordinary items are shown on preceding schedule.

The GNP Implicit Price Deflator increased by 5.4% from the first quarter of 1975 to the first quarter of 1976, and by 5.3% from the first quarter of 1976 to the first quarter of 1977.

SCHEDULE III (Continued)
Percent Increase (Decrease) in Financial Statement Items From 1975–1976

	Depreciation expense					Cost of goods sold				
	Conventional model	Model A	Model B	Model C	Model D	Conventional model	Model A	Model B	Model C	Model D
Transportation company	i	(12.4)	(5.4)	(5.4)	(6.4)	NA	NA	NA	NA	NA
Retailer	6.9	8.0	9.8	9.8	9.8	13.9	4.6	13.9	13.9	13.9
Manufacturers										
1	i	2.2	3.9	i	i	i	5.6	11.4	i	i
2	28.9	24.0	b	b	b	18.7	11.3	b	b	b
3	20.6	16.2	20.8	35.6	19.5	15.2	9.3	15.9	17.1	16.4
4	8.5	7.3	12.7	12.7	12.7	5.1	0.3	4.7	4.9	4.9
5	30.0	20.2	35.8	26.2	26.5	14.7	7.8	14.2	14.2	14.2
6	9.1	j	0.7	0.7	0.7	12.8	j	10.1	12.8	12.7
7	23.5	26.9	15.0	15.0	15.0	32.3	18.3	32.6	32.3	32.1
8	(5.4)	(9.9)	(5.4)	(5.4)	(5.4)	18.1	12.0	17.6	17.6	17.6
9	7.8	2.3	9.3	9.7	9.7	29.6	21.2	29.5	29.1	29.1
10	9.7	5.0	5.0	8.2	8.2	11.8	5.6	11.9	12.4	12.9
11	9.4	9.9	9.4	9.4	10.2	a	a	a	a	a
12	11.0	2.4	6.2	15.0	15.0	17.0	8.8	16.2	15.8	16.1
13	13.9	8.5	19.7	19.7	19.7	(3.2)	(7.9)	(3.2)	(3.9)	(3.9)
14	25.5	14.8	29.8	8.3	8.3	11.8	6.1	13.1	10.2	10.1
15	(0.5)	j	6.1	6.1	16.9	9.9	j	9.9	9.8	9.9
16	17.4	9.3	14.3	17.5	17.5	21.8	16.2	21.8	21.9	22.6
17	(1.7)	(1.1)	(0.2)	(0.2)	(0.2)	4.5	0.4	1.4	0.9	0.9
18	0.0	(7.5)	0.0	0.0	0.0	a	a	a	a	a

132

SCHEDULE III (Continued)
Percent Increase (Decrease) in Financial Statement Items From 1975–1976

| | Net interest expense | | | Value increase in property, plant, and equipment | | |
| | | | | Model C | | |
	Conventional model, models B and C	Model A	Model D	Unrealized	Realized	Model D
Transportation company	i	36.2	20.1	(29.3)	(1.2)	(34.5)
Retailer	(44.7)	(47.4)	(46.3)	14.5	106.8	21.7
Manufacturers						
1	i	9.2	21.8	(38.9)	15.7	(39.6)
2	3.8	(1.2)	b	b	b	b
3	(4.0)	(8.7)	(18.7)	(24.2)	49.5	(14.3)
4	(8.5)	(12.9)	(4.7)	(13.3)	18.8	6.1
5	(2.0)	(8.5)	(4.8)	34.6	37.7	54.7
6	(1.1)	j	(15.4)	(77.8)*	(21.0)	(90.4)
7	10.8	1.4	7.8	f	f	f
8	(23.2)	26.9	(23.2)	(29.0)	(4.1)	(11.2)
9	(12.1)	(16.3)	(13.0)	f	f	f
10	(11.4)	(15.9)	(9.7)	(10.5)	19.7	(14.9)
11	d	d	d	f	f	f
12	4.1	(1.4)	9.3	(6.3)	28.2	1.6
13	(12.5)	(17.0)	(12.5)	(42.7)	60.0	22.0
14	d	d	d	(20.0)	(10.9)	(16.1)
15	(3.3)	j	(2.8)	f	f	f
16	45.4	38.4	36.6	48.5	19.0	36.1
17	(21.0)	(24.8)	(26.0)	f	f	f
18	(6.2)	(11.3)	(5.5)	f	f	f

* Value decrease

SCHEDULE III (Continued)
Percent Increase (Decrease) in Financial Statement Items From 1975–1976

| | Value increase in inventories | | | Value increase in other assets | | |
| | Model C | | | Model C | | |
	Unrealized	Realized	Model D	Unrealized	Realized	Model D
Transportation company	NA	NA	NA	c	c	c
Retailer	10.3	10.3	10.3	NA	NA	NA
Manufacturers						
1	184.2	184.2	184.1	(44.6)	NA	c
2	b	b	b	b	b	b
3	39.6	117.2	41.2	54.7	108.1	60.7
4	c	(3.1)	200.0	c	c	c
5	c	c	c	97.6*	0.0	391.1*
6	c	59.1	c	(7.7)	23.4	(58.7)
7	f	f	f	f	f	f
8	198.7	19.9	84.6	(95.2)*	(95.2)	c
9	f	f	f	f	f	f
10	c	0.0	c	(64.2)*	c	218.6*
11	f	f	f	f	f	f
12	224.2	(49.4)	(3.9)	46.7	c	41.7
13	(40.1)	(53.1)	(52.1)	(33.3)	c	(37.5)
14	52.7	(7.6)	30.7	c	1.6	c
15	f	f	f	f	c	f
16	859.1	c	887.9	(15.3)	c	c
17	f	f	f	f	f	f
18	f	f	f	f	f	f

* Value decrease

SCHEDULE III (Continued)

Percent Increase (Decrease) in Financial Statement Items from 1975–1976

| | Model A | | Model D | | |
| | Net monetary | | Value change in obligations | | Impact of general price level |
	Gain	Loss	Increase	Decrease	
Transportation company	(31.4)		104.3		(31.1)
Retailer	(57.4)			(94.3)	(38.4)
Manufacturers					
1	(44.1)			(35.0)	(33.6)
2	(31.5)	565.1	b	b	b
3			c	c	(28.9)
4	(68.7)			(5.0)	(30.5)
5	(52.0)	j	c	c	(9.9)
6			c	c	(60.2)
7	(11.2)		f	f	f
8		4.9	c	c	(27.3)
9	(42.1)		f	f	f
10	(67.1)		(82.3)		(39.7)
11	(61.9)		f	f	f
12	(74.7)		63.6		(43.9)
13		86.2	84.0		(23.0)
14		(46.7)	c	c	(29.4)
15	j	j	f	f	f
16	(39.7)		c	c	(23.1)
17	c		f	f	f
18	c		f	f	f

11

Financial Statements Prepared by Two Participants

The financial statements prepared by two participants under each of the four experimental accounting models and the conventional model are presented in this chapter. The participants are identified as "manufacturer 5" and "retailer," the same identifications given to them in chapter 10 in the matrix schedules. The actual names of the participants that appeared in some places in the notes have been deleted and the deletions are indicated.

CONVENTIONAL MODEL
Manufacturer 5
Consolidated Balance Sheet

Assets	October 30, 1976	November 1, 1975
Current assets		
Cash (note 5)	$ 11,582,000	$ 12,368,000
Accounts receivable, less allowance for doubtful accounts of $1,400,000 and $1,200,000	89,019,000	85,035,000
Inventories (note 3)	38,199,000	33,346,000
Deferred tax benefit	2,139,000	—
Prepaid expenses	533,000	484,000
Total current assets	141,472,000	131,233,000
Other assets (note 4)	1,455,000	1,550,000
Property, plant, and equipment, at cost (note 6)		
Land and land improvements	11,696,000	8,893,000
Buildings and stockyards	43,480,000	37,005,000
Equipment	82,268,000	72,878,000
	137,444,000	118,776,000
Less accumulated depreciation	34,022,000	28,177,000
	103,422,000	90,599,000
Construction in progress	4,251,000	3,824,000
	107,673,000	94,423,000
Deferred financing costs, less amortization of $1,955,000 and $1,698,000	2,837,000	2,478,000
	$253,437,000	$229,684,000

Liabilities and Stockholders' Equity	October 30, 1976	November 1, 1975
Current liabilities		
Notes payable (note 5)	$ —	$ 11,000,000
Accounts payable and accrued expenses (note 9)	$23,242,000	21,285,000
Salaries, wages, bonuses, and amounts withheld from employees	9,889,000	9,106,000
Federal and state income taxes	16,514,000	6,186,000
Current maturities on long-term obligations	2,325,000	3,833,000
Total current liabilities	51,970,000	51,410,000
Deferred income taxes	11,460,000	9,459,000
Long-term obligations (notes 5 and 6)	55,715,000	61,258,000
Contingencies (note 11)		
Stockholders' equity (notes 6, 7, and 10)		
Common stock, par value $1.50 a share Authorized, 6,000,000 shares Issued, 1976—4,382,659	6,574,000	4,337,000
Additional paid-in capital	18,981,000	20,741,000
Retained earnings	109,508,000	82,479,000
	135,063,000	107,557,000
Less common stock in treasury, at cost, 40,200 shares; net shares outstanding, 1976—4,342,459	771,000	—
Stockholders' equity—net	134,292,000	107,557,000
	$253,437,000	$229,684,000

See notes to consolidated financial statements.

CONVENTIONAL MODEL

Manufacturer 5
Consolidated Statement of Earnings

	Year (52 weeks) ended	
	October 30, 1976	November 1, 1975
Sales	$2,077,158,000	$1,805,340,000
Cost of products sold	1,990,176,000	1,735,592,000
	86,982,000	69,748,000
Expenses		
Selling, general, and administrative	24,374,000	22,992,000
Interest costs incurred	3,666,000	4,636,000
Less interest capitalized on construction	—	(896,000)
	28,040,000	26,732,000
Earnings before income taxes	58,942,000	43,016,000
Income taxes (note 8)	30,164,000	19,779,000
Net earnings	$ 28,778,000	$ 23,237,000
Net earnings per common and common equivalent share (adjusted for three-for-two stock split) (note 10)	$6.17	$5.37

CONVENTIONAL MODEL
Manufacturer 5
Consolidated Statement of Stockholders' Equity
Years (52 Weeks) Ended October 30, 1976 and November 1, 1975

	Common stock		Additional paid-in capital	Retained earnings	Treasury stock
	Shares (note 10)	Amount			
Balance, November 3, 1974	2,579,699	$3,870,000	$14,505,000	$ 59,242,000	$ —
Common stock options exercised	12,070	17,000	195,000	—	—
Common stock warrants exercised	299,877	450,000	6,041,000	—	—
Net earnings	—	—	—	23,237,000	—
Balance, November 1, 1975	2,891,646	4,337,000	20,741,000	82,479,000	—
Common stock options exercised					
Qualified stock options	24,127	37,000	363,000	—	—
Nonqualified stock options	6,000	9,000	68,000	—	—
Shares (40,200) acquired for treasury	—	—	—	—	(771,000)
Cash dividends paid, $.40 per share (adjusted for three-for-two stock split) (note 10)	—	—	—	(1,749,000)	—
Three-for-two stock split (note 10)	1,460,886	2,191,000	(2,191,000)	—	—
Net earnings	—	—	—	28,778,000	—
Balance, October 30, 1976	4,382,659	$6,574,000	$18,981,000	$109,508,000	$(771,000)

See notes to consolidated financial statements.

CONVENTIONAL MODEL

Manufacturer 5
Consolidated Statement of Changes in Financial Position

	Year (52 weeks) ended	
	October 30, 1976	November 1, 1975
Source of Funds		
Operations		
Net earnings	$28,778,000	$23,237,000
Noncash charges to operations		
Depreciation and amortization	7,742,000	5,957,000
Deferred income taxes and write-down of investment	2,709,000	2,051,000
Total funds provided from operations	39,229,000	31,245,000
Proceeds from long-term borrowings	2,400,000	—
Property, plant, and equipment retirements	2,184,000	735,000
Proceeds from options and warrants	477,000	6,703,000
Other, net	—	189,000
	$44,290,000	$38,872,000
Application of Funds		
Reduction of long-term obligations	$15,098,000	$ 3,835,000
Acquisition of [name omitted] (note 2)	8,373,000	—
Additions to properties	7,982,000	24,366,000
Cash dividends paid	1,749,000	—
Purchase of common stock for treasury	771,000	—
Increase in other assets	638,000	
Increase in working capital	9,679,000	10,671,000
	$44,290,000	$38,872,000
Analysis of Working Capital Changes		
Increase (decrease) in current assets		
Cash	$ (786,000)	$(1,953,000)
Accounts receivable, net	3,984,000	13,719,000
Inventories	4,853,000	11,613,000
Deferred tax benefit	2,139,000	—
Prepaid expenses	49,000	(67,000)
Net increase in current assets	10,239,000	23,312,000
Increase (decrease) in current liabilities		
Notes payable	(11,000,000)	1,000,000
Accounts payable and accrued expenses	1,957,000	4,785,000
Salaries, wages, bonuses, and amounts withheld from employees	783,000	2,088,000
Federal and state income taxes	10,328,000	2,103,000
Current maturities on long-term debt	(1,508,000)	2,665,000
Net increase in current liabilities	560,000	12,641,000
Increase in working capital	$ 9,679,000	$10,671,000

See notes to consolidated financial statements.

Manufacturer 5
Notes to Consolidated Financial Statements
Years (52 Weeks) Ended October 30, 1976 and November 1, 1975

1. Summary of significant accounting policies

Principles of consolidation. All subsidiaries are wholly owned and are consolidated in the accompanying financial statements. All material intercompany balances, transactions, and profits have been eliminated.

Property, plant, and equipment. Depreciation is provided for property, plant, and equipment on the straight-line method over the useful lives of the respective classes of assets as follows.

Land improvements	10 to 20 years
Buildings and stockyards	20 to 40 years
Furniture and fixtures	4 to 10 years
Plant equipment	10 to 12 years
Automobiles and aircraft	3 to 8 years
Leasehold improvements	Life of lease or life of asset, whichever is shorter

Expenditures for maintenance and repairs are charged to operations when incurred, whereas those for renewals and betterments are capitalized.

It is the policy of the company to relieve the asset accounts and related depreciation accounts in respect of properties retired or otherwise disposed of. The resulting profits or losses from disposals are credited or charged to income.

Deferred financing costs. The company follows the policy of deferring financing costs and amortizing them on the bonds outstanding method over the life of the debt involved.

Capitalization of interest. The company follows the practice of capitalizing interest on major plant expansion funds during the construction period. The capitalized interest is charged to the property, plant, and equipment accounts and depreciated over the lives of the related assets.

Income taxes. Taxes are provided, at appropriate rates, for all taxable items included in the earnings statement regardless of the period when such items are reported for tax purposes. The principal items that result in timing differences for financial and tax reporting purposes are (1) accelerated depreciation and capitalized interest, which are reported as expenses for tax purposes in years earlier than reported for financial purposes, and (2) certain accrued liabilities and a valuation reserve for investments, both of which are not currently deductible for tax purposes. Federal income taxes have not been provided on the exempt earnings of the company's domestic international sales corporation (DISC) subsidiary since the company intends to reinvest such earnings permanently in export related activities.

Investment tax credits are accounted for using the flow-through method which recognizes the benefit in the year in which the assets are placed in service.

Earnings per share. Earnings per share have been computed based on the weighted average number of common and common equivalent shares outstanding during the year reduced by the number of shares assumed to have been purchased from the proceeds of the common equivalent shares. Common equivalent shares are common stock options and warrants. A fully diluted earnings per share computation results in no material dilution. All earnings per share amounts have been adjusted to reflect the three-for-two stock split declared in November, 1976.

2. Acquisition

During May 1976, the company acquired the outstanding stock and warrants of [name omitted] for $9.9 million. [Name omitted] with offices in [name omitted] owns and operates a pork plant at that location under an exclusive custom slaughtering agreement with [name omitted].

The acquisition has been accounted for as a purchase. The excess of purchase price over carrying value of net assets acquired will be allocated to these assets based on an appraisal. The excess has tentatively been allocated to property, plant, and equipment. Any reallocation would not have a significant effect on the financial statements. Transactions related to the acquisition are summarized below:

Assets acquired	
Net current assets	$ 1,504,000
Property, plant, and equipment	14,937,000
Other	591,000
	17,032,000
Less long-term debt assumed	(7,155,000)
	9,877,000
Less net current assets received	(1,504,000)
Net funds used in acquisition	$ 8,373,000

Operations of the acquired company from date of acquisition have been included in the accompanying consolidated statement of earnings. Information concerning the results of operations for periods prior to acquisition are not presented since they are not material to the consolidated results of operations.

3. Inventories

Inventories comprise the following.

	October 30, 1976	November 1, 1975
Lower of cost (FIFO method) or market		
Carcasses		
Slaughter division	$ 8,900,000	$ 6,399,000
Operating supplies	6,519,000	5,337,000
Cattle on feed	4,227,000	1,254,000
Approximate market less allowance for selling expenses		
Processed cuts	8,100,000	10,983,000
By-products	6,063,000	4,635,000
Carcasses		
Processing division	4,390,000	4,738,000
	$38,199,000	$33,346,000

4. Other assets

Other assets comprise the following.

	October 30, 1976	November 1, 1975
Notes receivable	$1,043,000	$ 216,000
Investments	303,000	1,011,000
Deposits	109,000	323,000
	$1,455,000	$1,550,000

The company's investment in [name omitted] (approximately 13 percent of the outstanding common shares) has been adjusted from cost to management's estimate of realizable value.

5. Credit arrangements

In May 1976, the company consummated a revolving credit and term loan agreement (the "Term Loan Agreement") and an unsecured short-term open line-of-credit arrangement with a group of banks that replaced similar credit arrangements that were outstanding at November 1, 1975.

Pursuant to the term loan agreement, the company may, on an unsecured basis, borrow and repay from time to time before January 1, 1978, for its general working capital and plant expansion, amounts that could aggregate, but not exceed, $30 million outstanding at any one time. The amounts borrowed under the agreement at December 31, 1977, may be converted to a term loan payable in twelve equal quarterly installments commencing March 31, 1978, and ending December 31, 1980.

Interest is payable monthly at 115.5 percent of the prime commercial rate through December 31, 1978, and thereafter at 119 percent of the prime rate. A commitment fee of ½ of 1 percent on the average unused portion of the commitment is payable quarterly. The company has informally agreed to maintain unrestricted compensating cash balances averaging 10 percent of the $30 million commitment.

During the year ended October 30, 1976, the highest month-end balance was $30 million, the average balance was $14,995,000 and the average effective interest rate was 10.47 percent.

The company's unsecured short-term open line-of-credit arrangement provides borrowing of up to $50 million with interest payable at the prime commercial rate. The company has informally agreed to maintain unrestricted compensating cash balances averaging 10 percent of the available line plus 10 percent of the amount borrowed. Only limited borrowings under the short-term arrangement were made during fiscal 1976 and 1975.

The company is required by the terms of the loan agreement to first borrow against the term loan agreement. This gives the company the option, in case of unexpected short-term cash needs, to repay this borrowing over a long-term period and still have the $50 million line-of-credit available for working capital.

On October 29, 1976, the company borrowed $15 million against its term loan agreement. This loan was repaid on November 1, 1976.

6. Long-term obligations

Long-term obligations consist of the following.

	October 30, 1976	November 1, 1975
Term loan agreement (note 5)	$15,000,000	$30,000,000
9⅞% secured bonds, due 1995, redeemable at 106½ decreasing to principal amount in 1990	14,681,000	14,981,000
Lease obligations to retire industrial development bonds, 4¾% to 6%, due 1988	11,512,000	11,905,000
6¼% subordinated debentures due in equal amounts in 1983 and 1984, callable at 101½ decreasing to principal amount in 1979	5,330,000	5,330,000
9¾% mortgage note due 1983	3,300,000	—
9% subordinated debentures due 1983	3,000,000	—
Other, 5.2% to 11%, due 1977 to 1991	5,217,000	2,875,000
	58,040,000	65,091,000
Less amounts due within one year	2,325,000	3,833,000
	$55,715,000	$61,258,000

Property, plant, and equipment with a carrying value of $69,579,000 is pledged as collateral under certain long-term debt instruments.

Restrictive covenants of the loan agreements provide, among other things, for (1) the maintenance of minimum working capital, current ratio, tangible net worth, and the ratio of earnings before taxes and interest to interest (all as defined), (2) certain restrictions on incurring additional indebtedness and the sale of assets, and (3) limitation on payment of cash dividends, other cash payments to shareholders, and acquisition of its own stock. Under the agreements, $109,150,000 of retained earnings was restricted as to the payment of cash dividends, payments to shareholders, and acquisition of its own stock at October 30, 1976. Aggregate maturities of long-term debt for each of the five years subsequent to October 30, 1976, are as follows.

Fiscal year	Amount
1977	$2,325,000
1978	6,195,000
1979	6,974,000
1980	7,039,000
1981	3,785,000

7. Capital stock and options

The company is authorized to issue 100,000 shares of $100 par value preferred stock. No shares had been issued at October 30, 1976.

Common stock options outstanding have been granted at 100 percent of the market value of the company's common stock at the date of grant. Options granted under the qualified plans become exercisable over a five-year period and expire five years from date of grant. Nonqualified options were immediately exercisable and expire no more than five years from date of grant.

Changes in options during the periods were as follows.

	Shares		
	Qualified		Nonqualified granted
	Reserved	Granted	
Balance at November 3, 1974	1,093,737	702,396	9,000
Granted	—	198,626	30,000
Exercised (aggregate pro-			
ceeds of $212,000)	(18,105)	(18,105)	—
Cancelled	—	(146,720)	—
Balance at November 1, 1975	1,075,632	736,197	39,000
Granted	—	242,074	15,000
Exercised (aggregate pro-			
ceeds of $400,000			
and $77,000)	(36,190)	(36,190)	(9,000)
Cancelled	—	(176,439)	—
Balance at October 30, 1976	1,039,442	765,642	45,000
Option prices per share at			
October 30, 1976	$7.00 to $22.17		$11.50 to $14.92
Options exercisable at			
October 30, 1976	13,165		45,000

Stock option data has been adjusted for the three-for-two stock split declared in November 1976.

8. Income taxes

Income tax expense consists of the following.

	Year (52 weeks) ended	
	October 30, '1976	November 1, 1975
Paid or currently payable	$30,939,000	$20,225,000
Deferred	(138,000)	1,692,000
Investment tax credits	(637,000)	(2,138,000)
	$30,164,000	$19,779,000

Total tax expense varies from the amount that would be provided by applying the U.S. income tax rate of 48 percent to earnings before income taxes. The major reasons for this difference (expressed as a percentage of pre-tax income) are as follows.

146

	1976	1975
Federal income tax rate	48.0%	48.0%
State income taxes	1.7	1.9
Investment tax credit	(1.1)	(5.0)
Taxes not provided on exempt earnings of the DISC subsidiary	(1.5)	(1.1)
Additional taxes provided in connection with tax examinations	3.9	1.8
Other	.2	.4
	51.2%	46.0%

The undistributed earnings of the company's DISC subsidiary on which federal income tax has not been provided amounted to $4,468,000 at October 30, 1976. Federal income tax returns through fiscal 1974 have been examined by the Internal Revenue Service. The service has concluded its examination through fiscal 1972 and various tax deficiencies have been proposed. In the opinion of management, adequate provision has been made for all tax liabilities.

9. Retirement agreements

In September 1974, the board of directors approved retirement agreements with three key executives. The agreements provide for monthly compensation following retirement. The present value of these benefits has been fully accrued at October 30, 1976.

The agreements further provide that the individuals have the option to sell to the company the equivalent of approximately 133,000 shares (after three-for-two stock split) of the company's common stock, owned by them, at a price that is the higher of fair market value or book value as of the date of the repurchase. The company makes periodic adjustments to reflect changes in the difference between fair market and book values of the common stock. The effect of these adjustments was to reduce net earnings in 1976 by $162,000 and increase net earnings in 1975 by $54,000. The company intends to treat any excess of book value over fair market value at the date of repurchase as compensation taxable to the individuals and deductible by the company.

10. Stockholders' equity

In November, 1976, the board of directors declared a three-for-two stock split effected in the form of a 50 percent stock dividend. The additional shares were issued on December 20, 1976, to shareholders of record on November 26, 1976. All share and per share data have been retroactively adjusted to give effect to the stock split including the transfer of additional paid-in capital to common stock of the par value of the additional shares which were not issued until after October 30, 1976.

11. Contingencies

The company is a defendant, along with three other beef slaughter and processing companies, in a suit instituted by a group of approximately 450 cattle feeders. The suit seeks treble damages under the antitrust laws. No amount of damages is specified in the suit. Pretrial discovery of relevant evidence is presently in a preliminary stage.

It is the opinion of management and the company's counsel that any liability for which provision has not been made relative to the above or other various law suits and claims pending against the company will not have a material adverse effect on its financial position.

12. Subsequent events

In December, 1976, the company acquired all the issued and outstanding capital stock of [name omitted], a privately held corporation in the state of Washington, for $500,000 in cash, plus [name omitted] common stock with a value of $250,000. An additional $3 million advance was made to [name omitted] that owns two beef slaughtering and processing plants.

The acquisition will be accounted for as a purchase. The excess of the purchase price over carrying value of net assets acquired will be allocated to these assets based on an appraisal. The excess has tentatively been allocated to property, plant, and equipment. Any reallocation will not have a significant effect on [name omitted] financial position. Transactions related to the acquisition are summarized below.

Assets acquired	
Property, plant, and equipment	$8,509,000
Other	3,000
	8,512,000
Liabilities assumed	
Net current liabilities	249,000
Long-term debt	4,513,000
	4,762,000
Net funds and [name omitted] stock used in acquisition	$3,750,000

[Name omitted], an officer and former shareholder of the [name omitted] company, is a former official of [name omitted]. Information concerning the results of operations of [name omitted] is not presented for fiscal 1976 and 1975 as it is not material to the [name omitted] consolidated results of operations.

MODEL A

Manufacturer 5
Consolidated Balance Sheets

	In $(1976)	
	October 30, 1976	*November 1, 1975*
Assets		
Current assets		
Cash	$ 11,582,000	$ 13,061,000
Accounts receivable	89,019,000	89,797,000
Inventories	38,199,000	35,213,000
Deferred tax benefit	2,139,000	—
Prepaid expenses	533,000	511,000
Total current assets	141,472,000	138,582,000
Other assets	1,455,000	1,637,000
Property, plant, and equipment	179,650,000	162,411,000
Less accumulated depreciation	(51,208,000)	(43,941,000)
	128,442,000	118,470,000
Construction in process	4,512,000	4,074,000
	132,954,000	122,544,000
Deferred financing costs	2,837,000	2,617,000
	$278,718,000	$265,380,000
Liabilities and Stockholders' Equity		
Current liabilities		
Notes payable	$ —	$ 11,616,000
Accounts payable and accrued expenses	23,242,000	22,477,000
Salaries, wages, and bonuses	9,889,000	9,616,000
Federal and state income taxes	16,514,000	6,534,000
Current maturities on long-term obligations	2,325,000	4,046,000
Total current liabilities	51,970,000	54,289,000
Deferred income taxes	11,460,000	9,990,000
Long-term obligations	55,715,000	64,688,000
Stockholders' equity	159,573,000	136,413,000
	$278,718,000	$265,380,000

See notes to financial statements.

MODEL A

Manufacturer 5
Consolidated Statements of Earnings

	In $(1976)	
	Year (52 weeks) ended	
	October 30, 1976	November 1, 1975
Sales	$2,127,010,000	$1,965,538,000
Operating expenses		
Cost of sales	2,031,971,000	1,884,805,000
Depreciation	9,775,000	8,132,000
Selling, general, and administrative	24,959,000	25,032,000
	2,066,705,000	1,917,969,000
Operating earnings before interest and taxes	60,305,000	47,569,000
Interest on debt	(3,754,000)	(4,104,000)
Income taxes	(30,786,000)	(21,785,000)
Operating earnings after interest and taxes	25,765,000	21,680,000
Losses from sale of assets after related income taxes of $143,000 and $375,000	(1,193,000)	(705,000)
General purchasing power loss on monetary items, excluding long-term debt	(2,634,000)	(4,068,000)
General purchasing power gain on long-term debt	3,275,000	5,403,000
Net earnings	25,213,000	22,310,000
Proceeds from exercise of warrants and options	488,000	7,086,000
Dividends	(1,770,000)	—
Acquisition of treasury shares	(771,000)	—
Balance added to stockholders' equity	23,160,000	29,396,000
Stockholders' equity at beginning of year	136,413,000	107,017,000
Stockholders' equity at end of year	$ 159,573,000	$ 136,413,000

See notes to financial statements.

MODEL A

Manufacturer 5
Reconciliation of Net Earnings in Units of Money

	Year (52 weeks) ended	
	October 30, 1976	November 1, 1975
Net earnings per earnings statements (in historical dollars)	$28,778,000	$ 23,237,000
Increase (decrease) from restatement in dollars of 1976 general purchasing power		
Sales	49,852,000	160,198,000
Cost of sales	(49,561,000)	(155,675,000)
Depreciation	(2,290,000)	(2,398,000)
Other costs and expenses, net	(1,295,000)	(4,410,000)
Gains (losses) on sales of property and equipment	(912,000)	23,000
Net general purchasing power gains on monetary items, including long-term debt	641,000	1,335,000
Net impact of restatement on results for the year	(3,565,000)	(927,000)
Price-level adjusted net earnings (in dollars of 1976 general purchasing power)	$25,213,000	$ 22,310,000

See notes to financial statements.

MODEL A

Manufacturer 5
Explanatory Note to Supplementary
General Purchasing Power Information
Years (52 Weeks) Ended October 30, 1976 and November 1, 1975

The accompanying general purchasing power information, expressed in units of the general purchasing power of the dollar at October 30, 1976, is based on the financial statements in units of money (historical dollars) and should be read in conjunction with them (including the notes). The historical dollar financial statements combine amounts expressed in dollars expended at various times in the past with amounts expressed in dollars expended more recently, regardless of changes in the general purchasing power of the dollar. Amortization of the expenditures of dollars in prior years is deducted from revenues received currently in determining net income. The result is a mixture of dollars that represents various amounts of general purchasing power. In the general purchasing power information, historical amounts have been restated to recognize the reductions that have occurred in the general purchasing power of the dollar (inflation). The amounts originally recorded are restated into units of the general purchasing power of the dollar at October 30, 1976, using the gross national product implicit price deflator (GNP deflator).

General purchasing power restatement does not change the underlying accounting principles; the same principles are used in both the historical dollar financial statements and the general purchasing power information. The latter retains the historical cost basis of accounting; only the unit is changed. That is, historical cost is expressed in amounts restated for changes in the general purchasing power of the dollar as measured by the GNP deflator. The restated amounts do not purport to be appraised value, replacement cost, or current value; nor do they purport to be based on prices at which transactions would take place currently. Establishing units of general purchasing power is a process of translation, not of valuation.

Changing to units of general purchasing power should not be confused with reporting the effects of changes in the prices of particular goods and services. Movements in specific prices are caused in part by changes in general purchasing power and in part by various other factors (for example, supply and demand and technological changes). Changes in the general price level may be more or less rapid than, and may even be counter to, changes in specific prices.

Inflation over a period of time has cumulative effects on historical dollar financial statements. The cumulative effect of inflation is particularly significant for long-lived nonmonetary assets such as property, plant, and equipment, shown by the restatement of these items in the supplementary balance sheet information and in the corresponding restatement of depreciation in the supplementary income statement information. Restatement of inventories significantly affects cost of sales. The resulting increases in the amounts at which nonmonetary assets are presented in the balance sheet are not included in income since they are merely the results of changing the measurement unit.

Holders of monetary assets, such as cash and receivables, lose general purchasing power during inflation because monetary assets buy fewer goods and services as the general level of prices rises. Conversely, those who own monetary liabilities gain general purchasing power because the liabilities will be payable with dollars that have less general purchasing power than those received when the liabilities were incurred. Information about general purchasing power gain or loss is necessary to evaluate the overall impact of inflation on the results of business operations. The accompanying general purchasing power income statement reflects a general purchasing power loss of $2,634,000 in 1976 ($4,068,000 in 1975) because of holding net monetary assets (before deducting gain on long-term debt) and a general purchasing power gain of $3,275,000 in 1976 ($5,403,000 in 1975) as a result of owing long-term debt.

The cumulative effect of inflation disclosed by the restatement of historical units of money to units of general purchasing power includes all the elements discussed in the preceding two paragraphs. The net impact of restatement on results for the years 1976 and 1975 and the relative importance of the various elements of inflationary effect for the years are shown in the reconciliation of net income in units of money with net income in units of October 30, 1976, general purchasing power.

No deferred tax charge or credit has been provided with respect to the restatement of assets or liabilities since the restatements do not affect income taxes.

MODEL B

Manufacturer 5
Consolidated Balance Sheets

	October 30, 1976	November 1, 1975
Assets		
Current assets		
Cash	$ 11,582,000	$ 12,368,000
Accounts receivable	89,019,000	85,035,000
Inventories at LIFO	39,299,000	30,446,000
Deferred tax benefit	2,139,000	—
Prepaid expenses	533,000	484,000
Total current assets	142,572,000	128,333,000
Other assets	1,455,000	1,550,000
Property, plant, and equipment	141,695,000	122,600,000
Less accumulated depreciation	(34,022,000)	(28,177,000)
	107,673,000	94,423,000
Deferred financing costs	2,837,000	2,478,000
	$254,537,000	$226,784,000
Liabilities and Stockholders' Equity		
Current liabilities		
Notes payable	$ —	$ 11,000,000
Accounts payable and accrued expenses	33,131,000	30,391,000
Federal and state income taxes	17,064,000	4,736,000
Current maturities on long-term obligations	2,325,000	3,833,000
Total current liabilities	52,520,000	49,960,000
Deferred income taxes	8,980,000	8,290,000
Long-term obligations	55,715,000	61,258,000
Stockholders' equity		
Common stock	6,574,000	4,337,000
Additional paid-in capital	18,981,000	20,741,000
Retained earnings	107,899,000	79,974,000
Accumulated current cost depreciation	4,639,000	2,224,000
Treasury stock	(771,000)	—
Total stockholders' equity	137,322,000	107,276,000
	$254,537,000	$226,784,000

See notes to financial statements.

MODEL B

Manufacturer 5
Consolidated Statements of Earnings

	Year (52 weeks) ended	
	October 30, 1976	November 1, 1975
Sales	$2,077,158,000	$1,805,340,000
Operating expenses		
Cost of sales	1,978,691,000	1,733,358,000
Depreciation	10,147,000	7,472,000
Selling, general, and administrative	24,374,000	22,992,000
	2,013,212,000	1,763,822,000
Operating earnings before interest and taxes	63,946,000	41,518,000
Interest on debt	(3,666,000)	(3,740,000)
Income taxes	(30,853,000)	(17,160,000)
Net earnings	$ 29,427,000	$ 20,618,000

MODEL B

Manufacturer 5
Consolidated Statements of Changes in
Retained Earnings and Accumulated Current Cost Depreciation

	Retained earnings	Accumulated current cost depreciation
Balance at November 3, 1974	$ 59,242,000	
Net earnings	20,618,000	
Excess of current cost depreciation over historical cost depreciation		$2,338,000
Current cost depreciation realized on sale or disposition of assets	114,000	(114,000)
Balance at November 1, 1975	79,974,000	2,224,000
Net earnings	29,427,000	
Excess of current cost depreciation over historical cost depreciation		2,662,000
Current cost depreciation realized on sale or disposition of assets	247,000	(247,000)
Dividend paid	(1,749,000)	
Balance at October 30, 1976	$107,899,000	$4,639,000

See notes to financial statements.

Manufacturer 5
Notes to Supplemental Consolidated Financial Statements
Years (52 Weeks) Ended October 30, 1976 and November 1, 1975

1. General

In the inflationary environment of the past several years, financial information reported on the conventional basis of historical costs fails to reflect fully economic reality of the results of operations of business enterprises. As a result, the company is presenting supplemental financial statements reflecting the following:

a. Depreciation expense that has been based on current replacement cost of its depreciable assets. Current replacement cost has been estimated using the Factory Mutual Building Cost Index to restate the historical cost depreciation. Depreciation expense for years prior to 1975 has not been restated. The excess current cost depreciation has been charged to operations and credited to accumulated current cost depreciation, a separate account shown in the stockholders' equity section of the balance sheet. Current cost depreciation expense for 1976 and 1975 was $2.662 million and $2.338 million respectively greater than historical cost depreciation.

b. Inventory that has been restated from FIFO cost to LIFO cost. LIFO inventory at October 31, 1976, was $1.1 million greater than FIFO inventory and at November 1, 1975, LIFO inventory was $2.9 million less than FIFO. Because of use of LIFO inventory cost, cost of sales was increased by $2.9 million in 1975 and reduced by $4 million in 1976.

c. Income tax expense that has been adjusted for the changes resulting from current cost depreciation and LIFO inventory. Income tax expense in the supplemental statements has been increased in 1976 by $.689 million and reduced in 1975 by $2.619 million.

2. Notes to historical cost basis financial statements

The supplemental financial statements should be read in conjunction with the notes to the historical cost basis financial statements.

MODEL C

Manufacturer 5
Consolidated Balance Sheets

	October 30, 1976	November 1, 1975
Assets		
Cash	$ 11,582,000	$ 12,368,000
Accounts receivable (net)	89,019,000	85,035,000
Inventories, at cost	38,199,000	33,346,000
Prepaid expenses	533,000	484,000
Total current assets	139,333,000	131,233,000
Property, plant, and equipment, at cost	141,695,000	122,600,000
Less accumulated depreciation, on cost	(34,022,000)	(28,177,000)
Valuation adjustment to net replacement cost	35,937,000	33,804,000
Total property, plant, and equipment	143,610,000	128,227,000
Investment held for disposition, at cost	2,008,000	2,008,000
Less valuation adjustment to net realizable value (net of imputed taxes)	(1,194,000)	(698,000)
Total investment held for disposition	814,000	1,310,000
Other assets	1,152,000	539,000
Deferred financing costs	2,837,000	2,478,000
	$287,746,000	$263,787,000
Liabilities and Stockholders' Equity		
Notes payable	$ —	$ 11,000,000
Accounts payable and accrued liabilities	30,992,000	29,668,000
Federal and state income taxes	16,514,000	6,186,000
Current maturities of long-term obligations	2,325,000	3,833,000
Total current liabilities	49,831,000	50,687,000
Long-term obligations	55,715,000	61,258,000
Stockholders' equity		
Contributed capital—common stock	6,574,000	4,337,000
—additional capital	18,981,000	20,741,000
Less common stock in treasury, at cost	(771,000)	—
Retained operating earnings	102,486,000	76,204,000
Unrealized value changes	46,714,000	43,587,000
Retained value changes realized since November 3, 1974	8,216,000	6,973,000
Total stockholders' equity	182,200,000	151,842,000
	$287,746,000	$263,787,000

See notes to financial statements.

MODEL C

Manufacturer 5
Consolidated Statements of Operating Earnings

	Year (52 weeks) ended	
	October 30, 1976	November 1, 1975
Sales	$2,077,158,000	$1,805,340,000
Cost of sales (replacement cost)	1,977,445,000	1,731,441,000
Selling, general, and administrative	24,374,000	22,992,000
Depreciation (replacement cost)	13,126,000	10,398,000
	2,014,945,000	1,764,831,000
Operating income before interest and taxes	62,213,000	40,509,000
Interest	(3,666,000)	(3,740,000)
Income taxes—on current cost income	(29,273,000)	(16,910,000)
—on taxable income in excess of current cost income	(1,243,000)	(3,344,000)
Net operating earnings	28,031,000	16,515,000
Retained operating earnings— balance beginning	76,204,000	59,689,000
Dividends paid	(1,749,000)	—
Retained operating earnings— balance ending	$ 102,486,000	$ 76,204,000

See notes to financial statements.

MODEL C

Manufacturer 5

Consolidated Statement of Unrealized Value Changes
Years (52 Weeks) Ended October 30, 1976 and November 1, 1975

	Inventory	Investment held for disposition	Plant and equipment	Total
Balance unrealized value changes, November 3, 1974	$ —	$ (447,000)	$41,506,000	$41,059,000
Net value increases (decreases) for the year	2,900,000	(251,000)	6,485,000	9,134,000
	2,900,000	(698,000)	47,991,000	50,193,000
Realized during the year				
Net gains (losses) realized on disposal	—	—	735,000	735,000
Capital maintenance allowance recovered through operations	(2,900,000)	—	(4,441,000)	(7,341,000)
Balance unrealized value changes, November 3, 1975	—	(698,000)	44,285,000	43,587,000
Net value increases (decreases) for the year	(4,000,000)	(496,000)	8,726,000	4,230,000
	(4,000,000)	(1,194,000)	53,011,000	47,817,000
Realized during the year				
Net gains (losses) realized on disposal	—	—	281,000	281,000
Capital maintenance allowance recovered through operations	4,000,000	—	(5,384,000)	(1,384,000)
Balance unrealized value changes, October 30, 1976	$ —	$(1,194,000)	$47,908,000	$46,714,000

See notes to financial statements.

158

MODEL C

Manufacturer 5
Consolidated Statements of Retained Realized Value Changes
Years (52 Weeks) Ended October 30, 1976 and November 1, 1975

Balance November 3, 1974	$ —
Capital maintenance allowances recovered from operations	4,441,000
Gains realized on inventory from operations	2,900,000
Capital (losses) on exchange of property, plant, and equipment	(735,000)
Less related income taxes	367,000
Realized value changes for the year	6,973,000
Balance November 1, 1975	6,973,000
Capital maintenance allowances recovered from operations	5,384,000
Losses realized on inventory from operations	(4,000,000)
Capital (losses) on exchange of property, plant, and equipment	(281,000)
Less related income taxes	140,000
Realized value changes for the year	1,243,000
Balance October 30, 1976	$8,216,000

See notes to financial statements.

MODEL C

Manufacturer 5
Consolidated Statement of Changes in Financial Position
Years (52 Weeks) Ended October 30, 1976 and November 1, 1975

	1976	1975
Sources of Current Financial Resources		
Sales	$2,077,158,000	$1,805,340,000
Property disposed of	2,184,000	735,000
Proceeds from long-term borrowings	2,400,000	—
Stock options and warrants exercised	477,000	6,703,000
	$2,082,219,000	$1,812,778,000
Uses of Current Financial Resources		
Expenses		
Cost of sales	$1,977,445,000	$1,731,441,000
Income taxes	29,167,000	18,770,000
Selling, general, and administrative	24,374,000	22,992,000
Interest	3,666,000	3,740,000
Increase (decrease) in replacement cost valuation of inventories	4,000,000	(2,900,000)
Increase in property, plant, and equipment	22,919,000	24,366,000
Payment of dividends	1,749,000	—
Increase in other assets	613,000	(189,000)
Increase in deferred financing costs	616,000	—
Reduction of long-term obligations	7,943,000	3,835,000
Payment for treasury shares	771,000	—
Increase in net current assets	8,956,000	10,723,000
	$2,082,219,000	$1,812,778,000

See notes to financial statements.

Manufacturer 5
Notes to Consolidated Financial Statements
Years (52 Weeks) Ended October 30, 1976 and November 1, 1975

1. General

In the inflationary environment of the past several years, financial information reported on the conventional basis of historical costs fails to reflect fully economic reality of the financial condition and results of operations of business enterprises. As a result, the company is presenting financial statements reflecting the current costs of its assets, operating results, and changes in value by estimating the current replacement cost for assets expected to be retained and net realizable value for assets expected to be disposed of.

2. Current assets and liabilities

Inventories at year-end are stated on the same basis as used in the historical cost financial statements since they are stated at amounts that approximate current replacement cost or net realizable value. Other current assets and liabilities are substantially the same as at historical cost except for imputed income taxes that have been deducted from accrued liabilities.

3. Property, plant, and equipment

Property, plant, and equipment are stated at current replacement cost less accumulated depreciation and historical deferred income taxes. Current replacement cost was developed principally by using engineering estimates for the cost of replacing existing productive capacity after giving recognition to technological changes. The costs so determined have not been adjusted for anticipated reductions in operating expenses since such reductions are not estimated to be significant. Accumulated depreciation has been restated to reflect depreciation that would have been incurred in 1976, 1975, and in prior years based on the current replacement costs. Current cost depreciation expenses for 1976 and 1975 were $5,384,000 and $4,441,000 greater than the respective historical cost amounts. The increase in replacement cost of property, plant, and equipment during the year is reported as a value change in the consolidated statement of unrealized value changes.

4. Income taxes

Income taxes have not been imputed on the differences between current cost and historical cost bases of plant, property, and equipment. At October 30, 1976, the current cost bases exceeded the historical cost bases of plant, property, and equipment by approximately $48,000,000.

Historical noncurrent deferred income taxes have been reclassified in the balance sheet and included with the respective asset's valuation account as follows.

	1976	1975
Plant, property, and equipment	$11,971,000	$10,481,000
Investment held for disposition	(511,000)	(299,000)
	$11,460,000	$10,182,000

5. Cost of products sold

Prices for live cattle, dressed carcasses, processed cuts, and by-products all fluctuated during the years. The inventory value changes as reported in the statements of unrealized value changes and retained realized value changes represent the net change in the value of inventories held throughout the respective years. The inventory value changes are measured from the date the product is received until the product is shipped.

6. Notes to historical cost basis financial statements

The current cost financial statements should be read in conjunction with the notes to the historical cost basis financial statements.

MODEL D
Manufacturer 5
Consolidated Balance Sheets

	October 30, 1976	November 1, 1975
Assets		
Current assets		
Cash	$ 11,582,000	$ 12,368,000
Accounts receivable	89,019,000	85,035,000
Inventories	38,199,000	33,346,000
Prepaid expenses	533,000	484,000
Total current assets	139,333,000	131,233,000
Other assets	1,966,000	1,849,000
Property, plant, and equipment	224,978,000	194,554,000
Less accumulated depreciation and imputed income tax	(105,322,000)	(88,469,000)
	119,656,000	106,085,000
	$260,955,000	$239,167,000
Liabilities and Stockholders' Equity		
Current liabilities		
Notes payable	$ —	$ 11,000,000
Accounts payable and accrued liabilities	30,992,000	29,668,000
Federal and state income taxes	16,514,000	6,186,000
Current maturities of long-term obligation	2,325,000	3,833,000
Total current liabilities	49,831,000	50,687,000
Long-term obligations	54,284,000	58,878,000
	104,115,000	109,565,000
Stockholders' equity	156,840,000	129,602,000
	$260,955,000	$239,167,000

See notes to current value consolidated financial statements.

MODEL D

Manufacturer 5
Consolidated Statement of Changes in Stockholders' Equity

	Year (52 weeks) ended	
	October 30, 1976	November 1, 1975
Results of operations		
Sales	$2,077,158,000	$1,805,340,000
Cost of sales	1,978,354,000	1,732,264,000
Depreciation expense	12,869,000	10,175,000
Selling, general, and administrative	23,722,000	22,392,000
Interest	3,703,000	3,890,000
Income taxes	30,230,000	18,320,000
	2,048,878,000	1,787,041,000
	28,280,000	18,299,000
Value changes		
Investments	(496,000)	(101,000)
Inventories	(4,000,000)	2,900,000
Property, plant, and equipment	5,352,000	3,459,000
Long-term debt including interest differential	(1,271,000)	(894,000)
Income tax	1,416,000	52,000
	1,001,000	5,416,000
Amount required to recognize impact on stockholders' equity of increase in the general price level during the year	(7,248,000)	(8,041,000)
	(6,247,000)	(2,625,000)
Net results of operations and value changes	22,033,000	15,674,000
Stockholders' equity—beginning of year	136,860,000	107,218,000
Stock options and warrants exercised	488,000	6,710,000
Treasury stock acquired	(771,000)	—
Dividends paid	(1,770,000)	—
Stockholders' equity—end of year	$ 156,840,000	$ 129,602,000

See notes to current value consolidated financial statements.

Manufacturer 5
Notes to Consolidated Financial Statements
Years (52 Weeks) Ended October 30, 1976 and November 1, 1975

1. General

In the inflationary environment of the past several years, financial information reported on the conventional basis of historical costs fails to reflect fully economic reality of the financial condition and results of operations of business enterprises. As a result, the company is presenting financial statements reflecting the current values of its assets, liabilities, operating results, and changes in value by estimating the following:

a. The current replacement cost for assets and resources expected to be retained and net realizable value for assets expected to be disposed of.

b. The present value of estimated future cash outflows for liabilities.

c. The imputed income taxes relative to the difference in current value and income tax basis of assets and liabilities.

d. The effects of changes in general purchasing power on the net resources of the company.

2. Current assets and liabilities

Inventories at year-end are stated on the same basis as used in the historical cost financial statements since they are stated at amounts that approximate current replacement cost or net realizable value. Other current assets and liabilities are substantially the same as historical cost except for imputed income taxes that have been deducted from accrued liabilities.

3. Property, plant, and equipment

Property, plant, and equipment is stated at current replacement cost less accumulated depreciation and imputed income taxes. Current replacement cost was developed principally by using engineering estimates for the cost of replacing existing productive capacity after giving recognition to technological changes. The costs so determined have not been adjusted for anticipated reductions in operating expenses since such reductions are not estimated to be significant. Accumulated depreciation has been restated to reflect depreciation that would have been incurred in 1976, 1975, and in prior years based on the current replacement costs. Current value depreciation expenses for 1976 and 1975 were $5,384,000 and $4,441,000 greater than the respective historical cost amounts. The increase in replacement cost (net of imputed income taxes) of property, plant, and equipment during the year is reported as a value change in the consolidated statement of changes in stockholders' equity.

4. Long-term debt

Long-term debt is stated at the present value of future cash flows (net of imputed income taxes) based on the current applicable interest rates at the statement dates. The rates include an element for estimated financing costs. Current value interest expense is calculated at average current rates for the year.

5. Income taxes

Income tax expense shown in the current value statements is the amount currently payable adjusted for current amounts related to disposition of property and equipment. Income taxes have been imputed on the differences between current value and income tax bases of assets and liabilities as follows.

	1976	1975
Property, plant, and equipment	$35,925,000	$32,623,000
Other assets	(511,000)	(299,000)
Accounts payable and accrued liabilities	(2,139,000)	(723,000)
Long-term obligations	(1,406,000)	(98,000)
	$31,869,000	$31,503,000

All changes in imputed taxes are reported as value changes in the statements of changes in stockholders' equity.

6. Cost of products sold

Prices for live cattle, dressed carcasses, processed cuts, and by-products all fluctuated during the years. The inventory value changes as reported in the statements of changes in stockholders' equity represent the net change in the value of inventories held throughout the respective years. The inventory value changes are measured from the date the product is received until the product is shipped.

7. Stockholders' equity

Stockholders' equity at the beginning of the year and the amounts shown for sales and purchases of stock and dividends paid during the years have been restated as appropriate to give effect to the increase in general price level during the year as measured by the GNP implicit price deflator.

The amount required to recognize the impact on stockholders' equity of the increase in the general price level during the years is composed of the following.

	1976	1975
Net nonmonetary assets	$8,415,000	$9,793,000
Net monetary liabilities	(375,000)	(1,011,000)
Operations	(792,000)	(741,000)
	$7,248,000	$8,041,000

8. Notes to historical cost basis financial statement

The current value financial statements and the historical cost basis information contained therein should be read in conjunction with the notes to the historical cost basis financial statements.

CONVENTIONAL
MODEL

Retailer
Consolidated Balance Sheets
July 31, 1976 and 1975

	1976	1975
Assets		
Current assets		
Cash and marketable securities	$ 3,374,845	$ 4,050,629
Receivables, less allowances ($2,263,674 in 1976 and $2,224,364 in 1975) for doubtful accounts	75,212,596	66,736,074
Inventories		
Finished and in-process goods	110,888,876	96,113,219
Raw materials	18,986,372	13,783,678
Total current assets	$208,462,689	$180,683,600
Property, plant, and equipment, at cost		
Land	$ 1,553,198	$ 1,253,098
Buildings	21,057,955	20,199,626
Machinery and equipment	35,867,690	33,979,163
Leasehold improvements	27,262,773	22,902,408
Construction in progress	524,688	166,992
	$ 86,266,304	$ 78,501,287
Accumulated depreciation and amortization	36,836,384	33,075,075
	$ 49,429,920	$ 45,426,212
Other assets		
Excess of cost of investments over book value of net assets acquired	$ 7,115,482	$ 7,115,482
Installment receivables, less current portion included in current assets	5,245,531	4,974,528
Prepaid expenses and deferred charges	3,981,503	3,036,421
Future tax benefits, net	861,559	1,842,170
Sundry investments	1,909,202	2,695,053
	$ 19,113,277	$ 19,663,654
	$277,005,886	$245,773,466

The accompanying notes are an integral part of these financial statements.

	1976	1975
Liabilities and Shareholders' Equity		
Current liabilities		
Unsecured notes payable and current portion of long-term debt	$ 6,363,595	$ 10,357,420
Accounts payable	38,871,869	27,348,161
Accrued expenses and employee deductions	17,630,111	17,421,200
Federal income taxes	15,471,127	5,396,045
Total current liabilities	$ 78,336,702	$ 60,522,826
Long-term debt, less portion due within one year included in current liabilities	$ 53,500,352	$ 59,880,116
Deferred credits and other provisions	$ 6,107,249	$ 5,873,741
Commitments and contingencies (note 7)		
Shareholders' investment		
Common shares, without par value— 10,000,000 shares authorized; 6,949,292 issued in 1976, 6,871,008 in 1975, of which 33,300 shares are held in treasury	$ 2,305,330	$ 2,279,235
Cumulative preferred shares, without par value—authorized 1,500,000 shares; none issued or outstanding	—	—
Capital surplus	26,252,891	25,480,475
Retained earnings	110,503,362	91,737,073
	$139,061,583	$119,496,783
	$277,005,886	$245,773,466

CONVENTIONAL MODEL

Retailer
Consolidated Statements of Earnings and Retained Earnings
Years Ended July 31, 1976 and 1975

	1976	1975
Earnings		
Net sales	$552,566,605	$473,423,783
Cost of sales	354,216,061	310,903,321
Gross profit	$198,350,544	$162,520,462
Selling, general, and administrative expenses	145,008,552	129,926,021
Earnings from operations	$ 53,341,992	$ 32,594,441
Other income (expense), net		
Interest	(4,217,240)	(7,632,020)
Other	925,322	428,937
Earnings before income taxes and effect of 1975 change in accounting method	$ 50,050,074	$ 25,391,358
Provision for income taxes	24,391,000	11,984,000
Earnings before effect of 1975 change in accounting method	$ 25,659,074	$ 13,407,358
Effect of 1975 change in accounting method, net of tax (note 8)	—	(835,506)
Net earnings for the year	$ 25,659,074	$ 12,571,852
Earnings per common and common equivalent share		
Before effect of 1975 change in accounting method	$3.68	$1.95
Effect of 1975 change in accounting method (note 8)	—	(.12)
After effect of 1975 change in accounting method	$3.68	$1.83
Retained Earnings		
Balance at beginning of year	$ 91,737,073	$ 85,661,089
Add (deduct)		
Net earnings for the year	25,659,074	12,571,852
Dividends paid on common shares ($1.00 in 1976 and $.95 in 1975)	(6,892,785)	(6,495,868)
Balance at end of year	$110,503,362	$ 91,737,073

The accompanying notes are an integral part of these financial statements.

CONVENTIONAL MODEL
Retailer
Consolidated Statement of Changes in Financial Position
Years Ended July 31, 1976 and 1975

	1976	1975
Working Capital Was Provided by		
Net earnings (before effect of 1975 change in accounting method)	$25,659,074	$13,407,358
Add—amounts deducted in determining net earnings that do not represent current fund expenditures		
Provisions for depreciation and amortization	6,154,648	5,756,926
Other, net	233,508	185,988
Working capital provided by operations	$32,047,230	$19,350,272
Increase in long-term debt	1,023,516	14,332,711
Proceeds from sale of common shares under stock option plans	818,876	—
Retirements of property, plant, and equipment	1,109,715	1,358,652
Total working capital provided	$34,999,337	$35,041,635
Working Capital Was Used for		
Effect of 1975 change in accounting method	$ —	$ 835,506
Additions to property, plant, and equipment	10,589,719	9,895,686
Retirements and repurchases of long-term debt	7,403,280	4,903,472
Dividends paid	6,892,785	6,495,868
Other, net	148,340	(905,592)
Total working capital used	$25,034,124	$21,224,940
Net increase (decrease) in working capital	$ 9,965,213	$13,816,695
Components of Working Capital Increase (Decrease)		
Cash and marketable securities	$ (675,784)	$ 660,154
Receivables	8,476,522	(4,305,439)
Inventories	19,978,351	(15,234,102)
Change in current assets	$27,779,089	$(18,879,387)
Notes payable	$ (3,993,825)	$(41,725,646)
Accounts payable	11,523,708	4,972,688
Accrued expenses	208,911	2,526,834
Federal income taxes	10,075,082	1,530,042
Change in current liabilities	$17,813,876	$(32,696,082)
Net increase (decrease) in working capital	$ 9,965,213	$13,816,695

The accompanying notes are an integral part of these financial statements.

1. Statement of major accounting policies

Principles of consolidation. The consolidated financial statements include the accounts of all subsidiaries; all significant intercompany transactions have been eliminated.

Inventories. Inventories are stated at the lower of cost or market; costs are determined using primarily moving averages, which approximate FIFO costs, and retail inventory methods (note 8).

Depreciation. Depreciation and amortization of property, plant, and equipment are provided over the estimated useful lives of the assets, or the remaining terms of leases, where applicable, on primarily a straight-line basis.

The excess of cost of investments over book value of net assets acquired arose primarily in connection with acquisitions in 1966 and 1968. This amount is not being amortized.

Store opening costs. The company follows the practice of charging new store opening costs against earnings as the stores are opened.

Employee retirement plans (fixed benefit). The company has noncontributory retirement plans that provide for pensions to eligible employees, upon retirement, based on length of service and compensation. Prior service costs are being amortized and funded over approximately thirty years.

Income taxes. The company provides for deferred income taxes and records future income tax benefits on tax timing differences. The flow-through method of accounting for investment tax credit is used.

2. Employee retirement plans (fixed benefit)

Provisions for pension expense charged against earnings during the year ended July 31, 1976, which include amortization of prior service cost over thirty years, totaled approximately $2.6 million ($2 million in 1975). The actuarially computed value of vested benefits for all plans as of July 31, 1976, using the basis followed by the Pension Benefit Guaranty Corporation, exceeded the total of the net assets in the pension fund and balance sheet reserves by approximately $1 million. Unfunded and unprovided prior service costs totaled $11.9 million at July 31, 1976 ($9.2 million in 1975).

The company amended certain of its employee retirement plans as of January 1, 1976, for the purpose of providing improved benefits to employees and to remain in compliance with the provisions of the Employee Retirement Income Security Act of 1974; assumptions used in the actuarial computations were also changed. These changes had the effect of increasing fiscal 1976 pension expense by $800,000.

3. Income taxes

The provision for income taxes consists of the following.

	1976	1975
Federal income taxes		
Currently payable	$20,592,000	$ 8,141,000
Deferred		
Utilization of future tax benefits		
on tax operating loss carryforwards	412,000	2,747,000
Other, net	569,000	(125,000)
State and local income taxes	3,320,000	1,719,000
Investment tax credit	(502,000)	(498,000)
	$24,391,000	$11,984,000

4. Short-term debt

The company's short-term debt at July 31, 1976, includes unsecured notes payable to banks ($2,016,000) and commercial paper ($3 million). These borrowings had an average remaining term of nineteen days and an average interest rate of 6.28 percent. Maturities under these obligations generally do not exceed ninety days.

During the fiscal year, the average short-term debt outstanding approximated $1,384,000 and reflected a weekly weighted average interest rate of 7.0 percent. The maximum amount of short-term debt outstanding at the end of any month during fiscal 1976 aggregated $6.5 million.

At year end, the company had unused lines of credit totaling $19 million available for short-term financing. Such lines are not extended for indefinite periods and are subject to termination periodically by either the company or the banks. Under informal agreements with participating banks, the company maintains compensating balances ranging up to 20 percent of the credit lines.

5. Long-term debt

Long-term debt at July 31, 1976, and 1975 consists of the following.

	1976	1975
7.85% notes, payable in annual installments of $1,500,000 commencing in 1979	$15,000,000	$15,000,000
7.125% debentures, payable in annual installments of $750,000	11,058,000	14,240,000
10.75% notes (additional $8,000,000 issued in August, 1976) payable in annual installments of $1,700,000 beginning in 1978 with the balance payable in 1990	14,000,000	14,000,000
5.35% notes, payable in semi-annual installments of $333,333	6,666,667	7,333,333
5.125% notes, payable in annual installments of $200,000 with the balance payable in 1985	2,600,000	2,800,000
7.50% term loan	—	4,200,000
9% notes	—	2,200,000
Other	5,523,280	5,000,289
	54,847,947	64,773,622
Less portion due within one year	1,347,595	4,893,506
	$53,500,352	$59,880,116

The 7.125 percent debentures have been reduced in 1976 by the purchase of $2,442,000 of such debentures now held in the treasury.

The agreements with respect to long-term debt include, among other things, provisions that limit total consolidated indebtedness, require the maintenance of minimum amounts of working capital, and limit capital stock repurchases and the payment of cash dividends by the company. Under the most restrictive of these various provisions, approximately $81.3 million of consolidated retained earnings at July 31, 1976, is restricted as to the payment of cash dividends.

6. Common shares and capital surplus

At July 31, 1976, of the authorized but unissued common shares, 240,266 were reserved for issuance to executives and key employees under the company's stock option plans. Of such reserved shares, 236,166 were subject to options outstanding at that date. A summary of the changes in options outstanding during the year is set forth below:

	Number of shares	Option price range (per share)
Outstanding, July 31, 1975	227,758	$ 7.50–$25.25
Add (deduct)		
Granted	81,550	32.75– 33.31
Exercised	(39,284)	10.56– 25.25
Cancelled		
Expirations	(27,000)	18.50
Terminations	(6,858)	10.56– 23.63
Outstanding, July 31, 1976	236,166	$ 7.50–$33.31

The changes in common shares and capital surplus during the year were as follows:

	Shares	Amount	Capital surplus
Balance at July 31, 1975	6,837,708	$2,279,235	$25,480,475
Proceeds from sale of shares issued under stock option plan	39,284	13,095	805,781
A company was acquired on a pooling of interests basis (restatement of prior years has not been reflected due to the immateriality of the transaction)	39,000	13,000	13,000
Treasury stock transactions in accordance with the provisions of certain deferred compensation plans, net	—	—	(104,295)
Other	—	—	57,930
Balance at July 31, 1976	6,915,992	$2,305,330	$26,252,891

7. Commitments and contingencies

Lease arrangements. The company leases various plant, warehouse, office, and retail store facilities under lease arrangements expiring between 1977 and 2001. Minimum annual rentals under such arrangements in effect at July 31, 1976, are as follows.

	Minimum rental	
Fiscal year(s) ended	*Plant, warehouse, and office facilities*	*Retail store facilities*
1977	$1,481,000	$12,322,000
1978	1,355,000	12,176,000
1979	1,261,000	12,135,000
1980	1,243,000	11,848,000
1981	1,243,000	11,547,000
1982–1986	5,560,000	52,017,000
1987–1991	4,018,000	35,052,000
1992–1996	3,173,000	1,865,000
1997–2001	1,585,000	82,000

Aggregate rental expense applicable to plant, warehouse, and office facilities amounted to $1,939,000 in fiscal 1976 ($1,417,000 in 1975). Aggregate rental expense applicable to retail store facilities, including "sales override" provisions, amounted to $12,996,000 in fiscal 1976 ($10,909,000 in 1975).

The company also leases certain production and data processing equipment. Aggregate rental expense for such equipment was $3,086,000 in fiscal 1976 ($2,659,000 in 1975). These lease arrangements are generally cancellable, on written notice, within three to six months and, therefore, do not represent a significant long-term commitment.

Noncapitalized financing leases (as defined by the SEC) are not material.

License arrangements. Several of the company's divisions operate departments under license arrangements whereby the stores provide not only space and certain other facilities, but also utilities, maintenance, credit administration, and other related services. These license arrangements usually involve periods of five years or less with the license fee generally being based on a percentage of the department sales. In certain instances a minimum license fee is guaranteed.

Fiscal 1976 license fees applicable to these departments (approximately one-half of which represent payments for service) aggregated $8,258,000 ($8,942,000 in 1975). Minimum annual fees under existing license arrangements range from $1,820,000 for fiscal 1977 to $378,000 in 1981 and aggregate $5,449,000.

Contingencies. The company is contingently liable under certain leases of facilities that are operated by customers but have been guaranteed by the company. Minimum annual rentals guaranteed under such leases aggregate approximately $3,233,000 in 1977 and $2.9 million in 1981.

Legal proceedings. A number of legal actions have been instituted against the company that involve ordinary routine matters as are incident to the kinds of businesses conducted by the company. In the opinion of management, the ultimate disposition of all such actions will not have a materially adverse effect upon the company's consolidated financial statements.

8. Change in accounting method

The company changed its method of accounting for certain of its retail inventories from the lower of average cost or market method to the retail method. This change was made in the fourth quarter of fiscal 1975 and applied retroactively to the beginning of the fiscal year, August 1, 1974. This change was made so that all company retail divisions would conform to a uniform inventory accounting method.

This change did not materially affect 1975 earnings from operations. The cumulative effect of such change at August 1, 1974, amounted to a reduction of $835,506 (net of related taxes of $694,000) or $.12 per share.

MODEL A

Retailer
Consolidated Balance Sheet Information
July 31, 1976 and 1975

	In $ (1976)	
	1976	*1975*
Current assets	$208,922,000	$191,317,000
Other assets	24,283,000	25,532,000
Current liabilities	(78,337,000)	(63,899,000)
Deferred credits	(6,647,000)	(6,812,000)
	$148,221,000	$146,138,000
Property, plant, and equipment	119,135,000	113,506,000
Accumulated depreciation	(57,386,000)	(52,959,000)
	$ 61,749,000	$ 60,547,000
Long-term debt	(53,500,000)	(63,221,000)
Shareholders' equity	$156,470,000	$143,464,000

MODEL A

Retailer
Consolidated Earnings Information
Years Ended July 31, 1976 and 1975

	In $ (1976)	
	1976	1975
Earnings (Condensed)		
Sales	$562,347,000	$513,711,000
Operating income after depreciation		
of $7,616 in 1976 and $7,052 in 1975	$ 42,917,000	$ 13,240,000
Loss on disposal of fixed assets	1,324,000	1,978,000
Federal income taxes		
On general purchasing power net		
income	21,135,000	8,154,000
On reported net income in excess		
of general purchasing power net		
income	3,688,000	4,850,000
Earnings (loss) from operating		
transactions	$ 16,770,000	$ (1,742,000)
Effect of 1975 change in accounting		
method, net of tax	—	(1,056,000)
General purchasing power gain (loss)		
On long-term debt	2,917,000	5,230,000
On all other monetary items	(478,000)	496,000
Net earnings for the year	$ 19,209,000	$ 2,928,000
Per Share		
Earnings from operating transactions	$2.41	$(.25)
Net earnings for the year	$2.76	$ .43
Retained Earnings		
Balance at beginning of year	$ 87,690,000	$ 91,811,000
Add (deduct)		
Net earnings for the year	19,209,000	2,928,000
Dividends paid on common shares		
($1.01 in 1976 and $1.03 in 1975)	(7,015,000)	(7,049,000)
Balance at end of year	$ 99,884,000	$ 87,690,000

MODEL A

Retailer
Reconciliation of "Unit-of-Money" Net Income With
"Unit-of-Purchasing-Power" Net Income

	1976	1975
Net income in units of money	$25,659,000	$12,572,000
Increase (decrease) to net income resulting from restatement to units of 1976 purchasing power		
Sales	9,780,000	40,287,000
Cost of sales	(12,848,000)	(40,027,000)
Depreciation	(2,140,000)	(2,064,000)
Other expenses, net	(2,844,000)	(12,104,000)
Loss on disposal of equipment	(838,000)	(1,243,000)
General purchasing power gains on monetary items	2,440,000	5,727,000
Effect of change in accounting method, net	—	(220,000)
Net income in units of 7/31/76 general purchasing power	$19,209,000	$ 2,928,000

MODEL A

Retailer
Explanatory Note to Supplementary
General Purchasing Power Information

The accompanying general purchasing power information, expressed in units of the general purchasing power of the dollar at July 31, 1976, is based on the financial statements in units of money (historical dollars) and should be read in conjunction with them (including the notes). The historical dollar financial statements combine amounts expressed in dollars expended at various times in the past with amounts expressed in dollars expended more recently, regardless of changes in the general purchasing power of the dollar. Amortization of the expenditures of dollars in prior years is deducted from revenues received currently in determining net income. The result is a mixture of dollars that represent various amounts of general purchasing power. In the general purchasing power information, historical amounts have been restated to recognize the reductions that have occurred in the general purchasing power of the dollar (inflation). The amounts originally recorded are restated into units of the general purchasing power of the dollar at July 31, 1976, using the gross national product implicit price deflator (GNP deflator).

General purchasing power restatement does not change the underlying accounting principles; the same principles are used in both the historical dollar financial statements and the general purchasing power information. The latter retains the historical cost basis of accounting; only the unit is changed. That is, historical cost is expressed in amounts restated for changes in the general purchasing power of the dollar as measured by the GNP deflator. The restated amounts do not purport to be appraised value, replacement cost, or current value; nor do they purport to be based on prices at which transactions would take place currently. Establishing units of general purchasing power is a process of translation, not of valuation.

Changing to units of general purchasing power should not be confused with reporting the effects of changes in the prices of particular goods and services. Movements in specific prices are caused in part by changes in general purchasing power and in part by various other factors (for example, supply and demand and technological changes). Changes in the general price level may be more or less rapid than, and may even be counter to, changes in specific prices.

Inflation over a period of time has cumulative effects on historical dollar financial statements. The cumulative effect of inflation is particularly significant for long-lived nonmonetary assets such as property, plant, and equipment, shown by the restatement of these items in the supplementary balance sheet information and in the corresponding restatement of depreciation in the supplementary income statement information. Restatement of inventories significantly affects cost of sales. The resulting increases in the amounts at which nonmonetary assets are presented in the balance sheet are not included in income since they are merely the results of changing the measurement unit.

Holders of monetary assets, such as cash and receivables, lose general purchasing power during inflation because monetary assets buy fewer goods and services as the general level of prices rises. Conversely, those who owe monetary liabilities gain general purchasing power because the liabilities will be payable with dollars that have less general purchasing power than those expended when the liabilities were incurred. Information as to general purchasing power gain or loss is necessary to evaluate the overall impact of inflation on the results of business operations. The accompanying general purchasing power income statement reflects a general purchasing power loss of $478,000 in 1976 because of holding net monetary assets (before deducting gain on long-term debt) and a general purchasing power gain of $2,917,000 in 1976 as a result of owing long-term debt.

The cumulative effect of inflation disclosed by the restatement of historical units of money to units of general purchasing power includes all the elements discussed in the preceding two paragraphs. The net impact of restatement on results for the years 1976 and 1975 and the relative importance of the various elements of inflationary effect for the years are shown in the reconciliation of net income in units of money with net income in units of July 31, 1976, general purchasing power.

No deferred tax charge or credit has been provided with respect to the restatement of assets or liabilities since the restatements do not affect income taxes.

MODEL B

Retailer
Consolidated Statements of Earnings and Changes in Retained Earnings
Years Ended July 31, 1976 and 1975

	1976	1975
Earnings		
Net Sales	$552,566,605	$473,423,783
Cost of sales	360,761,061	316,839,321
Gross profit	$191,805,544	$156,584,462
Selling, general and administrative expenses	146,941,552	131,535,021
Earnings from operations	$ 44,863,992	$ 25,049,441
Other income (expense), net		
Interest	(4,217,240)	(7,632,020)
Other	925,322	428,937
Earnings before income taxes and effect of 1975 change in accounting method	$ 41,572,074	$ 17,846,358
Provision for income taxes	20,370,000	8,433,000
Earnings before effect of 1975 change in accounting method	$ 21,202,074	$ 9,413,358
Effect of 1975 change in accounting method, net of tax (note 8)	—	(835,506)
Net earnings for the year	$ 21,202,074	$ 8,577,852
Earnings per common and common equivalent share		
Before effect of 1975 change in accounting method	$3.04	$1.37
Effect of 1975 change in accounting method (note 8)	—	(.12)
After effect of 1975 change in accounting method	$3.04	$1.25
Retained Earnings		
Balance at beginning of year	$ 87,743,073	$ 85,661,089
Add (deduct)		
Net earnings for the year	21,202,074	8,577,852
Dividends paid on common shares ($1.00 in 1976 and $.95 in 1975)	(6,892,785)	(6,495,868)
Balance at end of year	$102,052,362	$ 87,743,073

The accompanying notes are an integral part of these financial statements.

MODEL B

Retailer
Consolidated Balance Sheets
July 31, 1976 and 1975

Assets	1976	1975
Current assets		
Cash and marketable securities	$ 3,374,845	$ 4,050,629
Receivables, less allowances ($2,263,674 in 1976 and $2,224,364 in 1975) for doubtful accounts	75,212,596	66,736,074
Inventories		
Finished and in-process goods	100,935,876	91,218,219
Raw materials	16,458,372	12,742,678
Total current assets	$195,981,689	$174,747,600
Property, plant, and equipment, at cost		
Land	$ 1,553,198	$ 1,253,098
Buildings	21,057,955	20,199,626
Machinery and equipment	35,867,690	33,979,163
Leasehold improvements	27,262,773	22,902,408
Construction in progress	524,688	166,992
	$ 86,266,304	$ 78,501,287
Accumulated depreciation and amortization	36,836,384	33,075,075
	$ 49,429,920	$ 45,426,212

Liabilities and Shareholders' Equity	1976	1975
Current liabilities		
Unsecured notes payable and current portion of long-term debt	$ 6,363,595	$ 10,357,420
Accounts payable	38,871,869	27,348,161
Accrued expenses and employee deductions	17,630,111	17,421,200
Federal income taxes	9,480,127	2,547,045
Total current liabilities	$ 72,345,702	$ 57,673,826
Long-term debt, less portion due within one year included in current liabilities	$ 53,500,352	$ 59,880,116
Deferred credits and other provisions	$ 6,107,249	$ 5,873,741
Shareholders' equity		
Common shares, without par value—10,000,000 shares authorized; 6,949,292 issued in 1976, 6,871,008 in 1975, of which 33,300 shares are held in treasury	$ 2,305,330	$ 2,279,235

Other assets		
Excess of cost of investments over book value of net assets acquired	$ 7,115,482	$ 7,115,482
Installment receivables, less current portion included in current assets	5,245,531	4,974,528
Prepaid expenses and deferred charges	3,981,503	3,036,421
Future tax benefits, net	2,442,559	2,544,170
Sundry investments	1,909,202	2,695,053
	$ 20,694,277	$ 20,365,654
	$266,105,886	$240,539,466

Cumulative preferred shares, without par value—authorized 1,500,000 shares; none issued or outstanding	—	—
Capital surplus	26,252,891	25,480,475
Retained earnings	102,052,362	87,743,073
Accumulated current cost depreciation	3,542,000	1,609,000
	$134,152,583	$117,111,783
	$266,105,886	$240,539,466

The accompanying notes are an integral part of these financial statements.

MODEL B

Retailer
Consolidated Statement of Changes in Financial Position
Years Ended July 31, 1976 and 1975

	1976	1975
Working Capital Was Provided by		
Net earnings (before effect of 1975 change in accounting method)	$21,202,074	$ 9,413,358
Add—amounts deducted in determining net earnings that do not represent current fund expenditures		
Provisions for replacement cost depreciation and amortization	8,087,648	7,365,926
Other, net	233,508	185,988
Working capital provided by operations	29,523,230	16,965,272
Increase in long-term debt	1,023,516	14,332,711
Proceeds from sale of common shares under stock option plans	818,876	—
Retirements of property, plant, and equipment	1,109,715	1,358,652
Total working capital provided	$32,475,337	$32,656,635
Working Capital Was Used for		
Effect of 1975 change in accounting method	$ —	$ 835,506
Additions to property, plant, and equipment	10,589,719	9,895,686
Retirements and repurchases of long-term debt	7,403,280	4,903,472
Dividends paid	6,892,785	6,495,868
Other, net	1,027,340	(203,592)
Total working capital used	25,913,124	21,926,940
Net increase in working capital	$ 6,562,213	$10,729,695
Components of Working Capital Increase (Decrease)		
Cash and marketable securities	$ (675,784)	$ 660,154
Receivables	8,476,522	(4,305,439)
Inventories	13,433,351	(21,170,102)
Change in current assets	21,234,089	(24,815,387)
Notes payable	(3,993,825)	(41,725,646)
Accounts payable	11,523,708	4,972,688
Accrued expenses	208,911	2,526,834
Federal income taxes	6,933,082	(1,318,958)
Change in current liabilities	14,671,876	(35,545,082)
Net increase in working capital	$ 6,562,213	$10,729,695

The accompanying notes are an integral part of these financial statements.

MODEL B

Retailer
Notes to Consolidated Financial Statements
Years Ended July 31, 1976 and 1975

1. Statement of major accounting policies

Principles of consolidation. The consolidated financial statements include the accounts of all subsidiaries; all significant intercompany transactions have been eliminated.

Inventories. Inventories are valued by the LIFO method of inventory valuation. The LIFO reserve was $12,481,000 in 1976 and $5,936,000 in 1975.

Depreciation. Provision is made for depreciation of property, plant, and equipment based on the charge necessary each year to provide the replacement cost of those assets in that year over the assets' useful life or the remaining terms of leases. The company primarily uses the straight line method of depreciation.

The excess of cost of investments over book value of net assets acquired arose primarily in connection with acquisitions in 1966 and 1968. This amount is not being amortized.

Store opening costs. The company follows the practice of charging new store opening costs against earnings as the stores are opened.

Employee retirement plans (fixed benefit). The company has noncontributory retirement plans that provide for pensions to eligible employees, on retirement, based on length of service and compensation. Prior service costs are being amortized and funded over approximately thirty years.

Income taxes. The company provides for deferred income taxes and records future income tax benefits on tax timing differences. The "flow-through" method of accounting for investment tax credit is used.

2. Employee retirement plans (fixed benefits)

Provisions for pension expense charged against earnings during the year ended July 31, 1976, which include amortization of prior service cost over thirty years, totaled approximately $2 million ($2 million in 1975). The actuarially computed value of vested benefits for all plans as of July 31, 1976, using the basis followed by the Pension Benefit Guaranty Corporation, exceeded the total of the net assets in the pension fund and balance sheet reserves by approximately $1.1 million. Unfunded and unprovided prior service costs totaled $11.9 million at July 31, 1976 ($9.2 million in 1975).

The company amended certain of its employee retirement plans as of January 1, 1976, for the purpose of providing improved benefits to employees and to remain in compliance with the provisions of the Employee Retirement Income Security Act of 1974; assumptions used in the actuarial computations were also changed. These changes had the effect of increasing fiscal 1976 pension expense by $800,000.

3. Income taxes

The provision for income taxes consists of the following:

	1976	1975
Federal income taxes		
Currently payable	$17,450,000	$5,292,000
Deferred		
Utilization of future tax benefits on tax operating loss carryforwards	412,000	2,747,000
Other, net	(310,000)	(827,000)
State and local income taxes	3,320,000	1,719,000
Investment tax credit	(502,000)	(498,000)
	$20,370,000	$8,433,000

4. Short-term debt

The company's short-term debt at July 31, 1976, includes unsecured notes payable to banks ($2,016,000) and commercial paper ($3 million). These borrowings had an average remaining term of nineteen days and an average interest rate of 6.28 percent. Maturities under these obligations generally do not exceed ninety days.

During the fiscal year, the average short-term debt outstanding approximated $1,384,000 and reflected a weekly weighted average interest rate of 7.0 percent. The maximum amount of short-term debt outstanding at the end of any month during the fiscal 1976 aggregated $6.5 million.

At year end, the company had unused lines of credit totaling $19 million available for short-term financing. Such lines are not extended for indefinite periods and are subject to termination periodically by either the company or the banks. Under informal agreements with participating banks, the company maintains compensating balances ranging up to 20 percent of the credit lines.

5. Long-term debt

Long-term debt at July 31, 1976, and 1975 consists of the following:

	1976	1975
7.85% notes, payable in annual installments of $1,500,000 commencing in 1979	$15,000,000	$15,000,000
7.125% debentures, payable in annual installments of $750,000	11,058,000	14,240,000
10.75% notes (additional $8,000,000 issued in August, 1976) payable in annual installments of $1,700,000 beginning in 1978 with the balance payable in 1990	14,000,000	14,000,000
5.35% notes, payable in semi-annual installments of $333,333	6,666,667	7,333,333
5.125% notes, payable in annual installments of $200,000 with the balance payable in 1985	2,600,000	2,800,000
7.50% term loan	—	4,200,000
9% notes	—	2,200,000
Other	5,523,280	5,000,289
	$54,847,947	$64,773,622
Less portion due within one year	1,347,595	4,893,506
	$53,500,352	$59,880,116

The 7.125 percent debentures have been reduced in 1976 by the purchase of $2,442,000 of such debentures now held in the treasury.

The agreements with respect to long-term debt include, among other things, provisions that limit total consolidated indebtedness, require the maintenance of minimum amounts of working capital, and limit capital stock repurchases and the payment of cash dividends by the company. Under the most restrictive of these various provisions, approximately $81.3 million of consolidated retained earnings at July 31, 1976, is restricted as to the payment of cash dividends. These loan covenant restrictions do not take into account the fact that the LIFO inventory method is used or that depreciation is charged on a replacement cost basis. The covenants would require renegotiation to provide a more meaningful restriction.

6. Common shares and capital surplus

At July 31, 1976, of the authorized but unissued common shares, 240,266 were reserved for issuance to executives and key employees under the company's stock option plans. Of such reserved shares, 236,166 were subject to options outstanding at that date. A summary of the changes in options outstanding during the year is set forth below.

	Number of shares	Option price range (per share)
Outstanding, at July 31, 1975	227,758	$ 7.50–$25.25
Add (deduct)		
Granted	81,550	32.75– 33.31
Exercised	(39,284)	10.56– 25.25
Cancelled		
Expirations	(27,000)	18.50
Terminations	(6,858)	10.56– 23.63
Outstanding, at July 31, 1976	236,166	$ 7.50–$33.31

The changes in common shares and capital surplus during the year were as follows.

	Common shares		Capital surplus
	Shares	Amount	
Balance at July 31, 1975	6,837,708	$2,279,235	$25,480,475
Proceeds from sale of shares issued under stock option plan	39,284	13,095	805,781
A company was acquired on a pooling of interests basis (restatement of prior years has not been reflected due to the immateriality of the transaction)	39,000	13,000	13,000
Treasury stock transactions in accordance with the provisions of certain deferred compensation plans, net	—	—	(104,295)
Other	—	—	57,930
Balance at July 31, 1976	6,915,992	$2,305,330	$26,252,891

7. Commitments and contingencies

Lease arrangements. The company leases various plant, warehouse, office, and retail store facilities under lease arrangements expiring between 1977 and 2001. Minimum annual rentals under such arrangements in effect at July 31, 1976, are as follows:

	Minimum rental	
For fiscal year(s) ended	Plant, warehouse, and office facilities	Retail store facilities
1977	$1,481,000	$12,322,000
1978	1,355,000	12,176,000
1979	1,261,000	12,135,000
1980	1,243,000	11,848,000
1981	1,243,000	11,547,000
1982–1986	5,560,000	52,017,000
1987–1991	4,018,000	35,052,000
1992–1996	3,173,000	1,865,000
1997–2001	1,585,000	82,000

Aggregate rental expense applicable to plant, warehouse, and office facilities amounted to $1,939,000 in fiscal 1976 ($1,417,000 in 1975). Aggregate rental expense applicable to retail store facilities, including "sales override" provisions, amounted to $12,996,000 in fiscal 1976 ($10,909,000 in 1975).

The company also leases certain production and data processing equipment. Aggregate rental expense for such equipment was $3,086,000 in fiscal 1976 ($2,659,000 in 1975). These lease arrangements are generally cancellable, on written notice, within three to six months and, therefore, do not represent a significant long-term commitment.

Noncapitalized financing leases (as defined by the SEC) are not material.

Licensing arrangements. Several of the company's divisions operate departments under license arrangements whereby the stores provide not only space and certain other facilities, but also utilities, maintenance, credit administration, and other related services. These license arrangements usually involve periods of five years or less with the license fee generally being based on a percentage of the department sales. In certain instances a minimum license fee is guaranteed.

Fiscal 1976 license fees applicable to these departments (approximately one-half of which represent payments for service) aggregated $8,258,000 ($8,942,000 in 1975). Minimum annual fees under existing license arrangements range from $1,820,000 for fiscal 1977 to $378,000 in 1981 and aggregate $5,449,000.

Contingencies. The company is contingently liable under certain leases of facilities that are operated by customers but have been guaranteed by the company. Minimum annual rentals guaranteed under such leases aggregate approximately $3,233,000 in 1977 and $2.9 million in 1981.

Legal proceedings. A number of legal actions have been instituted against the company that involve ordinary routine matters as are incident to the kinds of businesses conducted by the company. In the opinion of management, the ultimate disposition of all such actions will not have a materially adverse effect on the company's consolidated financial statements.

8. Change in accounting method

The company changed its method of accounting for certain of its retail inventories from the lower of average cost or market method to the retail method. This change was made in the fourth quarter of fiscal 1975 and applied retroactively to the beginning of the fiscal year, August 1, 1974. This change was made so that all company retail divisions would conform to a uniform inventory accounting method.

This change did not materially affect 1975 earnings from operations. The cumulative effect of such change at August 1, 1974, amounted to a reduction of $835,506 (net of related taxes of $694,000) or $.12 per share.

MODEL C

Retailer
Statement of Retained Realized Value Changes
Years Ended July 31, 1976 and 1975

	1976	1975
Balance at beginning of year	$ 6,813,000	$ —
Capital maintenance allowances recovered through operations		
Cost of sales	6,545,000	5,936,000
Depreciation	1,936,000	1,609,000
	8,481,000	7,545,000
Capital (losses) realized on disposal of property, plant, and equipment*	(122,000)	(732,000)
Balance at end of year	$15,172,000	$6,813,000

* No tax benefit is recognized on the capital losses because of the uncertainty of the existence of capital gains.

The accompanying notes are an integral part of these financial statements.

MODEL C

Retailer
Consolidated Statements of Operating Income and Retained Operating Income
Years Ended July 31, 1976 and 1975

	1976	1975
Operating Income		
Net sales	$552,566,605	$473,423,783
Cost of sales	360,761,061	316,839,321
Gross profit	191,805,544	156,584,462
Selling, general and administrative		
expenses	146,944,552	131,535,021
Earnings from operations	44,860,992	25,049,441
Other income (expense), net		
Interest	(4,217,240)	(7,632,020)
Other	1,047,322	1,160,937
Operating income before income taxes and effect of 1975 change in accounting method	41,691,074	18,578,358
Provision for income taxes	24,391,000	11,984,000
Operating income before effect of 1975 change in accounting method	17,300,074	6,594,358
Effect of 1975 change in accounting method, net of tax (note 8)	—	(835,506)
Net operating income for the year	$ 17,300,074	$ 5,758,852
Operating income per common and common equivalent share		
Before effect of 1975 change in accounting method	$2.48	$.96
Effect of 1975 change in accounting method (note 8)	—	(.12)
After effect of 1975 change in accounting method	$2.48	$.84
Retained Operating Income		
Balance at beginning of year	$ 84,924,073	$ 85,661,089
Add (deduct)		
Net operating income for the year	17,300,074	5,758,852
Dividends paid on common shares ($1.00 in 1976 and $.95 in 1975)	(6,892,785)	(6,495,868)
Balance at end of year	$ 95,331,362	$ 84,924,073

The accompanying notes are an integral part of these financial statements.

MODEL C
Retailer
Statement of Value Changes*
Years Ended July 31, 1976 and 1975

	1976				1975			
	Inventories	Land	Property, plant, and equipment, net	Total	Inventories	Land	Property, plant, and equipment, net	Total
Balance of unrealized value changes at beginning of year	$ —	$1,665,000	$12,519,000	$14,184,000	$ —	$1,519,000	$10,301,000	$11,820,000
Net value increases (decreases) for the year	6,545,000	76,000	3,545,000	10,166,000	5,936,000	146,000	3,095,000	9,177,000
	6,545,000	1,741,000	16,064,000	24,350,000	5,936,000	1,665,000	13,396,000	20,997,000
Realized during the year								
Capital maintenance allowance recovered through operations	(6,545,000)	—	(1,936,000)	(8,481,000)	(5,936,000)	—	(1,609,000)	(7,545,000)
Net (gains) losses realized through disposal	—	—	122,000	122,000	—	—	732,000	732,000
	(6,545,000)	—	(1,814,000)	(8,359,000)	(5,936,000)	—	(877,000)	(6,813,000)
Balance of unrealized value changes at end of year	—	$1,741,000	$14,250,000	$15,991,000	—	$1,665,000	$12,519,000	$14,184,000

* Sundry investments have not been revalued because of their hedge nature.

The accompanying notes are an integral part of these financial statements.

MODEL C

Retailer
Consolidated Statements of Changes in Financial Position
Years Ended July 31, 1976 and 1975

	1976	1975
Working Capital Was Provided by		
Operating income (before effect of 1975 change in accounting method)	$17,300,074	$ 6,594,358
Add—amounts considered in determining operating income that do not represent current fund expenditures		
Provisions for replacement value depreciation and amortization	8,090,648	7,365,926
Replacement cost of sales adjustment	6,545,000	5,936,000
Other, net	111,508	(546,012)
Working capital provided by operations	$32,047,230	$19,350,272
Revaluation of property, plant, and equipment, net to replacement cost	1,807,000	2,364,000
Increase in long-term debt	1,023,516	14,332,711
Proceeds from sale of common shares under stock option plans	818,876	—
Retirements of property, plant, and equipment	1,109,715	1,358,652
Total working capital provided	$36,806,337	$37,405,635
Working Capital Was Used for		
Unrealized property, plant, and equipment value change	$ 1,807,000	$ 2,364,000
Effect of 1975 change in accounting method	—	835,506
Additions to property, plant, and equipment	10,589,719	9,895,686
Retirements and repurchases of long-term debt	7,403,280	4,903,472
Dividends paid	6,892,785	6,495,868
Other, net	148,340	(905,592)
Total working capital used	$26,841,124	$23,588,940
Net increase in working capital	$ 9,965,213	$13,816,695
Components of Working Capital Increase (Decrease)		
Cash and marketable securities	$ (675,784)	$ 660,154
Receivables	8,476,522	(4,305,439)
Inventories	19,978,351	(15,234,102)
Change in current assets	$27,779,089	$(18,879,387)
Notes payable	$ (3,993,825)	$(41,725,646)
Accounts payable	11,523,708	4,972,688
Accrued expenses	208,911	2,526,834
Federal income taxes	10,075,082	1,530,042
Change in current liabilities	$17,813,876	$(32,696,082)
Net increase in working capital	$ 9,965,213	$ 13,816,695

The accompanying notes are an integral part of these financial statements.

MODEL C

Retailer

Consolidated Balance Sheet
July 31, 1976 and 1975

	1976	1975
Assets		
Current assets		
Cash and marketable securities	$ 3,374,845	$ 4,050,629
Receivables, less allowances ($2,263,674 in 1976 and $2,224,364 in 1975) for doubtful accounts	75,212,596	66,736,074
Inventories		
Finished and in-process goods	110,888,876	96,113,219
Raw materials	18,986,372	13,783,678
Total current assets	$208,462,689	$180,683,600
Property, plant, and equipment		
Land	$ 3,294,198	$ 2,918,098
Buildings	38,548,955	34,367,626
Machinery and equipment	46,213,690	43,276,163
Leasehold improvements	34,160,773	28,991,408
Construction in progress	524,688	166,992
	$122,742,304	$109,720,287
	1976	1975
Liabilities and Shareholders' Equity		
Current liabilities		
Unsecured notes payable and current portion of long-term debt	$ 6,363,595	$ 10,357,420
Accounts payable	38,871,869	27,348,161
Accrued expenses and employee deductions	17,630,111	17,421,200
Federal income taxes	15,471,127	5,396,045
Total current liabilities	$ 78,336,702	$ 60,522,826
Long-term debt, less portion due within one year included in current liabilities	$ 53,500,352	$ 59,880,116
Deferred credits and other provisions	$ 6,107,249	$ 5,873,741

Accumulated depreciation and amortization

	1976	1975
	58,670,384	50,998,075
	$ 64,071,920	$ 58,722,212
Other assets		
Excess of cost of investments over book value of net assets acquired	$ 7,115,482	$ 7,115,482
Installment receivables, less current portion included in current assets	5,245,531	4,974,528
Prepaid expenses and deferred charges	3,981,503	3,036,421
Future tax benefits, net	2,210,559	2,730,170
Sundry investments	1,909,202	2,695,053
	$ 20,462,277	$ 20,551,654
	$292,996,886	$259,957,466

Shareholders' equity

	1976	1975
Common shares, without par value—10,000,000 shares authorized; 6,949,292 issued in 1976, 6,871,008 in 1975, of which 33,300 shares are held in treasury	$ 2,305,330	$ 2,279,235
Cumulative preferred shares, without par value— authorized 1,500,000 shares; none issued or outstanding		
Capital surplus	26,252,891	25,480,475
Retained operating income	95,331,362	84,924,073
Retained realized value changes	15,172,000	6,813,000
Unrealized value changes	15,991,000	14,184,000
	$155,052,583	$133,680,783
	$292,996,886	$259,957,466

The accompanying notes are an integral part of these financial statements.

193

Retailer
Notes to Consolidated Financial Statements
Years Ended July 31, 1976 and 1975

1. Statement of major accounting policies

Accounting principles. For the most part, assets and liabilities are stated on the balance sheet at their historical cost or net realizable value. Inventories, land and property, plant and equipment (net) are restated annually to an approximation of their replacement cost, as measured in that year. To the extent that the effect of the restatement is not recovered currently through operations, the credit (or charge) is accumulated in an equity account entitled "unrealized value changes." As the effects of the restatements are eventually recovered through operations, they are transferred into an equity account entitled "realized value changes." This account is intended to assure the reservation of sufficient company resources to replace the company's existing level of productive capacity at such time it is necessary to be replaced and at the higher costs that will then be incurred. Although these accounts are considered to be shareholders' equity, their balances are not available for distribution to shareholders as dividends in the normal course of business.

Principles of consolidation. The consolidated financial statements include the accounts of all subsidiaries; all significant intercompany transactions have been eliminated.

Inventories. Inventories are stated at the lower of cost or market; costs are determined using primarily moving averages and retail inventory methods that approximate FIFO costs, as well as replacement costs (note 8). Cost of sales for each period is charged with the amounts that were incurred in the replacement of the products sold during the period.

Depreciation. Provision is made for depreciation of property, plant, and equipment based on the charge necessary each year to provide the replacement cost of those assets, in that year, over the assets' useful life or the remaining terms of leases. The company primarily uses the straight-line method of depreciation.

The excess of cost of investments over book value of net assets acquired arose primarily in connection with acquisitions in 1966 and 1968. This amount is not being amortized.

Store opening costs. The company follows the practice of charging new store opening costs against earnings as the stores are opened.

Employee retirement plans (fixed benefit). The company has noncontributory retirement plans that provide for pensions to eligible employees, on retirement, based on length of service and compensation. Prior service costs are being amortized and funded over approximately thirty years.

Income taxes. The company provides for deferred income taxes and records future income tax benefits on tax timing differences. The flow-through method of accounting for investment tax credit is used.

2. Employee retirement plans (fixed benefit)

Provisions for pension expense charged against operating income during the year ended July 31, 1976, which include amortization of prior service cost over thirty years, totaled approximately $2.6 million ($2 million in 1975). The actuarially computed value of vested benefits for all plans as of July 31, 1976, using the basis followed by the Pension Benefit Guaranty Corporation, exceeded the total of the net assets in the pension fund and balance sheet reserves by approximately $1 million. Unfunded and unprovided prior service costs totaled $11.9 million at July 31, 1976 ($9.2 million in 1975).

The company amended certain of its employee retirement plans as of January 1, 1976, for the purpose of providing improved benefits to employees and to remain in compliance with the provisions of the Employee Retirement Income Security Act of 1974; assumptions used in the actuarial computations were also changed. These changes had the effect of increasing fiscal 1976 pension expense by $800,000.

3. Income taxes

The provision for income taxes consists of the following.

	1976	1975
Federal income taxes		
Currently payable	$20,592,000	$ 8,141,000
Deferred		
Utilization of future tax benefits on tax operating loss carryforwards	412,000	2,747,000
Other, net	569,000	(125,000)
State and local income taxes	3,320,000	1,719,000
Investment tax credit	(502,000)	(498,000)
	$24,391,000	$11,984,000

4. Short-term indebtedness

The company's short-term debt at July 31, 1976, includes unsecured notes payable to banks ($2,016,000) and commercial paper ($3 million). These borrowings had an average remaining term of nineteen days and an average interest rate of 6.28 percent. Maturities under these obligations generally do not exceed ninety days.

During the fiscal year, the average short-term debt outstanding approximated $1,384,000 and reflected a weekly weighted average interest rate of 7.0 percent. The maximum amount of short-term debt outstanding at the end of any month during fiscal 1976 aggregated $6.5 million.

At year-end, the company had unused lines of credit totaling $19 million available for short-term financing. Such lines are not extended for indefinite periods and are subject to termination periodically by either the company or the banks. Under informal agreements with participating banks, the company maintains compensating balances ranging up to 20 percent of the credit lines.

5. Long-term debt

Long-term debt at July 31, 1976, and 1975 consists of the following.

	1976	1975
7.85% notes, payable in annual installments of $1,500,000 commencing in 1979	$15,000,000	$15,000,000
7.125% debentures, payable in annual installments of $750,000	11,058,000	14,240,000
10.75% notes (additional $8,000,000 issued in August, 1976) payable in annual installments of $1,700,000 beginning in 1978 with the balance payable in 1990	14,000,000	14,000,000
5.35% notes, payable in semi-annual installments of $333,333	6,666,667	7,333,333
5.125% notes, payable in annual installments of $200,000 with the balance payable in 1985	2,600,000	2,800,000
7.50% term loan	—	4,200,000
9% notes	—	2,200,000
Other	5,523,280	5,000,289
	$54,847,947	$64,773,622
Less portion due within one year	1,347,595	4,893,506
	$53,500,352	$59,880,116

The 7.125 percent debentures were reduced in 1976 by the purchase of $2,442,000 of such debentures now held in the treasury.

The agreements with respect to long-term debt include, among other things, provisions that limit total consolidated indebtedness, require the maintenance of minimum amounts of working capital, and limit capital stock repurchases and the payment of cash dividends by the company. Under the most restrictive of these various provisions, approximately $81.3 million of consolidated retained operating income at July 31, 1976, is restricted as to the payment of cash dividends. These loan covenant restrictions are not based on the conceptual framework underlying the company's financial statements as presented and would require renegotiation to generate a more meaningful restriction.

6. Common shares and capital surplus

At July 31, 1976, of the authorized but unissued common shares, 240,266 were reserved for issuance to executives and key employees under the company's stock option plans. Of such reserved shares, 236,166 were subject to options outstanding at that date. A summary of the changes in options outstanding during the year is set forth below.

	Number of shares	Option price range (per share)
Outstanding at July 31, 1975	227,758	$ 7.50–$25.25
Add (deduct)		
Granted	81,550	32.75– 33.31
Exercised	(39,284)	10.56– 25.25
Cancelled		
Expirations	(27,000)	18.50
Terminations	(6,858)	10.56– 23.63
Outstanding at July 31, 1976	236,166	$ 7.50–$33.31

The changes in common shares and capital surplus during fiscal 1976 were as follows.

	Common shares		Capital surplus
	Shares	Amount	
Balance at July 31, 1975	6,837,708	$2,279,235	$25,480,475
Proceeds from sale of shares issued under stock option plans	39,284	13,095	805,781
A company was acquired on a pooling of interests basis (restatement of prior years has not been reflected due to the immateriality of the transaction)	39,000	13,000	13,000
Treasury stock transactions in accordance with the provisions of certain deferred compensation plans, net	—	—	(104,295)
Other	—	—	57,930
Balance at July 31, 1976	6,915,992	$2,305,330	$26,252,891

7. Commitments and contingencies

Lease arrangements. The company leases various plant, warehouse, office, and retail store facilities under lease arrangements expiring between 1977 and 2001. Minimum annual rentals under such arrangements in effect at July 31, 1976, are as follows.

	Minimum rental	
For fiscal year(s) ended	*Plant, warehouse, and office facilities*	*Retail store facilities*
1977	$1,481,000	$12,322,000
1978	1,355,000	12,176,000
1979	1,261,000	12,135,000
1980	1,243,000	11,848,000
1981	1,243,000	11,547,000
1982–1986	5,560,000	52,017,000
1987–1991	4,018,000	35,052,000
1992–1996	3,173,000	1,865,000
1997–2001	1,585,000	82,000

Aggregate rental expense applicable to plant, warehouse, and office facilities amounted to $1,939,000 in fiscal 1976 ($1,417,000 in 1975). Aggregate rental expense applicable to retail store facilities, including "sales override" provisions, amounted to $12,996,000 in fiscal 1976 ($10,909,000 in 1975).

The company also leases certain production and data processing equipment. Aggregate rental expense for such equipment was $3,086,000 in fiscal 1976 ($2,659,000 in 1975). These lease arrangements are generally cancellable, on written notice, within three to six months and, therefore, do not represent a significant long-term commitment.

Noncapitalized financing leases (as defined by the SEC) are not material.

License arrangements. Several of the company's divisions operate departments under license arrangements whereby the stores provide not only space and certain other facilities, but also utilities, maintenance, credit administration, and other related services. These license arrangements usually involve periods of five years or less with the license fee generally being based on a percentage of the department sales. In certain instances a minimum license fee is guaranteed.

Fiscal 1976 license fees applicable to these departments (approximately one-half of which represent payments for service) aggregated $8,258,000 ($8,942,000 in 1975). Minimum annual fees under existing license arrangements range from $1,820,000 for fiscal 1977 to $378,000 in 1981 and aggregate $5,449,000.

Contingencies. The company is contingently liable under certain leases of facilities that are operated by customers but have been guaranteed by the company. Minimum annual rentals guaranteed under such leases aggregate approximately $3,233,000 in 1977 and $2,900,000 in 1981.

Legal proceedings. A number of legal actions have been instituted against the company that involve ordinary routine matters as are incident to the kinds of businesses conducted by the company. In the opinion of management, the ultimate disposition of all such actions will not have a materially adverse effect upon the company's consolidated financial statements.

8. Change in accounting method

The company changed its method of accounting for certain of its retail inventories from the lower of average cost or market method to the retail method. This change was made in the fourth quarter of fiscal 1975 and applied retroactively to the beginning of the fiscal year, August 1, 1974. This change was made so that all company retail divisions would conform to a uniform inventory accounting method.

This change did not materially affect 1975 earnings from operations. The cumulative effect of such change at August 1, 1974, amounted to a reduction of $835,506 (net of related taxes of $694,000) or $.12 per share.

MODEL D

Retailer

Consolidated Statements of Changes in Shareholders' Equity
Years Ended July 31, 1976 and 1975

	1976	1975
Results of Ordinary Operations		
Sales	$552,566,605	$473,423,783
Other income, net	928,322	1,015,937
Cost of sales	(360,761,061)	(316,839,321)
Selling, general and administrative expense	(147,044,552)	(131,562,021)
Interest expense, net	(4,723,240)	(8,798,020)
Provision for income taxes	(24,771,000)	(12,491,000)
	16,195,074	4,749,358
Unusual Events		
Change in accounting method (note 8)	—	(835,506)
Computational change for pension liability	2,195,000	—

Value Changes

Land	53,000	102,000
Inventory	6,545,000	5,936,000
Property, plant, and equipment, net	3,118,000	2,561,000
Long-term debt		
General market element	(1,208,000)	(459,000)
Risk change element	—	—
Interest expense differential	506,000	1,166,000
Pension plans	754,000	204,000
	9,768,000	9,510,000
Impact on shareholders' equity resulting from increases in the general price level during the year	(6,577,000)	(10,673,000)
	$ 21,581,074	$ 2,750,852
Shareholders' equity at beginning of year	125,956,783	123,913,368
Common stock and other equity transactions	815,511	65,431
Dividends paid	(7,012,785)	(6,680,868)
Shareholders' equity at end of year	$141,340,583	$120,048,783

MODEL D
Retailer
Consolidated Balance Sheet
July 31, 1976 and 1975

Assets

	1976	1975
Current assets		
Cash and marketable securities	$ 3,374,845	$ 4,050,629
Receivables, less allowances ($2,263,674 in 1976 and $2,224,364 in 1975) for doubtful accounts	75,212,596	66,736,074
Inventories		
Finished and in process goods	110,888,876	96,113,219
Raw materials	18,986,372	13,783,678
Total current assets	$208,462,689	$180,683,600
Property, plant, and equipment		
Land	$ 2,771,198	$ 2,418,098
Buildings	38,548,955	34,367,626
Machinery and equipment	47,022,690	43,814,163
Leasehold improvements	34,700,773	29,341,408
Construction in progress	524,688	166,992
	$123,568,304	$110,108,287

Liabilities and Shareholders' Equity

	1976	1975
Current liabilities		
Unsecured notes payable and current portion of long-term debt	$ 6,363,595	$ 10,357,420
Accounts payable	38,871,869	27,348,161
Accrued expenses and employee deductions	17,630,111	17,421,200
Federal income taxes	15,423,127	5,372,045
Total current liabilities	$ 78,288,702	$ 60,498,826
Long-term debt, less portion due within one year included in current liabilities	$ 51,013,352	$ 56,185,116

Accumulated depreciation and amortization	67,631,384	57,895,075
	$ 55,936,920	$ 52,213,212
Other assets		
Installment receivables, less current portion included in current assets	$ 5,245,531	$ 4,974,528
Prepaid expenses and deferred charges	3,981,985	3,036,903
Future tax benefits	—	400,000
Sundry investments	1,909,202	2,695,053
	$ 11,136,718	$ 11,106,484
	$275,536,327	$244,003,296

Deferred credits and other provisions	$ 4,893,690	$ 7,270,571
Shareholders' equity	$141,340,583	$120,048,783
	$275,536,327	$244,003,296

The accompanying notes are an integral part of these financial statements.

MODEL D

Retailer
Consolidated Statements of Changes in Financial Position
Years Ended July 31, 1976 and 1975

	1976	1975
Working Capital Was Provided by		
Results of ordinary operations	$16,195,074	$ 4,749,358
Add—amounts considered in determining results of ordinary operations that do not represent current fund expenditures		
Provision for replacement value depreciation and amortization	8,090,648	7,365,926
Replacement cost of sales adjustment	6,595,000	5,936,000
Replacement interest expense adjustment	506,000	1,166,000
Other, net	660,508	132,988
Working capital provided by ordinary operations	$32,047,230	$ 19,350,272
Increase in long-term debt	1,023,516	14,332,711
Proceeds from sale of common shares under stock option plans	818,876	—
Retirements of property, plant, and equipment	1,109,715	1,358,652
Total working capital provided	$34,999,337	$ 35,041,635
Working Capital Was Used for		
Effect of 1975 change in accounting method	$ —	$ 835,506
Additions to property, plant, and equipment	10,589,719	9,895,686
Retirements and repurchases of long-term debt	7,403,280	4,903,472
Dividends paid	6,892,785	6,495,868
Other, net	148,340	(905,592)
Total working capital used	$25,034,124	$ 21,224,940
Net increase in working capital	$ 9,965,213	$ 13,816,695
Components of Working Capital Increase (Decrease)		
Cash and marketable securities	$ (675,784)	$ 660,154
Receivables	8,476,522	(4,305,439)
Inventories	19,978,351	(15,234,102)
Change in current assets	$27,779,089	$(18,879,387)
Notes payable	(3,993,825)	(41,725,646)
Accounts payable	11,523,708	4,972,688
Accrued expenses	208,911	2,526,834
Federal income taxes	10,075,082	1,530,042
Change in current liabilities	$17,813,876	$(32,696,082)
Net increase in working capital	$ 9,965,213	$ 13,816,695

The accompanying notes are an integral part of these financial statements.

MODEL D

Retailer
Notes to Consolidated Financial Statements
Years Ended July 31, 1976 and 1975

1. Statement of major accounting policies

Accounting principles. The amounts presented in the financial statements represent the current values, and changes in these values, of the economic resources and obligations of the company. The determination of current values is made, for the most part, through an assessment of the value of each resource to the continuing operations of the company and also by reference to the external markets in which the resource might be traded.

Principles of consolidation. The consolidated financial statements include the accounts of all subsidiaries; all significant intercompany transactions have been eliminated.

Inventories. Inventories are stated at the lower of cost or market; costs are determined using primarily moving averages and retail inventory methods that approximate FIFO costs, as well as replacement costs (note 8). Cost of sales for each period is charged with the amounts that were incurred in the replacement of the products sold during the period.

Depreciation. Provision is made for depreciation of property, plant, and equipment based on the charge necessary each year to provide the replacement cost of those assets, in that year, over the assets' useful life or the remaining terms of leases. The company primarily uses the straight-line method of depreciation.

Store opening costs. The company follows the practice of charging new store opening costs against earnings as the stores are opened.

Employee retirement plans (fixed benefits). The company has noncontributory retirement plans that provide for pensions to eligible employees, on retirement, based on length of service and compensation. Prior service costs are being funded over approximately thirty years.

Income taxes. The company provides for deferred income taxes and records future income tax benefits on tax timing differences arising from differences between the current value results of operations as reported for financial statement purposes and taxable income reported to the IRS. Deferred taxes are also provided on all other current value adjustments and the resulting tax benefit or liability adjusts the current value basis of the appropriate asset or liability. The "flow-through" method of accounting for investment tax credit is used.

2. Employee retirement plans (fixed benefit)

Provisions for pension expense charged against shareholders' investment during the year ended July 31, 1976, totaled approximately $2.6 million ($2 million in 1975). The actuarially computed value of total benefits for all plans as of July 31, 1976, using the basis followed by the Pension Benefit Guaranty Corporation is equal to the total of the net assets in the pension fund and balance sheet reserves. Unfunded prior service costs totaled $11.9 million at July 31, 1976 ($9.2 million in 1975).

The company amended certain of its employee retirement plans as of January 1, 1976, for the purpose of providing improved benefits to employees and to remain in compliance with the provisions of the Employee Retirement Income Security Act of

1974; assumptions used in the actuarial computations were also changed. These changes had the effect of increasing fiscal 1976 pension expense by $800,000.

3. Income taxes
The provision for income taxes consists of the following:

	1976	1975
Federal income taxes		
Currently payable	$20,592,000	$ 8,141,000
Deferred		
Utilization of future tax benefits on tax operating loss carryforwards	412,000	2,747,000
Other, net	949,000	382,000
State and local income taxes	3,320,000	1,719,000
Investment tax credit	(502,000)	(498,000)
	$24,771,000	$12,491,000

4. Short-term debt
The company's short-term debt at July 31, 1976, includes unsecured notes payable to banks ($2,016,000) and commercial paper ($3 million). These borrowings had an average remaining term of nineteen days and an average interest rate of 6.28 percent. Maturities under these obligations generally do not exceed ninety days.

During the fiscal year, the average short-term debt outstanding approximated $1,384,000 and reflected a weekly weighted average interest rate of 7.0 percent. The maximum amount of short-term debt outstanding at the end of any month during fiscal 1976 aggregated $6.5 million.

At year-end, the company had unused lines of credit totaling $19 million available for short-term financing. Such lines are not extended for indefinite periods and are subject to termination periodically by either the company or the banks. Under informal agreements with participating banks, the company maintains compensating balances ranging up to 20 percent of the credit lines.

5. Long-term debt

The principal amounts shown below are those amounts that would be totally amortized in accordance with the repayment terms of each of the original debt instruments if the original instruments required interest to be computed at the market interest rate in effect in the current year. The market interest rate for long-term debt was approximately 10 percent in 1976 (11 percent in 1975).

	1976	1975
7.85% notes, payable in annual installments of $1,500,000 commencing in 1979	$13,412,000	$12,456,000
7.125% debentures, payable in annual installments of $750,000	9,321,000	11,002,000
10.75% notes (additional $8,000,000 issued in August, 1976) payable in annual installments of $1,700,000 beginning in 1978 with the balance payable in 1990	14,520,000	13,818,000
5.35% notes, payable in semi-annual installments of $333,333	4,997,000	5,261,000
5.125% notes, payable in annual installments of $200,000 with the balance payable in 1985	1,916,000	1,954,000
7.50% term loan	—	4,068,000
Other	4,552,352	4,216,116
	$48,718,352	$52,775,116
Add income tax deferred on the gain realized through the reduction from historical principal amounts to current value	2,295,000	3,410,000
	$51,013,352	$56,185,116

The 7.125 percent debentures were reduced in 1976 by the purchase of $2,442,000 of such debentures now held in the treasury.

The agreements with respect to long-term debt include, among other things, provisions that limit total consolidated indebtedness, require the maintenance of minimum amounts of working capital, and limit capital stock repurchases and the payment of cash dividends by the company. Under the most restrictive of these various provisions, approximately $81.3 million of consolidated shareholders' equity at July 31, 1976, is restricted as to the payment of cash dividends. These loan covenant restrictions are not based on the conceptual framework underlying the company's financial statements as presented and would require renegotiation to generate a more meaningful restriction.

6. Common shares and capital surplus

At July 31, 1976, 240,266 of the authorized but unissued common shares were reserved for issuance to executives and key employees under the company's stock option plans. Of such reserved shares, 236,166 were subject to options outstanding at that date. A summary of the changes in options outstanding during the year is set forth below:

	Number of shares	Option price range (per share)
Outstanding at July 31, 1975	227,758	$ 7.50–$25.25
Add (deduct)		
Granted	81,550	32.75– 33.31
Exercised	(39,284)	10.56– 25.25
Cancelled		
Expirations	(27,000)	18.50
Terminations	(6,858)	10.56– 23.63
Outstanding at July 31, 1976	236,166	$ 7.50–$33.31

The changes in the number of common shares during fiscal 1976 were as follows:

	Common shares
Balance at July 31, 1975	6,837,708
Proceeds from sale of shares issued under stock option plan	39,284
A company was acquired on a pooling of interests basis (restatement of prior years has not been reflected due to the immateriality of the transaction)	39,000
Balance at July 31, 1976	6,915,992

7. Commitments and contingencies

Lease arrangements. The company leases various plant, warehouse, office, and retail store facilities under lease arrangements expiring between 1977 and 2001. Minimum annual rentals under such arrangement in effect at July 31, 1976, are as follows:

	Minimum rental	
For fiscal year(s) ended	*Plant, warehouse, and office facilities*	*Retail store facilities*
1977	$1,481,000	$12,322,000
1978	1,355,000	12,176,000
1979	1,261,000	12,135,000
1980	1,243,000	11,848,000
1981	1,243,000	11,547,000
1982–1986	5,560,000	52,017,000
1987–1991	4,018,000	35,052,000
1992–1996	3,173,000	1,865,000
1997–2001	1,585,000	82,000

Aggregate rental expense applicable to plant, warehouse, and office facilities amounted to $1,939,000 in fiscal 1976 ($1,417,000 in 1975). Aggregate rental expense applicable to retail store facilities, including "sales override" provisions, amounted to $12,996,000 in fiscal 1976 ($10,909,000 in 1975).

The company also leases certain production and data processing equipment. Aggregate rental expense for such equipment was $3,086,000 in fiscal 1976 ($2,659,000 in 1975). These lease arrangements are generally cancellable, on written notice, within three to six months and, therefore, do not represent a significant long-term commitment.

Noncapitalized financing leases (as defined by the SEC) are not material.

License arrangements. Several of the company's divisions operate departments under license arrangements whereby the stores provide not only space and certain other facilities, but also utilities, maintenance, credit administration, and other related services. These license arrangements usually involve periods of five years or less with the license fee generally being based on a percentage of the department sales. In certain instances a minimum license fee is guaranteed.

Fiscal 1976 license fees applicable to these departments (approximately one-half of which represent payments for service) aggregated $8,258,000 ($8,942,000 in 1975). Minimum annual fees under existing license arrangements range from $1,820,000 for fiscal 1977 to $378,000 in 1981 and aggregate $5,449,000.

Contingencies. The company is contingently liable under certain leases of facilities that are operated by customers, but have been guaranteed by the company. Minimum annual rentals guaranteed under such leases aggregate approximately $3,233,000 in 1977 and $2.9 million in 1981.

Legal proceedings. A number of legal actions have been instituted against the company that involve ordinary routine matters as are incident to the kinds of businesses conducted by the company. In the opinion of management, the ultimate disposition of all such actions will not have a materially adverse effect upon the company's consolidated financial statements.

8. Change in accounting method

The company changed its method of accounting for certain of its retail inventories from the lower of average cost or market method to the retail method. This change was made in the fourth quarter of fiscal 1975 and applied retroactively to the beginning of the fiscal year, August 1, 1974. This change was made so that all company retail divisions would conform to a uniform inventory accounting method.

This change did not materially affect 1975 results of operations. The cumulative effect of such change at August 1, 1974, amounted to a reduction of $835,506 (net of related taxes of $694,000) or $.12 per share.

Bibliography

Canadian Institute of Chartered Accountants, Accounting Research Committee. Accounting Guidelines. *Accounting for the Effects of Changes in the General Purchasing Power of Money*. November, 1976.

————. Discussion Paper. Current Value Accounting. August, 1976.

Financial Accounting Standards Board. Exposure Draft. *Financial Reporting in Units of General Purchasing Power*. December, 1974.

————. Discussion Memorandum. *An Analysis of Issues Related to Conceptual Framework for Accounting and Reporting: Elements of Financial Statements and Their Measurement*. December, 1976.

————. *Tentative Conclusions on Objectives of Financial Statements of Business Enterprises*. December, 1976.

————. Exposure Draft. *Objectives of Financial Reporting and Elements of Financial Statements of Business Enterprises*. December, 1977.

————. Statement of Financial Accounting Concepts no. 1. *Objectives of Financial Reporting by Business Enterprises*. November, 1978.

Inflation Committee. F. E. P. Sandilands, Chairman. *Report of the Inflation Committee*. Her Majesty's Stationery Office, London. September, 1975.

Institute of Chartered Accountants in Australia and Australian Society of Accountants. Statement of Provisional Accounting Standards. *Current Cost Accounting*. October, 1976.

Institutes of Chartered Accountants in England and Wales, Scotland, and Ireland; Association of Certified Accountants; Institute of Cost and Management Accountants; Chartered Institute of Public Finance and Accountancy. Provisional Statement of Standard Accounting Practice no. 7. *Accounting for Changes in the Purchasing Power of Money*. 1974.

Institute of Chartered Accountants in England and Wales, Accounting Standards Committee. Proposed Statement of Standard Accounting Practice 18. *Current Cost Accounting*. November, 1976.

Securities and Exchange Commission. Accounting Series Release no. 190. *Amendments to Regulation S-X Requiring Disclosure of Certain Replacement Cost Data*. March, 1976.

Questionnaire for the Experiment of the Conceptual Framework Task Force

This questionnaire should be completed by all participants in the experiment conducted by the AICPA Task Force on Conceptual Framework for Accounting and Reporting. The questionnaire is essential to accomplish one of the major purposes of the experiment, which is to assess the usefulness, practicality, and practicability of each of the four models specified in the experimentation program. The questions cover (1) preparation time, (2) implementation problems, (3) improvements suggested for the models, and (4) the participants' evaluations of the usefulness of the models. The task force believes the answers obtained from the questionnaire will be just as important as the financial statements prepared under each of the models.

The questions should be answered in the space provided or on a separate sheet of paper if more space is needed. If separate sheets are used, please identify at the top of each sheet the question being answered and the model to which it applies.

The questionnaire is not intended to take the place of the notes to the financial statements for each model, although some overlapping may occur. If the answer to a particular question can be found in a financial statement note, the question may be answered by cross-referencing to the note.

General

Preparation Time

1. Did your company previously prepare financial statements in units of general purchasing power for the Financial Accounting Standards Board?

2. If so, how many hours were spent on the FASB project?

	Fiscal year		
	1972	1973	1974
Managerial hours			
Staff accounting hours			
Computer programming hours			
Computer running hours	———	———	———
Total			

3. How many hours were spent by company employees in preparing the information on replacement cost called for under SEC Accounting Series Release no. 190 in addition to time spent keeping inventory and plant and equipment records and calculating amounts for those items under the conventional accounting model? Answer only if you prepared that information.

Managerial hours
Staff accounting hours
Computer programming hours
Computer running hours ———
    Total

4. How many hours were spent by consultants in preparing the information on replacement cost called for under ASR 190? If time data were not furnished by consultants, please estimate.

Engineering hours (external)
Engineering hours (internal)
Accounting hours (external) ———
    Total

5. Assuming continuation of the requirement to file replacement cost information under ASR 190, how many hours do you estimate will be required annually by company employees to prepare that information?

Managerial hours
Staff accounting hours
Computer programming hours
Computer running hours ———
    Total

Implementation

6.   How would you rank the four models in terms of simplicity to apply? Rank them from 1 (simplest) to 4 (most complex). (Ignore preparation time as an element of simplicity; preparation time is covered under each model.)

Model A
Model B
Model C
Model D

7.   Assume that the improvements, if any, of the models you recommended in other sections of the questionnaire (pages 219, 221, 224, and 227) were adopted. How would you then rank the four models in terms of simplicity to apply? Rank them from 1 (simplest) to 4 (most complex). Answer only if you recommended improvements for one or more of the four models.

Model A
Model B
Model C
Model D

Evaluation

8.   How would you rank information produced under the four models with respect to usefulness to outsiders in making decisions to buy or sell shares in the company or lend money to the company? Rank the four models both in terms of overall usefulness and under each of the following four qualitative characteristics from 1 (most useful) to 4 (least useful). The four characteristics are described fully in paragraphs 329–365 of the FASB discussion memorandum of December 2, 1976.

Overall usefulness	*Measurability*	*Comparability*
Model A	Model A	Model A
Model B	Model B	Model B
Model C	Model C	Model C
Model D	Model D	Model D

Relevance	*Reliability*
Model A	Model A
Model B	Model B
Model C	Model C
Model D	Model D

9.   Assume that the improvements, if any, of the models you recommended in other sections of the questionnaire were adopted. How would you then rank information produced under the four models with respect to usefulness to outsiders in making decisions to buy or sell shares in the company or lend money to the company? Rank the four models both in terms of overall usefulness and under each of the following

four qualitative characteristics from 1 (most useful) to 4 (least useful). Answer only if you recommended improvements for one or more of the four models.

Overall usefulness	*Measurability*	*Comparability*
Model A	Model A	Model A
Model B	Model B	Model B
Model C	Model C	Model C
Model D	Model D	Model D

Relevance	*Reliability*
Model A	Model A
Model B	Model B
Model C	Model C
Model D	Model D

Other

10. How many people are employed by the following:

(*a*) The entity for which financial statements under each model were prepared? (Answer only if the experiment was limited to a segment.)

(*b*) The entity for which consolidated financial statements are published?

11. Identify the industry in which the entity operates. If the entity operates in more than one industry, identify each industry and state the percent of total entity sales that applies to each.

12. Did you file replacement cost information under ASR 190? If so, attach a copy of it.

13. For purposes of preparing financial statements under models C and D, did you consider modifying the information filed under ASR 190 to give effect to operating cost savings (as discussed on pages 113–114 of the Experimentation Program booklet)?

14. If you decided not to modify the information filed under ASR 190 to give effect to operating cost savings, please explain why you did not.

15. If you did modify the information filed under ASR 190 to give effect to operating cost savings, please give the monetary amount of the modification, and explain how you developed the modified amounts and any problems encountered in doing so. If the information was modified differently for model C than for model D, explain the difference and give the monetary amount of it.

16. If you modified the information filed under ASR 190 for models C and D purposes for any reasons other than to give effect to operating cost savings, give the monetary amount of each modification and describe the nature of the modifications. If the information was modified differently for model C than for model D, explain the difference and give the monetary amount of it.

17. Did your company submit comments to the FASB on the section of the discussion memorandum dealing with the objectives and elements of financial statements? If you answer yes, attach a copy of your response.

18. If your company did submit comments, did participation in this experiment change any of the company's views on the objectives and elements after you submitted comments? If you answer yes, explain the change. (If answering this question entails delay while awaiting clearance by company officials, omit answering this question now but submit an answer at a later date.)

19. If your company did not submit comments, state here any opinion on the objectives and elements that your company has. (If answering this question entails delay while awaiting clearance by company officials, omit answering this question now but submit an answer at a later date.)

20. State the opinion of your company on the issues covered in part 2 ("Qualitative Characteristics") and part 3 ("Measurement of the Elements of Financial Statements") of the FASB discussion memorandum. (If answering this question entails delay while awaiting clearance by company officials, omit answering this question now but submit an answer at a later date.)

21. If you stated an opinion under question 20 above, did participation in this experiment help in forming it? If you answer yes, explain how it helped.

22. What unforeseen problems did participation in the experiment uncover, other than implementation problems covered in other sections of this questionnaire?

23. Please give general comments on the meaningfulness and benefits of the experiment.

24. What additional experimentation, if any, do you suggest for the future?

Model A

Preparation Time

1. If your company previously prepared financial statements in units of general purchasing power for the FASB, did you continue to prepare financial statements after the conclusion of the project in accordance with the concepts set forth in the exposure draft on general purchasing power accounting?

2. If so, how many hours were spent in each year of restatement?

	Fiscal Year		
	1975	1976	1977
Managerial hours			
Staff accounting hours			
Computer programming hours			
Computer running hours	_____	_____	_____
Total			

3. How many hours were spent in preparing the financial statements called for under model A, in addition to time spent preparing the conventional financial statements? If you previously prepared financial statements in units of general purchasing power under FASB concepts for either of the two years for which you prepared

217

financial statements under model A concepts, confine your answer to the year for which statements under FASB concepts were not prepared.

	1975	1976
Managerial hours		
Staff accounting hours		
Computer programming hours		
Computer running hours	_____	_____
Total		

4. How many hours do you estimate would be required each year to continue preparing the financial statements called for under model A in addition to time spent preparing conventional financial statements?

Managerial hours	
Staff accounting hours	
Computer programming hours	
Computer running hours	_____
Total	

5. If you have suggested improvements for model A (see page 219) of the questionnaire), how many hours do you estimate would be required each year to continue preparing the financial statements called for under model A, including the improvements, in addition to time spent preparing conventional financial statements?

Managerial hours	
Staff accounting hours	
Computer programming hours	
Computer running hours	_____
Total	

6. Suppose that you continue in the future to prepare financial statements in units of general purchasing power but that you prepare them under the requirements of the FASB exposure draft instead of under the requirements of model A. How many hours do you estimate would be required each year in addition to the time spent preparing conventional financial statements? Do not answer if you did not participate in the FASB experiment.

Managerial hours	
Staff accounting hours	
Computer programming hours	
Computer running hours	_____
Total	

Implementation

7. Did you find the material in the experimental program booklet and the appendix sufficient to enable you to understand how to apply model A?

8. If you found the material in the booklet and the appendix insufficient, were you able to obtain enough guidance in the application of model A from other sources? Name the sources.

The following two questions need not be answered by those who participated in the FASB field test and submitted answers to essentially the same questions to the FASB:

9. Please describe any "shortcut" procedures that you used to save time in applying model A that were not used in preparing the financial statements presented in Appendix E of the FASB exposure draft. Do not include any departures from Appendix E called for in the experimental program.

10. Please describe any procedures of general purchasing power accounting that you used in applying model A that were not used in the financial statements in Appendix E, other than shortcut procedures, and give the reasons for using them. Do not include any departures called for in the experimental program.

Improvements and Variations

11. Suppose the FASB were to require that financial statements under model A be presented in place of or supplementary to financial statements prepared under the conventional model presently in use. Would you recommend changes in the principles described for model A in the experimentation program booklet or appendix?

12. If you answered yes to question 11, describe and give reasons for the changes you recommend.

13. If you recommended one or more changes in principles, state the effect on model A net income for your company of each change for 1975 and 1976.

14. If you recommended more than one change in principles, state the combined effect on model A net income of all changes for 1975 and 1976.

Evaluation

15. To what extent do you believe financial statements produced under model A should be reported? Answer only if you have an opinion on the subject.

_____ Not at all.

_____ Together with the conventional financial statements.

_____ As the only set of financial statements reported.

_____ Another presentation (please describe).

16. Assuming the improvements you recommended, if any, for model A or any of the other three models were adopted, to what extent do you believe financial statements produced under model A should be reported? Answer only if you have an opinion on the subject and if you recommended improvements for one or more of the four models.

_____ Not at all.

_____ Together with the conventional financial statements.

_____ As the only set of financial statements reported.

_____ Another presentation (please describe).

Model B

Preparation Time

1. How many hours were spent in preparing the financial statements called for under model B in addition to preparing the conventional financial statements? Do not include time spent preparing the replacement cost information required under ASR 190 even if you used that information in applying model B.

	1975	1976
Managerial hours		
Staff accounting hours		
Computer programming hours		
Computer running hours	_____	_____
Total		

2. How many hours do you estimate would be required each year to continue preparing the financial statements called for under model B in addition to time spent preparing conventional financial statements?. Do not include time spent preparing the replacement cost information required under ASR 190, but assume that you continue to use that information in applying model B.

Managerial hours	
Staff accounting hours	
Computer programming hours	
Computer running hours	_____
Total	

3. If you have suggested improvements for model B (see page 221 of the questionnaire), how many hours do you estimate would be required each year to continue preparing the financial statements called for under model B, including the improvements, in addition to time spent preparing conventional financial statements. Do not include time spent preparing the replacement cost information required under ASR 190, but assume that you continue to use that information in applying model B.

Managerial hours	
Staff accounting hours	
Computer programming hours	
Computer running hours	_____
Total	

4. Is your company now on LIFO? If not, estimate the monetary cost or number of hours of employee and machine time that would be required to change to LIFO.

	Hours	Monetary cost
Managerial time		
Staff accounting time		
Computer programming time		
Computer running time	_____	_____
Total		

Implementation

5. Did you find the material in the experimental program booklet and the appendix sufficient to enable you to understand how to apply model B?

6. If you found the material in the booklet and appendix insufficient, were you able to obtain enough guidance in the application of model B from other sources? Name the sources.

7. Describe any procedures that you used to save time in applying model B that were not discussed in the experimental program booklet or appendix.

8. Describe any procedures that you used in applying model B, other than time-saving expedients, that were not discussed in the booklet or appendix, and give the reasons for using them.

Improvements and Variations

9. Suppose the FASB were to require that financial statements under model B be presented in place of or supplementary to financial statements prepared under the conventional model presently in use. Would you recommend changes in the principles described for model B in the experimentation program booklet or appendix?

10. If you answered yes to question 9, describe and give reasons for the changes you recommend.

11. If you recommended one or more changes in principles, state the effect on model B net income for your company of each change for 1975 and 1976.

12. If you recommended more than one change in principles, state the combined effect on model B net income of all changes for 1975 and 1976.

Evaluation

13. To what extent do you believe financial statements produced under model B should be reported? Answer only if you have an opinion on the subject.

_____ Not at all.

_____ Together with the conventional financial statements.

_____ As the only set of financial statements reported.

_____ Another presentation (please describe).

14. Assuming the improvements you recommended, if any, for model B or any of the other models were adopted, to what extent do you believe financial statements produced under model B should be reported? Answer only if you have an opinion on the subject.

_____ Not at all.

_____ Together with the conventional financial statements.

_____ As the only set of financial statements reported.

_____ Another presentation (please describe).

Model C

Preparation Time

1. If you filed with the SEC the information on replacement cost required under ASR 190, how many hours did you spend additionally, if any, to modify that information to arrive at the replacement cost of inventory and productive capacity used in applying model C? Include hours spent jointly in modifying the information for both models C and D and in jointly calculating replacement cost at the beginning of fiscal year 1975 for both models C and D. (Unless replacement cost for models C and D differs, the answer to this question should be the same as the answer to question 1 on page 225.)

Managerial hours
Staff accounting hours
Computer programming hours
Computer running hours   _____
      Total

2. If you did not file the information required under ASR 190, how many hours were spent in developing the replacement cost information for inventories and productive capacity called for under model C? Include hours spent jointly in developing the information for both models C and D. (Unless replacement cost for models C and D differs, the answer to this question should be the same as the answer to question 2 on page 225.)

Managerial hours
Staff accounting hours
Computer programming hours
Computer running hours   _____
      Total

3. How many hours were spent in preparing the financial statements called for under model C, in addition to the time spent in calculating replacement cost information and in preparing the conventional financial statements? (Time spent in calculating replacement cost information consists of time spent developing information

for ASR 190 purposes and modifying it for models C and D purposes or developing replacement cost information solely for models C and D purposes.)

Managerial hours
Staff accounting hours
Computer programming hours
Computer running hours _____
      Total

4. How many hours do you estimate would be required each year to continue modifying or developing the information on replacement cost as described in questions 1 and 2 above, assuming continuance of the ASR 190 reporting requirement? Include hours that would be spent jointly developing or modifying the information for both models C and D. (Unless replacement cost for models C and D differs, the answer to this question should be the same as the answer to question 4 on page 226.)

Managerial hours
Staff accounting hours
Computer programming hours
Computer running hours _____
      Total

5. How many hours do you estimate would be required each year to continue preparing the financial statements called for under model C, in addition to time spent in calculating replacement cost information and in preparing conventional financial statements? (Time spent in calculating replacement cost information consists of time spent developing information for ASR 190 purposes and modifying it for models C and D purposes or developing replacement cost information solely for models C and D purposes.)

Managerial hours
Staff accounting hours
Computer programming hours
Computer running hours _____
      Total

6. If you have suggested improvements for model C (see page 224), how many hours do you estimate would be required each year to continue preparing the financial statements called for under model C, including the improvements, in addition to time spent in calculating replacement cost information (as described in question 5 above) and in preparing conventional financial statements?

Managerial hours
Staff accounting hours
Computer programming hours
Computer running hours _____
      Total

223

7. Suppose model C were to supersede the conventional accounting model presently in use, and only financial statements under model C had to be prepared. By what percent do you estimate that preparation time each year under model C, including all time spent in calculating replacement cost information, would be greater than or less than preparation time under the conventional accounting model? (Indicate whether the percent given means "greater than" or "less than.")

Without the improvements suggested by you

Managerial time
Staff accounting time
Computer programming time
Computer running time

With the improvements suggested by you, if any

Managerial time
Staff accounting time
Computer programming time
Computer running time

Implementation

8. Did you find the material in the experimental program booklet and the appendix sufficient to enable you to understand how to apply model C?

9. If you found the material in the booklet and the appendix insufficient, were you able to obtain enough guidance in the application of model C from other sources? Name the sources.

10. Describe any procedures that you used to save time in applying model C that were not discussed in the experimental program booklet or appendix.

11. Describe any procedures that you used in applying model C, other than time-saving expedients, that were not discussed in the experimental program booklet or appendix, and give the reasons for using them.

Improvements and Variations

12. Suppose the FASB were to require that financial statements under model C be presented in place of or supplementary to financial statements prepared under the conventional model presently in use. Would you recommend changes in the principles described for model C in the experimentation program booklet or appendix?

13. If you answered yes to question 12, describe and give reasons for the changes you recommend.

14. If you recommended one or more changes in principles, state the effect on model C net income of your company of each change for 1975 and 1976.

15. If you recommended more than one change in principles, state the combined effect on model C net income of all changes for 1975 and 1976.

Evaluation

16. To what extent do you believe financial statements produced under model C should be reported? Answer only if you have an opinion on the subject.

_____ Not at all.

_____ Together with the conventional financial statements.

_____ As the only set of financial statements reported.

_____ Another presentation (please describe).

17. Assuming the improvements you recommended, if any, for model C or any of the other models were adopted, to what extent do you believe financial statements produced under model C should be reported? Answer only if you have an opinion on the subject.

_____ Not at all.

_____ Together with the conventional financial statements.

_____ As the only set of financial statements reported.

_____ Another presentation (please describe).

Model D

Preparation Time

1. If you filed with the SEC the information on replacement cost required under ASR 190, how many hours did you spend additionally, if any, to modify that information to arrive at the replacement cost of inventory and productive capacity used in applying model D? Include hours spent jointly in modifying the information for both models C and D and in jointly calculating replacement cost at the beginning of fiscal year 1975 for both models C and D. (Unless replacement cost for models C and D differs, the answer to this question should be the same as the answer to question 1 on page 222.)

Managerial hours
Staff accounting hours
Computer programming hours
Computer running hours _____
Total

2. If you did not file the information required under ASR 190, how many hours were spent in developing the replacement cost information for inventories and productive capacity called for under model D? Include hours spent jointly in developing the information for both models C and D. (Unless replacement cost for models C and D differs, the answer to this question should be the same as the answer to question 2 on page 222.)

Managerial hours
Staff accounting hours
Computer programming hours
Computer running hours _____
Total

3. How many hours were spent in preparing the financial statements called for under model D, in addition to the time spent in calculating replacement cost information and in preparing the conventional financial statements? (Time spent in calculating replacement cost information consists of time spent developing information for ASR 190 purposes and modifying it for models C and D purposes or developing replacement cost information solely for models C and D purposes.)

Managerial hours
Staff accounting hours
Computer programming hours
Computer running hours   _____
      Total

---

4. How many hours do you estimate would be required each year to continue modifying or developing the information on replacement cost as described in questions 1 and 2 above, assuming continuance of the ASR 190 reporting requirement? Include hours that would be spent jointly developing or modifying the information for both models C and D. (Unless replacement cost for models C and D differs, the answer to this question should be the same as the answer to question 4 on page 223.)

Managerial hours
Staff accounting hours
Computer programming hours
Computer running hours   _____
      Total

---

5. How many hours do you estimate would be required each year to continue preparing the financial statements called for under model D, in addition to time spent in calculating replacement cost information and in preparing conventional financial statements? (Time spent in calculating replacement cost information consists of time spent developing information for ASR 190 purposes and modifying it for models C and D purposes or developing replacement cost information solely for models C and D purposes.)

Managerial hours
Staff accounting hours
Computer programming hours
Computer running hours   _____
      Total

---

6. If you have suggested improvements for model D (see page 227), how many hours do you estimate would be required each year to continue preparing the financial statements called for under model D, including the improvements, in addition to time spent in calculating replacement cost information (as described in question 5 above) and in preparing conventional financial statements?

Managerial hours	
Staff accounting hours	
Computer programming hours	
Computer running hours	_____
Total	

7.   Suppose model D were to supersede the conventional accounting model presently in use, and only financial statements under model D had to be prepared. By what percent do you estimate that preparation time each year under model D, including all time spent in calculating replacement cost information, would be greater than or less than preparation time under the conventional accounting model? (Indicate whether the percent given means "greater than" or "less than.")

Without the improvements suggested by you

Managerial time
Staff accounting time
Computer programming time
Computer running time

With the improvements suggested by you, if any

Managerial time
Staff accounting time
Computer programming time
Computer running time

Implementation

8.   Did you find the material in the experimental program booklet and the appendix sufficient to enable you to understand how to apply model D?

9.   If you found the material in the booklet and the appendix insufficient, were you able to obtain enough guidance in the application of model D from other sources? Name the sources.

10. Describe any procedures that you used to save time in applying model D that were not discussed in the experimental program booklet or appendix.

11. Describe any procedures that you used in applying model D, other than time-saving expedients, that were not discussed in the experimental program booklet or appendix, and give the reasons for using them.

Improvements and Variations

12. Suppose the FASB were to require that financial statements under model D be presented in place of or supplementary to financial statements prepared under the conventional model presently in use. Would you recommend changes in the principles described for model D in the experimentation program booklet or appendix?

13. If you answered yes to question 12, describe and give reasons for the changes you recommend.

14. If you recommended one or more changes in principles, state the effect on model D net income of your company of each change for 1975 and 1976.

15. If you recommended more than one change in principles, state the combined effect on model D net income of all changes for 1975 and 1976.

Evaluation

16. To what extent do you believe financial statements produced under model D should be reported? Answer only if you have an opinion on the subject.

    _____ Not at all.

    _____ Together with the conventional financial statements.

    _____ As the only set of financial statements reported.

    _____ Another presentation (please describe).

17. Assuming the improvements you recommended, if any, for model D or any of the other models were adopted, to what extent do you believe financial statements produced under model D should be reported? Answer only if you have an opinion on the subject.

    _____ Not at all.

    _____ Together with the conventional financial statements.

    _____ As the only set of financial statements reported.

    _____ Another presentation (please describe).